Evaluating Economic Instruments for Environmental Policy

ORGANISATION FOR ECONOMIC CO-OPERATION AND DEVELOPMENT

ORGANISATION FOR ECONOMIC CO-OPERATION AND DEVELOPMENT

Pursuant to Article 1 of the Convention signed in Paris on 14th December 1960, and which came into force on 30th September 1961, the Organisation for Economic Co-operation and Development (OECD) shall promote policies designed:

- to achieve the highest sustainable economic growth and employment and a rising standard of living in Member countries, while maintaining financial stability, and thus to contribute to the development of the world economy;
- to contribute to sound economic expansion in Member as well as non-member countries in the process of economic development; and
- to contribute to the expansion of world trade on a multilateral, non-discriminatory basis in accordance with international obligations.

The original Member countries of the OECD are Austria, Belgium, Canada, Denmark, France, Germany, Greece, Iceland, Ireland, Italy, Luxembourg, the Netherlands, Norway, Portugal, Spain, Sweden, Switzerland, Turkey, the United Kingdom and the United States. The following countries became Members subsequently through accession at the dates indicated hereafter: Japan (28th April 1964), Finland (28th January 1969), Australia (7th June 1971), New Zealand (29th May 1973), Mexico (18th May 1994), the Czech Republic (21st December 1995), Hungary (7th May 1996), Poland (22nd November 1996) and the Republic of Korea (12th December 1996). The Commission of the European Communities takes part in the work of the OECD (Article 13 of the OECD Convention).

Publié en français sous le titre :

ÉVALUER LES INSTRUMENTS ÉCONOMIQUES DES POLITIQUES DE L'ENVIRONNEMENT

FOREWORD

The Recommendation of the OECD Council "on the Use of Economic Instruments in Environmental Policy" (January 1991) asks that Member countries "make a greater and more consistent use of economic instruments" and instructs the Environment Policy Committee "to provide information regarding their effectiveness in achieving specific environmental objectives". During the first half of the 1990s, the use of economic instruments has grown considerably in OECD countries. Following a comprehensive review of the situation,* the Secretariat, under the supervision of the Group on Economic and Environmental Policy Integration, carried out a review of the efficiency and effectiveness of economic instruments, based on experience in a number of Member countries.

This report was prepared by **Dr. St. Smith** (Institute for fiscal Studies and University College, London), **Dr. H.B. Vos** (DHV Consultants) and the Secretariat. It is published on the responsibility of the Secretary-General of the OECD.

---

* *Managing the Environment: the Role of Economic Instruments*, OECD, 1994.

3

TABLE OF CONTENTS

Part I
THE CASE FOR EVALUATION

Chapter 1
THE CASE FOR EVALUATING ECONOMIC INSTRUMENTS

Chapter 2
THE CASE FOR ECONOMIC INSTRUMENTS – TYPES OF EVIDENCE

Part II
AVAILABLE EVIDENCE

Chapter 3
CHARGES AND TAXES: WATER

Chapter 4
CHARGES AND TAXES: AIR

Chapter 5
TRADEABLE PERMITS

Chapter 6
OTHER MARKET MECHANISMS (WASTE)

Part III
AN EVALUATION FRAMEWORK

Chapter 7
EVALUATION CRITERIA FOR ENVIRONMENTAL POLICY INSTRUMENTS

Chapter 8
THE INSTITUTIONAL CONTEXT OF EVALUATION STUDIES

Chapter 9
AN IN-BUILT EVALUATION FRAMEWORK

Chapter 10
KEY ISSUES IN EVALUATION

Chapter 11
CONCLUSIONS

TABLES

BOXES

FIGURES

EXECUTIVE SUMMARY

The OECD has been actively encouraging the use of economic instruments in environmental policy for a long time. As citizens' demands for a cleaner environment grows, it becomes increasingly important that environmental policies should be employed that provide the desired standard of environmental protection without incurring excessive economic cost.

In comparison with existing "command-and-control" regulatory policies, economic instruments could in principle contribute to improving the efficiency and effectiveness of environmental policy in at least three main ways:

- They could reduce the economic cost of achieving a given level of environmental protection, by allowing polluters greater flexibility in how they achieve the required reduction in pollution. Viewed another way, economic instruments can permit a greater standard of environmental protection to be achieved without increasing the economic costs incurred.

- They may stimulate more rapid innovation in pollution abatement technologies because they provide an incentive for polluters to seek ways to reduce pollution by more than required for compliance with current regulatory standards.

- Also, in some cases, such as taxes, charges and auctioned permits, economic instruments may raise revenues which may allow other taxes to be reduced, or can be used to finance environmental policy measures or other government spending.

The last OECD comprehensive survey of the use of economic instruments in Member countries' environmental policies found a wide range of applications, including charges of various types, subsidies, deposit-refund systems and tradeable permits, and a growing tendency for such instruments to be employed, especially in the form of environmentally-motivated taxes on products and deposit-refund systems. In many cases, the primary purpose of the use of economic instruments appears to have been a growing interest in their potential incentive role.

The growing number of practical applications of economic instruments in OECD countries provides the opportunity to learn more about how these instruments function, and about the circumstances in which they appear to be most effective.

Systematic analysis, or "evaluation", of practical experience with economic instruments can perform a number of different functions:

- Evaluation evidence on the performance of policy instruments can help to improve the administration of current policy.
- Evaluations of practical experiences can also improve the choice of instruments in future policy, by showing the advantages and disadvantages of particular instruments in actual operation.
- In addition, evaluations can provide evidence on the functioning of the political and policy processes, to ensure that they translate policy intentions into practice as effectively as possible.

– Evaluation may also contribute to better communication with and information of stakeholders and the public on the purpose, operation and effects of the policy.

In each of these ways, evaluation studies can contribute to a better design and implementation of environmental policies in the countries concerned. There may also be important benefits to other countries, which can learn from the practical experience of countries which have implemented particular policies.

What do we know about economic instruments?

Despite the benefits that could be gained from systematic evaluation of practical policy, few formal evaluations of economic instruments have been conducted in Member countries. However, there is considerable evidence on various aspects of the performance of economic instruments. Some of the evidence has been summarised in this report, although it is certainly not comprehensive, either in its coverage of the economic instruments employed in the OECD area, or in the extent to which it has been able to identify all relevant data on performance held by governments, agencies and researchers.

The evidence reviewed in this report does indicate that in relation to some of the relevant criteria, in many instances economic instruments can be shown to have been effective. Thus, the *charging and taxation measures* described have generally led to changes in emissions levels, and have not simply been absorbed as a cost by polluters, without any environmental improvement resulting. This appears true, even for some charging systems, such as the Dutch water charges, which were initially designed for revenue raising, rather than as incentive mechanisms.

There is also evidence on the extent to which *tradeable permit mechanisms* function according to theoretical expectations. In this case, much seems to turn on the restrictions imposed on trading, and on the extent to which rights and future entitlements are clearly defined. There are indications, too, from some of the studies (*e.g.* some of the fisheries quota markets, and the early Fox River tradeable permit system in the US) that permit trading may be affected by monopoly power in the permit market where there are too few participants.

However, whilst permit trading volumes may be an indication that economic efficiency gains are being achieved, relative to the same allocation of rights without trading, little of the evidence seeks directly to relate the observed outcomes from economic instruments to the underlying criterion of economic efficiency, which is the central theoretical justification for preferring economic instruments to conventional command-and-control regulation. In particular, there is little detailed evidence on the scale of the efficiency gains from permit trading, or on the extent to which charging systems succeed in equalising marginal abatement costs across polluters.

More could be done to investigate some of these key issues. In particular, a number of *ex ante* studies exist, which use data on the pattern of abatement costs across polluters in some particular situation to indicate the scale of efficiency gains which could result from achieving an efficient pattern of abatement across polluters, instead of the inefficient pattern resulting from some administrative rule. In principle, given appropriate data, such studies could also be carried out *ex post*, to assess the extent to which the actual pattern of abatement from using economic instruments achieved the efficient, optimal, distribution of abatement.

The major difficulty in conducting such studies is, of course, the availability of suitable data on individual emissions sources. Often this is difficult to obtain for reasons of commercial confidentiality. Also, however, retrospective analysis faces the further difficulty that relevant data about the costs involved in past abatement investments can no longer be found, due to the lack of detailed records, changes in personnel in firms and agencies through retirement and other causes, etc. Effective *ex post* evaluation thus requires advance planning, to ensure that appropriate data is collected, and records kept, to provide the necessary information base for later evaluation.

Recommendations for future action

The report argues that there would be gains from more widespread evaluation of the outcome from the use of economic instruments, and indeed from the use of environmental policy instruments more generally. "Ex *post*" evaluation of actual practice can provide a valuable supplement of what is already known from theoretical arguments and simulation studies about the relative advantages and disadvantages of different instruments. It can also provide evidence on performance which can help improve the design and the administration of current policy.

The functions which an evaluation aims to perform will vary; in some cases, the main purpose will be to find ways to *modify current policy* to make it function better, and in other cases, the primary purpose of evaluation will be to *provide information* which can be used in designing future policies. Also, the political and policy systems and cultures of countries differ. For both these reasons, a single "blueprint", or set of principles, for evaluation of economic instruments is unlikely to apply to all cases. Evaluations will need to be designed to reflect the purpose of the evaluation, and the political and administrative context within which it will be conducted. Nevertheless, there are a number of general ideas which may be helpful:

- In general, the sooner the decision is taken to evaluate, the better. If evaluations are not to be hampered by lack of the necessary data, there is a need for forethought and advance planning. Consideration needs to be given to the data requirements for future evaluation at the time initial decisions are being taken about the introduction of a new instrument. The most persuasive information on the performance of an economic instrument will come from analysing the changes that resulted from its introduction. A comparison of "before" and "after" data requires that data is collected before the policy is introduced; once the policy has been in operation for some time, it will be too late to consider evaluations of this form.

- The report recommends an "in-built" approach to evaluation. With "in-built" evaluation approach, decisions on future evaluation are made *at the start* of the policy process, and provision is made for collecting data and keeping records in a way which will facilitate the later evaluation of the policy.

- An in-built evaluation approach, in which a commitment is made at an early stage to later evaluation of the policy, has the further advantage that it smoothes many of the potential institutional obstacles to evaluation. The individuals and agencies implementing the policy are aware from the outset that an evaluation will take place. When the evaluation comes to be undertaken, it is likely to meet less institutional opposition, and to be seen as less of a threat to those involved in the policy, than if proposals for evaluation are suddenly raised, after the policy has been up and running for some time.

- Evaluations which are conducted independently may find it easier to be objective, and critical where this is appropriate. The perception of objectivity can often be important if the evaluation is to influence future policy. However, independent "outsiders" will often be less well-informed about key aspects of the policy than "insiders", and will therefore need to co-operate closely with those operating the policy.

- Publication of the findings of the evaluation may ensure effective dissemination of findings into the political domain. However, selective publication decisions, taken once the evaluation findings are known, are likely to be viewed with more skepticism than if a prior commitment is made to publication, before the results are known. However, publication may not always be appropriate, and will need to be judged in the light of the political and administrative structures in each country. Excessive controversy over adverse evaluation findings could, for example, harden attitudes, and make reforms more difficult to introduce than where a more low-key approach had been taken to the dissemination of the evaluation results.

– Greater efforts to evaluate the efficiency and effectiveness of economic instruments in actual practice would contribute greatly to improving future policy, by identifying the circumstances in which economic instruments are most likely to prove effective, and by providing information on the advantages and disadvantages in practice of employing the various different forms of economic instrument – taxes, charges, tradeable permits, etc. Greater experience with evaluation will also contribute to better evaluation design and practice. Although there are undoubtedly difficulties in conducting evaluation studies, and in integrating the results of evaluation research into administrative and policy processes, more extensive experience of evaluation of a range of policies, and in a range of institutional situations, will provide lessons which will help to improve the practice, and policy impact, of future evaluation work. Efficient and effective evaluation will, in turn, contribute to efficient and effective policy.

Part I

THE CASE FOR EVALUATION

Do economic instruments work when used in environmental policy? Do they really achieve significant reductions in polluting emissions, or do they simply increase the financial burdens on polluters without securing any environmental benefits? Are the theoretical predictions of efficiency gains from such instruments borne out in practice, and do they prove cost-effective from an administrative point of view? Although the theoretical merits of economic instruments in environmental policy have been discussed at length, only now is a sufficient body of evidence accumulating, from the growing number of applications of economic instruments in OECD countries, about how they perform when introduced in the real world.

Chapter 1

THE CASE FOR EVALUATING ECONOMIC INSTRUMENTS

1.1 OECD Studies on economic instruments

Since the 1984 OECD Conference on "Environment and Economics", the OECD has actively encouraged the use of economic instruments in environmental policy. The conclusions of the 1984 Conference had stressed the potential benefits that could accrue from greater use of economic instruments, noting, firstly, that such instruments should promote efficiency, and secondly, that they should provide a stimulus for innovation in pollution-control technologies. It was observed that as environmental policies moved in the direction of pollution prevention, rather than the earlier emphasis on cleaning-up existing pollution damage, economic instruments were likely to become more important.

Subsequent OECD work on economic instruments has included the development of agreed guidelines for the application of economic instruments in Member states (OECD, 1991), the collection and dissemination of comparative information and assessments regarding the role played by economic instruments in OECD Member countries (OECD, 1989a, 1994a), and analyses of their potential and application in particular areas, including climate change (OECD, 1994b), waste management (OECD, 1992) and taxation (OECD, 1993, 1995, 1996).

The OECD has recently reiterated the potential advantages of this approach to environmental policy. The Recommendation of the Council on the Use of Economic Instruments in Environmental Policy, adopted on 31 January 1991, recommended, inter alia, that Member countries:

1. make greater and more consistent use of economic instruments as a complement or a substitute to other policy instruments such as regulations, taking into account national socio-economic conditions;
2. work towards improving the allocation and efficient use of natural and environmental resources by means of economic instruments so as to better reflect the social cost of using these resources;
3. make effort to reach further agreement at international level on the use of environmental policy instruments with respect to solving regional or global environmental problems as well as ensuring sustainable development;
4. develop better modelling, forecasting and monitoring techniques to provide information on environmental consequences of alternative policy actions and their economic effects.

1.2 Types of economic instruments

OECD surveys and other sources have discussed definitions and classifications of economic instruments. The 1994 survey labels instruments "economic" when "they affect estimates of costs and benefits of alternative actions open to economic agents".[1] We distinguish: 1) charges/taxes, 2) subsidies, 3) tradeable emission permits, 4) deposit-refund systems. Some of these categories could be further subdivided into specific instruments. Some of the instruments, notably charges/taxes, may have various purposes.

Apart from the distinction between emission charges and product charges, which relates to the charge base, charges/taxes could also be divided into systems according to their purpose. Earlier surveys of economic instruments by OECD[2] distinguished incentive systems and revenue-raising or earmarked systems, in accordance to their stated purpose. The rise of new fiscal taxes on an environmental basis requires the definition of a third category: eco-taxes. They differ from earmarked charges as regards the allocation of the revenues, and from incentive charges when the primary function of the tax is fiscal, not environmental. In many cases, a mix of incentive, earmarked and fiscal functions can be observed.

In view of the polluter-pays principle, financial aid is permitted under certain conditions.[3] Such financial aid is found in different forms. OECD (1989) distinguished: 1) grants, non-repayable forms of financial assistance; 2) soft loans, whereby interest rates are set below market prices; 3) tax allowances, including tax exemptions, rebates and accelerated depreciation. In many instances, "hidden" subsidies exist, for example in case of user charges which do not fully cover the costs of the associated environmental service.

Deposit-refund systems may be divided in systems for short-cycle goods (like food packaging) and systems for durables.

Economic instruments for natural resource management are not dealt with in this paper, since they raise different issues to those applying to instruments aimed at pollution control. The criteria for efficiency and effectiveness that would be relevant for natural resource taxes and other market mechanisms for natural resource management differ sufficiently from those appropriate to environmental market mechanisms directed at pollution so that separate consideration of their evaluation would be appropriate.

Box 1. **Charges/Taxes**

Types

- Emission charges/taxes: charges to be paid on discharges into the environment, based in principle on (a proxy of) the quantity and/or quality of discharged pollutants
- User charges/taxes: charges that are payments for the costs of collective or public treatment of effluent or waste (tariffs either flat rate tariffs or based on discharges)
- Product charges/taxes: charges on products that are polluting in the manufacturing or consumption phase or for which a disposal system has been organised; resource use charges (water, minerals) an tax differentiation systems are special cases

Functions

- Incentive: some of the applied systems; all fiscal taxes and some of the earmarked charges have a secondary incentive function
- Earmarked: half of applied systems (all user charges)
- Fiscal: increasingly applied to shift the tax burden by offsetting non-environmental taxes

Fields of applications

- Water effluent charges are major examples
- Also applied in air quality policy, waste management and in policies to reduce aircraft noise
- User charges are common financing systems in waste and wastewater management
- Product charges are applied to a range of products, including energy products, packaging, fertiliser, pesticides, batteries, cars and car tires, light bulbs and plastic bags and tableware
- Tax differentiation is applied with regard to leaded and unleaded petrol, other energy products (*e.g.* on carbon and sulphur), and formerly to cars with and without specific air pollution characteristics
- Resource use charges are found with respect to raw materials such as water, sand, gravel, peat, stone, crude oil

Policy role

- In practically all cases emission and product charges are adjuncts to direct regulation
- User charges have a financing role
- Fiscally motivated taxes have a secondary environmental role

The only aspect of market mechanisms for natural resource management that we consider here is the operation of tradeable quotas in fisheries policy. We include this, since it sheds useful light on the functioning of tradeable permits.

The four categories of instruments mentioned, are successively and briefly dealt with in Boxes 1 to 4, in terms of types of instruments, functions, application aspects, and their role as a policy instrument.[4]

Box 2. **Subsidies**

Types

- **Grants:** non-repayable forms of financial assistance
- **Soft loans:** loans with interest rates below market rates
- **Tax allowances:** tax exemptions, tax rebates and accelerated depreciation

Function and conditions[5]

- To assist polluters in bearing the costs of pollution control in those parts of the economy, where otherwise severe difficulties would occur
- Limited to well-defined transitional periods
- Not to create significant distortions in international trade and investment

Applications

- wide range of applications

Policy role

- Adjuncts to direct regulation, *e.g.* licensing, product standards and bans
- Subsidies sometimes financed through environmental charges
- To create better conditions for market penetration of new technology

---

Box 3. **Tradeable emission permits**

Structure

- Dischargers operate under a multi-source emission limit and trade is allowed in permits adding up to that limit
- In cases of single source permits: if a discharger releases less pollution than its limit allows, the firm can sell or trade the differences between its actual discharges and its allowable discharges to another firm which then has the right to release more than its initial limit allows
- Trades can take place within a plant, within a firm (bubbling) or among different firms (offsetting)
- Earned credits may be saved for later use (banking)

Functions

- Incentive, as the instrument should contribute to attaining ambient environmental standards
- A major characteristic of this instrument is its cost-saving potential

Applications

- Important cases are found in the field of air pollution control in the USA, mainly regarding SO_2, VOC and ozone
- Also some cases in water quality policy

Policy role

- Emissions trading programmes are adjuncts to direct regulations, including technical requirements for modified and new industrial equipment

---

Box 4. **Deposit-refund systems**

Structure and types

- A surcharge is laid on the price of potentially polluting products. When pollution is avoided by returning these products or its residuals to a collection system, a refund of the surcharge follows
- Deposit-refund on short-cycle goods (packaging and batteries)
- Deposit-refund on durables (cars)

Functions

- Short-cycle goods: to facilitate reuse or recycling; durables: mainly to facilitate recycling and proper scrapping
- The performance of deposit-refund systems mainly is measured by the percentage of return of the related products
- Results of 40 to 100% were reported, and are 80% on average

Applications

- Number of applications is increasing
- Greater variety of short-cycle products under a DRS, extending from glass bottles and cans to plastic bottles, batteries, light bulbs and paint cans

Policy role

- DRS are components in environmental policy (waste management) programmes

---

1.3 Current practice in the use of economic instruments

A comprehensive survey of the use of economic instruments in OECD Member countries' environmental policies was presented in OECD (1989*a*). This found a wide range of applications of economic instruments in the environmental policies of OECD countries. These included charges (of various types, including emissions charges, product charges, administrative charges and tax differentiation), subsidies, deposit-refund systems, market creation instruments (including tradeable permits, market intervention and liability insurance), and financial enforcement incentives (including non-compliance fees and performance bonds).

In total, there were over 150 instances in 14 OECD countries where "some form of economic arrangement had been made for the sake of improving environmental quality". Defining the measures to be counted as economic instruments more narrowly, to exclude subsidies, liability and administrative charges, the number of economic instruments in the fourteen countries is reduced to about 100, or an average of seven per country surveyed (OECD, 1994*a*). However, many of these instruments were of little significance, and only a small proportion could be categorised as economic instruments in the stricter sense of measures which use financial incentives to encourage more appropriate environmental behaviour. Indeed, the study found, economic efficiency was seldom a stated goal of the economic instruments in Member countries, except in the case of the emissions trading systems, which were largely confined to the United States; the principal objective of the charging systems operated, for example, appeared to be to raise revenues. Broadly speaking, therefore, the way in which environmental policies in OECD countries achieved changes in polluting behaviour, and consequent improvements in the environment, was through measures of the command-and-control type.

A second survey, published in 1994, covering the situation in 1992/93, found a rising trend in the use made of economic instruments in OECD countries. Comparing the eight best-documented countries, the number of economic instruments in 1992 was some 25 per cent higher than in 1987; even more economic instruments were put into operation in these countries after 1992, raising the percentage increase since 1987 to almost 50 per cent. Over all of the countries surveyed in 1987 and 1992/93, the growth in reported use of economic instruments is even larger, although the study noted that this may reflect less-than-comprehensive reporting of the 1987 position in some countries. The greatest increases were in product charges and deposit-refund systems; there appeared to be little increase in the use made of emissions charges.

As regards the intended function of the economic instruments, the majority of emissions charges still seemed to be designed mainly as revenue-raising devices, but, overall, the incentive role of economic instruments appeared to have become more prominent; in some 45 per cent of cases, economic instruments appeared to be intended to have an incentive effect (as compared to 30 per cent of cases where an incentive effect was explicitly not sought). As far as the performance of the instruments is concerned, however, the study found little evidence about the existence of incentive effects; in 90 per cent of cases, information on incentive effects was inconclusive or unavailable.

One of the main conclusions of the study concerned the absence of clear evidence on the incentive performance of economic instruments in practice. Whilst quantitative or partly quantitative performance criteria were regularly employed for *ex ante* evaluation of environmental policy instruments, "there is far too little empirical evidence to arrive at a systematic *ex post* evaluation of the significance of instruments as used in practice". Much of the available evidence reflects "incidental observations" and "observation-driven intuitions" (OECD, 1994*a*, page 181). Further work to develop evaluation methodologies and collect evidence is needed, the study argued. Without such work, "the often-heard arguments of ineffectiveness or low elasticity will continue to be heard and constitute obstacles to a rational application of economic incentives. The same holds for the issue of administrative implementability; there is no *a priori* case that economic incentives are more difficult to implement, but this could be supported by much more empirical evidence" (OECD, 1994*a*, page 189).

Subsequent OECD work (OECD, 1996) has looked at strategies for implementing environmental taxes. How have these taxes been introduced in OECD countries, and what role do they play in environmental and fiscal policies? The report concludes that increasing use in being made of environmental taxes, including environmental taxes designed to provide incentives to achieve particular environmental policy objectives. Environmental tax policies are also, increasingly, being implemented as part of an integrated approach to tax reform, in which revenues from environmental taxes are used to permit reductions in labour taxes and/or other existing taxes.

Box 5. **Economic instruments in OECD countries' environmental policy: some examples**

Charges and Taxes

- Water pollution charges in France, Germany and the Netherlands
- Nitrogen oxides charge in Sweden
- Sulphur tax in Sweden
- Carbon taxes in Finland, Sweden, Denmark, the Netherlands

Tradeable permits systems

- Tradeable water pollution permits in the USA (Fox River, Wisconsin; Dillon Reservoir, Colorado; Tar-Pamlico River, North Carolina)
- Emissions trading in the USA
- Inter-refinery lead trading in the USA (expired)

User charges

- "Pay-per-bag" for domestic refuse collection: in some municipalities in USA, Germany, Switzerland

Deposit-refund systems

- Mandatory or negotiated deposit-refund systems in parts of the USA (*e.g.* Michigan), Sweden, Norway, Denmark, Germany

Table 1. **Overview of environmentally-related taxes/charges in OECD countries** (as of January 1997)[a]

Environmental Tax Measures	Australia	Austria	Belgium	Canada	Czech Republic	Denmark	Finland	France	Germany	Greece	Hungary	Iceland	Ireland	Italy	Japan	Luxembourg	Mexico	Netherlands	New Zealand	Norway	Poland	Portugal	Spain	Sweden	Switzerland	Turkey	United Kingdom	United States
Motor Fuels:																												
Leaded/Unleaded (differential)	●	●	●			●	●	●	●	●	●	●	●	●		●	●	●	●	●	●	●	●	●	●	●	●	
Gasoline (quality differential)							●																	●				
Diesel (quality differential)						●	●				●						●			●	●			●				
Carbon/energy taxation						●	●											●		●				●				
Sulphur tax																				●				●				
Other excise taxes (other than VAT)	●	●	●	●	●	●	●	●	●	●	●	●	●	●	●	●	●	●	●	●	●	●	●	●	●	●	●	●
Other Energy Products:																												
Other excise taxes	●	●	●			●	●	●	●	●	●		●	●	●	●	●	●		●			●	●	●		●	●
Carbon/Energy tax		●	●			●	●											●		●	●			●				
Sulphur tax or charge			●			●		●							●					●	●			●				
NO$_x$ charge					●			●													●							
Vehicle Related Taxation:																												
Sales/Excise/Regist. tax diff. (cars)		●	●	●	●	●	●			●	●	●	●	●	●		●	●		●		●		●	●	●		●
Road/Registration tax diff. (cars)		●	●	●	●	●			●	●	●	●	●	●			●	●		●			●	●	●	●		●
Agricultural Inputs:																												
Taxes or charges on fertilisers																				●				●				
Taxes or charges on pesticides						●	●													●				●				

a) This table does not include taxes/charges levied at state or regional level.

Table 1. **Overview of environmentally-related taxes/charges in OECD countries** (as of January 1997)[a] *(continued)*

Environmental Tax Measures	Australia	Austria	Belgium	Canada	Czech Republic	Denmark	Finland	France	Germany	Greece	Hungary	Iceland	Ireland	Italy	Japan	Luxembourg	Mexico	Netherlands	New Zealand	Norway	Poland	Portugal	Spain	Sweden	Switzerland	Turkey	United Kingdom	United States
Other goods:																												
Batteries			●			●					●													●	●			
Plastic carrier bags						●					●	●									●							
Disposable containers			●			●	●				●	●								●	●							
Tyres				●		●	●				●																	●
CFCs and/or halons					●	●					●										●							●
Disposable razors			●																									
Disposable cameras			●																									
Lubricant Oil Charge							●													●								
Oil Pollution Charge	●						●																					
Solvents						●																						
Direct Tax Provisions:																												
Env. Investments/Accelerated depreciation	●	●	●	●	●	●	●	●			●				●		●	●		●	●	●						●
Free company car part of taxable income							●		●																			
Employer-paid commuting expenses part of taxable income	●		●			●	●		●													●	●	●			●	●
Free parking part of taxable income	●																											●
Commuting expenses deductible from tax. income *only* if pub. transport used																												●

a) This table does not include taxes/charges levied at state or regional level.

Table I. **Overview of environmentally-related taxes/charges in OECD countries** (as of January 1997)[a] *(continued)*

Environmental Tax Measures	Australia	Austria	Belgium	Canada	Czech Republic	Denmark	Finland	France	Germany	Greece	Hungary	Iceland	Ireland	Italy	Japan	Luxembourg	Mexico	Netherlands	New Zealand	Norway	Poland	Portugal	Spain	Sweden	Switzerland	Turkey	United Kingdom	United States
Air transport:																												
Noise charges	●		●					●	●		●				●			●		●	●			●	●			
Other taxes				●																●		●		●				●
Water:																												
Water charges	●		●		●	●	●	●	●		●						●	●		●	●			●	●		●	●
Sewage charges	●		●		●	●	●		●		●						●	●		●	●	●	●	●	●	●	●	●
Water effluent charges	●		●		●	●		●	●			●					●	●			●	●			●			
Manure charges																		●										
Waste Disposal and Management:																												
Municipal waste charges	●			●	●	●	●	●	●		●	●						●		●	●	●	●	●	●			●
Waste disposal charges	●	●	●		●	●	●	●	●		●		●	●				●		●	●	●	●		●	●	●	
Hazardous waste charges	●	●	●		●		●		●		●	●								●	●	●						
Landfill tax or charges																		●									●	

a) This table does not include taxes/charges levied at state or regional level.

1.4 The potential contribution of evaluation evidence

In principle, the case for using economic instruments in environmental policies may be supported by analysis of three main sorts.

Theoretical arguments

First, much of the initial advocacy of economic instruments has been based on *theoretical or conceptual argument*. Economic theory may be used to evaluate the costs and benefits of economic instruments and conventional "command-and-control" regulations, in the context of a theoretical model, representing the behaviour of profit-maximising firms and a set of defined objectives for environmental policy. Analysis of this sort can indicate the range of relevant costs and benefits which will arise in the choice between different policy instruments, for the given set of assumptions about polluter behaviour. In some circumstances it may be possible to derive unambiguous conclusions about the merits of particular policy instruments, but more generally theoretical analysis can only indicate the range of conditions in which one set of policy would be preferable to another. Whether the particular conditions which would favour a particular instrument are satisfied in practice is an issue which cannot be resolved by theoretical argument, but depends on empirical evidence about the conditions existing in the practical application.

Ex ante *assessments*

A second form of analysis regarding the costs and benefits of using economic instruments takes the form of *ex ante quantification* of the potential benefits of different policy options, on the basis of data about the relevant environmental problems and economic context. Thus, it may be possible to evaluate some of the key parameters in advance of actual experience with economic instruments in environmental policy. The basis on which such *ex ante* quantifications may be made can include evidence of a number of different sorts. Thus, it may include data on the relative significance of various key magnitudes – for example, the "static efficiency" case for economic instruments will be stronger, relative to command-and-control regulation, the greater the differences between polluters in the marginal costs of pollution abatement. It may also be possible to assess the likely strength of polluter responses to policy measures from evidence about polluter behaviour in similar economic circumstances. Thus, for example, evidence about the price elasticity of demand for energy, resulting from periods when the price of energy fluctuated as a result of changes in market supplies and demands may be used to assess the likely response of energy users to imposition of higher energy taxes in the form of a carbon tax.

Ex post *evidence*

Third, the case for using economic instruments in environmental policy may also be analysed on the basis of *ex post evidence* of the performance of such instruments in practice. Such analysis can answer questions which cannot be definitively assessed by analyses of the first two sorts. Both theory and *ex ante* quantitative analysis can only suggest the likely consequences of using economic instruments, on given assumptions about behavioural responses, and other relevant factors. Theoretical analyses depend on assumptions that the behaviour of polluters and other relevant parties will conform to the assumptions of a particular theoretical model of behaviour. Quantitative analyses based on *ex ante* data, likewise, have to assume that responses will conform to predictions of theory, or to the patterns observed in response to other, analogous, episodes. Ex *post* analysis of the experience of using economic instruments in practice can provide evidence of a fundamentally different sort, in that it can show the pattern of actual responses to economic instruments, and can provide data, based on experience, regarding a number of other issues (such as costs of administration and compliance) which are not easily evaluated on the basis of theoretical argument or *ex ante* quantification.

1.5 Why is evaluation needed?

Assessment of the effectiveness and efficiency of economic instruments for environmental protection is a building block of comprehensive environmental policy evaluation. The project launched by OECD on effectiveness and efficiency of economic instruments has a number of objectives:

- increase awareness about the need to evaluate policy instruments in general, and economic instruments in particular;
- devise a methodological approach for obtaining data for evaluation;
- collect and analyse such data.

The general background of this initiative is the observation that *there is little tradition in policy evaluation*. To put it more exactly, there is little tradition in *ex post* evaluation, if compared with *ex ante* evaluation, or project and policy appraisal, that has extensively been studied since the early days of cost-benefit analysis.[6] Ex *post* policy evaluation is a common activity in the field of government finance, where accounting conventions facilitate policy assessment. Ex *post* policy evaluation is less common in other policy fields, including environmental policy, although some initiatives can be recorded.

Advantages and functions of evaluations

Policy evaluation may have several functions. A first and important function *is the review of policy instruments in practice*. It is usually taken for granted that instruments, once their implementation has been decided on, are implemented, and are correctly implemented.[7] The road from the political decision for implementation to operationality is full of pitfalls. This could end up in incorrect, or even completely ineffective implementation.

A second function is the review of the *performance* of policy instruments. Are introduced measures achieving what they were meant to achieve, for example in terms of effectiveness, and in terms of efficiency?

A third function is the *comparison of the performance* of introduced instruments with the assessed impact of alternative instruments that were not chosen in the *ex ante* policy appraisal. Retrospective analysis might reveal the need for other, or additional, policy measures.

A fourth function of policy evaluation is *improving the policy instrument design and implementation*. Environmental policy still is an extending policy field, and the policy instrument mix is further developing. Although direct regulation still is the dominant type of instrument, economic instruments and communicative instruments, such as covenants, are gaining ground.[8] The latter types of instruments are relatively young, and there might be room for improvement in the design as well as in implementation, once their functioning has been properly evaluated. Particularly mixes of (different types of) instruments may benefit from evaluation as to their design and implementation, if feedback could be established.

Other pros of policy evaluation include *providing information* for stakeholders, and providing a vehicle for *consultation and negotiation* on specific instruments.

Drawbacks

Policy evaluation, however, is not without drawbacks. If executed properly, evaluation requires considerable amounts of time and money. Many technical difficulties have to be surmounted. One of these difficulties concerns adequate data collection. Improper, partial or superficial, evaluation may result in incomplete, or even incorrect, conclusions, which may decrease the reliance of parties concerned on the evaluation process, and impede successful instrument practice. Focusing on evaluation of economic instruments runs the risk of putting this type of instruments at a disadvantage, compared with other instruments. Evaluation necessarily uses simplified models which are easy to criticise.

Box 6. **CO_2 taxes in the Netherlands**

One of the elements in the preparation of CO_2/energy taxes concerned the institution of a Steering Committee on Regulatory Energy Taxes. This committee was established by the Ministers of Economic Affairs and of the Environment. Its instruction was to co-ordinate research into regulatory energy taxes. The primary goal of such taxes was formulated as "to realise additional energy conservation, with a view to its favourable impact on sustainable development in general and CO_2 emissions in particular". The Committee had not been asked to advise on the desirability of such taxes from the instrumental point of view.

In its final report, the Committee concluded that an OECD-wide tax of 100 per cent would result in a reduction of energy use of 32 per cent in 2000 and 36 per cent in 2015, of which 25 to 30 per cent would be the result of replacement of economic activities. Thus, energy conservation through better efficiency would amount to 5 to 10 per cent. A tax on the national level would result in slightly higher conservation, the charge on small-scale users would have considerably lower effects. Macro-economic effects would be larger if the tax is levied on the national level only. Macro effects are smaller if the tax is levied at small-scale users only, but it will have a more significant distributional impact.

Observations were made that extensive *ex ante* evaluation of the tax system lead to overexposure of the role of economic instruments, which became a drawback in the preparation of the tax system. As a matter of fact, the Commission did not investigate the impact on energy conservation and on economic parameters of alternative policy instruments.

Source: *Final Report of the Steering Committee on Regulatory Energy Taxes*, 1992

Policy evaluation might be able to uncover in detail the policy making process, or the process in which instruments are brought to operationality. This is not always a positive result, as it may weaken positions of policy makers in related policy decision processes. Apart from that, policy makers may be inclined to ignore evaluations, if the results do not suit their targets. Ignoring review results is possible since the recommendations of policy reviews are normally not enforceable.

Regarding evaluation of economic instruments, the need for data is another case in point. One of the textbook advantages of economic instruments is the reduced need of information by authorities. This advantage might be questioned if the evaluation framework should increase data requirements.

In summary, adequate policy evaluation could be a helpful tool for assessing the performance of instruments and for improving instrument design and implementation, if possible drawbacks are taken into account, in other words if the value of evaluation results is correctly assessed.

It is important, however, not to overexpose economic instruments compared to other approaches to environmental policy.

Where there is insufficient data for assessing the qualities of economic instruments, *vis-à-vis* other policy instruments, a rational application of such instruments is impeded. If theoretical claims of effectiveness and efficiency are not empirically illustrated, practical considerations may favour the use of existing policy instruments, without thoroughly investigating their adequacy. H*owever, one should also be careful not to overexpose one type of instruments, compared with other types*. Indeed, promoting evaluation of economic instruments could result in increased attention for assessing the effects of applied and potential policy instruments in terms of their ability to contribute to realisation of the goals of environmental policy. But comparing positive, theoretical aspects of one instrument with negative, practical points of other instruments should be avoided. Anyhow, prospective planning of evaluation by means of an in-built evaluation framework could contribute to appropriate appraisal of environmental policy and of its results.

Like in the case of evaluation of policy instruments in general, evaluation of economic instruments as part of the package may encounter several drawbacks. One point in case is that industry and consumers tend to object against economic instruments, notably charges and taxes, which obviously give rise to cost or price increases. They will follow government policy evaluation and conclusions thereof with more than the usual suspicion. This is the more important since focusing on evaluation of economic instruments, more than on instruments in general, may raise suspicion in itself, drawing too much attention to the performance of this type of instrument.

Chapter 2

THE CASE FOR ECONOMIC INSTRUMENTS – TYPES OF EVIDENCE

This chapter briefly reviews the arguments in favour of using economic instruments in environmental policy. The intention is not simply to repeat well-known arguments, but to provide a reminder of the expectations which existing arguments have prompted regarding the efficiency and effectiveness of economic instruments.

2.1 Theoretical arguments

a) Advantages of economic instruments

Advocates of market mechanisms have stressed the potential for efficiency gains (greater cost-effectiveness) in environmental policy when the price mechanism is used to encourage reduced pollution.[9] These potential efficiency gains would have both a static and a dynamic dimension.

Static efficiency

The static efficiency gains from the use of market-based instruments arise in situations where polluters face different opportunities for pollution abatement, or different marginal abatement costs. The efficient, cost-minimising, pattern of pollution abatement would require greater reductions in pollution by those polluters for which the cost of each unit of pollution abatement was low, and would impose less stringent levels of abatement on polluters facing a high marginal cost of abatement.

In theory, a fully-informed regulatory agency could tailor regulatory requirements to the circumstances of each polluter so as to achieve this outcome. However, regulatory agencies rarely have access to the kinds of information necessary to design the efficient allocation of abatement across polluters; much of the necessary information concerning relative abatement costs is in the hands of individual firms, who may not wish to reveal it to the regulator. Given these informational limitations on regulatory policy, it is more likely that regulatory rules will be applied uniformly to all polluters. Polluters with high abatement costs will be required to undertake as much abatement as those with lower costs, and pollution abatement will be more costly than the efficient minimum.

Market mechanisms have the attraction that they may induce polluters to choose the efficient, cost-minimising, pattern of abatement in response to the price signal they provide (Baumol, 1972). A pollution tax, for example, that is imposed on each unit of emissions will mean that polluters with low abatement costs will be more likely to choose to abate, and to make larger reductions in emissions, than polluters for whom the costs of abatement are high. Polluters with low abatement costs will, in effect, volunteer to contribute higher levels of abatement, because the emissions tax makes additional abatement profitable for them. Conversely, the tax puts an upper limit on the cost of any abatement which takes place; polluters for which unit abatement costs exceed the potential tax saving will not find it worthwhile to undertake abatement measures.

Dynamic efficiency

In addition to the potential static efficiency advantages of market mechanisms, they may also confer dynamic efficiency gains, by providing an incentive for research and development in pollution abatement technologies (Wenders, 1975; Magat, 1978; Milliman and Prince, 1989). Even at the level of emissions which constitutes the current cost-minimising level, polluters will continue to face an incentive to look for further cost-effective ways of achieving emissions reductions; with an emissions tax, for example, this incentive arises because polluters pay the tax on any remaining units of pollution. There is thus a potential gain to be made from the development of new technologies which would allow the level of pollution to be reduced still further. Market mechanisms may thus hold out the possibility of a more rapid rate of development of pollution-control technologies than regulatory policies, which provide polluters with little incentive to abate pollution by more than the minimum required to comply with regulatory requirements.

Revenues

Both the static and dynamic efficiency arguments apply to market mechanisms in general. A further potential benefit of using market-based environmental policies may arise where these raise revenues (for example, the cases of emissions taxes or auctioned tradeable permits). The revenues raised from environmental taxes could allow other taxes, with possible distortionary effects on labour supply, investment or consumption, to be reduced. Empirical studies of the marginal distortionary costs (excess burden) of existing taxes show that these costs can be appreciable. For example, Ballard, Shoven and Whalley (1985) estimate the marginal excess burden of public revenues in the US at 20-30 cents for each extra dollar of tax revenue. Terkla (1984) compares the environmental benefits from pollution abatement using emissions taxes with estimates of the dead-weight loss that would be incurred in raising the same revenue through general taxation, and concludes that the reduction in excess burden permitted by the revenues from the emissions taxes could be of the same order of magnitude as their environmental benefits.

b) Issues raised by economic instruments

Monopoly power

Against these potential advantages of market mechanisms need to be set some potential disadvantages, and limitations on their applicability. One noted by Buchanan (1969) concerns the case where polluters have some degree of monopoly power in the output market. Firms may make use of their monopoly power to increase profits by reducing output below the competitive level; imposition of a pollution tax may then have the effect of inducing further reductions in output, below the socially optimal level. Regulatory policies, on the other hand, may not induce reductions in output on the same scale, and therefore may not add to the existing costs of monopoly power. Whilst this drawback of market mechanisms is recognised as a theoretical possibility, it has been demonstrated that in practice its quantitative significance may be low (Oates and Strassmann, 1984).

Uncertainty

A major difference between economic instruments which use the price mechanism to discourage pollution and regulatory policies which set quantitative emissions limits for individual polluters is the impact of uncertainty on the pollution outcome and the costs of abatement. Using a pollution tax, for example, the amount of pollution is the result of individual polluters' decisions in response to the incentive provided by the tax; this can turn out to be greater or less than envisaged when the rate of tax was set. With quantitative regulation, it may be possible to achieve greater certainty about the level of pollution abatement that will be achieved (assuming, of course, that regulations are properly enforced, which may not always be the case).

This does not, however, mean that quantitative regulation should always be preferred to market mechanisms in situations of uncertainty, for two reasons. First, the counterpart of the reduced uncertainty about polluting emissions under regulation is greater uncertainty about the economic costs of achieving the required level of abatement. These two potential costs of uncertainty thus have to be balanced one against the other, and certainty about pollution levels will not always be more important than placing an upper limit on the costs of pollution abatement. Second, even where the pattern of uncertainty points in the direction of choosing instruments which deliver a certain pollution outcome, market mechanisms are available, in the form of *tradeable permits*, which limit the aggregate pollution quantity to a fixed level rather than limiting aggregate pollution through price. The impact of uncertainty on policy does not therefore rule out the use of economic instruments, although it may affect the choice made between the different possible economic instruments which could be employed.

Tax burden

The obstacles to implementing environmental policies based on market incentives have also included concerns about the level of the financial burden that certain types of market incentives may place on polluters; these have included concern about the burden of environmental taxes and charges on both households and industry.

c)   *Balancing pros and cons*

Theoretical arguments thus point to a range of relevant considerations, some of which are likely to favour the use of economic instruments; other of which signal the circumstances where conventional regulatory policies based on command-and-control may be superior to the use of economic instruments. There are also further relevant issues, such as the costs of administration, the ease and effectiveness of enforcement, and the likely level of public acceptance, about which theory can provide little guide to policy. The balance of the argument between market mechanisms and conventional regulation, in any particular case, is unlikely to be settled purely by the theoretical arguments; the relative significance of the various considerations will need to be evaluated, and a balance drawn between costs and benefits. This generally will require various forms of empirical evidence, in addition to theoretical argumentation.

Empirical evidence will also be important in *choosing between the various possible forms* of economic instrument – taxes, charges, tradeable permits, etc. Theoretical arguments may provide even less conclusive guidance in choosing between the various types of economic instrument; what may matter much more are judgements about how far different instruments are likely to perform in practice, about the administrative and compliance costs they would impose, and about the public acceptability of different mechanism.

2.2 Ex ante analysis (forecasting and simulation studies)

Ex *ante* quantification of the costs and benefits of employing economic instruments in environmental policy tend to fall into one of two general categories.

First, there are studies which seek to quantify key magnitudes, on the basis of given assumptions about the way in which polluters and other individuals involved in the process will respond. Typically, these assumptions involve some form of "optimising" behaviour, in the form of an assumption of profit maximisation for enterprises, or utility maximisation for individuals. Second, there are studies based on inferences drawn from "analogous" episodes, such as for example, econometric studies of the effects of past changes in energy prices on patterns of energy use and consumption. Typically, these studies provide evidence on the consequences of using economic instruments in environmental policy on the basis of an

Table 2. **Empirical studies of the potential gains from least-cost air pollution control**

	Pollutants covered	Area covered	"Command-and-control" policy benchmark	Ratio of CAC cost to least-cost policy
Atkinson and Lewis (1974)	Particulates	St Louis	State Implementation Plan (SIP) regulations	6.00
Roach *et al.* (1981)	Sulphur dioxide	For Corners, Utah, Colorado, Arizona, New Mexico	State Implementation Plan (SIP) regulations	4.25
Hahn and Noll (1982)	Sulphates standards	Los Angeles	California emission standards	1.07
Krupnick (1986)	Nitrogen dioxide regulations	Baltimore	Proposed RACT (technology requirements)	5.96
Seskin *et al.* (1983)	Nitrogen dioxide regulations	Chicago	Proposed RACT (technology requirements)	14.40
McGartland (1984)	Particulates	Baltimore	State Implementation Plan (SIP) regulations	4.18
Spofford (1984)	Sulphur dioxide	Lower Delaware Valley	Uniform percentage reductions	1.78
	Particulates	Lower Delaware Valley	Uniform percentage reductions	22.00
Harrison (1983)	Airport noise	United States	Mandatory retrofit	1.72
Maloney and Yandle (1984)	Hydrocarbons	US DuPont plants	Uniform percentage reduction	4.15
Palmer *et al.* (1980)	CFC emissions excl. aerosols	United States	Proposed emission standards	1.96

Note: Methodological footnotes omitted here; for details see original source.
Source: T.H. Tietenberg, (1990), Economic Instruments for Environmental Regulation, *Oxford Review of Economic Policy*, Vol. 6, No. 1, p. 24.

assumption that individuals will respond in the same way to the economic instrument as to the analogous economic conditions observed in the past.

One influential group of studies based on optimising assumptions have been empirical studies using data on the pattern of abatement costs across different polluters to calculate the total costs of achieving a given level of pollution abatement, on different assumptions about how the aggregate abatement requirement is divided amongst different polluters. Typically, these studies compare the costs of achieving the efficient (in the sense of cost-minimising) pattern of abatement across polluters, with the total abatement costs when the reductions in pollution are distributed across polluters according to particular rules, representing the operation of certain types of command-and-control policies. Thus, for example, policies may compare the efficient pattern of abatement with the costs of achieving the same reduction in pollution by requiring all polluters to reduce emissions by the same percentage. Where polluters face widely-differing marginal costs of abatement, the costs of the equal-abatement policy will be substantially higher than the costs of the efficient policy. If market instruments were to achieve the cost-minimising pattern of abatement, then these studies would show the net economic benefit from achieving the given level of abatement using economic instruments. However, this depends on the assumption that economic instruments would be effective at securing the optimal, cost-minimising abatement pattern. If, in practice, polluters respond to economic instruments in ways which depart from the optimising model, then this will overstate the gains from using economic instruments.

Ex *ante* empirical studies of the costs of pollution abatement using this general methodology have included key papers by Krupnick (1986), Atkinson and Lewis (1974) and Seskin, Anderson and Reid (1983). Tietenberg (1990) surveys a range of estimates, and concludes that these studies generally show that there are substantial potential economic gains from using a policy instrument which would efficiently allocate emissions reductions between polluters, rather than the type of equal-abatement rule which frequently results from conventional command-and-control regulation.

A second way in which optimising assumptions can be used as the basis for *ex ante* assessment of the potential quantitative costs and benefits from using economic instruments is through the use of *linear programming models* of polluter behaviour. (Similar issues and possibilities arise in the case of other numerically-calibrated optimising models, such as computable general-equilibrium models recently employed on a wide scale to assess the effects of carbon taxes on energy use). Linear programming models take as a starting point a particular representation of the technological options facing a firm, and then calculate the cost-minimising pattern of inputs required to achieve a given pattern of production. If input prices change, for example as a result of the taxation of a particular input, then the optimal pattern of input use will change, generally substituting away from the taxed input. The linear programming model can show the size of the substitution, on the assumption of continuing cost minimisation. Using linear programming analyses to assess the consequences of policy measures which change the costs of a particular input, or otherwise restrict its use, rests on a clear assumption of optimising behaviour on the part of firms – it is assumed that they adjust, in response to policy, to use the new cost-minimising pattern of inputs and production.

Examples of studies using linear programming techniques to assess *ex ante* the likely effects of economic instruments include a number of studies of the effects of taxes on fertilisers or pesticides in agriculture. Given a linear programming model of the production of a typical farm, it is possible to see how the optimal (cost-minimising) level of fertiliser or pesticides inputs changes, in response to changes in their price. A number of studies of this sort for the case of fertiliser taxes are surveyed by Burrell (1989). Given that the calculations depend on the assumption of optimal adjustment to the changes in input prices, it is possible that these analyses may tend to overstate the likely scale of response, if producers respond, in practice, rather less sensitively to changes in input prices.

There are also a wide range of studies which seek to infer the likely quantitative consequences of using economic instruments in environmental policy on the basis of evidence from "analogous" economic changes or policy measures. The historical experience of the effects of large fluctuations in energy prices following the two OPEC oil price hikes in the 1970s has provided a good basis for assessing, using econometric techniques, the level and pattern of industrial and consumer responses to changes in energy prices. This, in turn, has provided important evidence on the likely consequences of future policy measures designed to tackle global warming through energy pricing measures. Similarly, econometric studies have assessed the effects of price changes for fertilisers and pesticides on the use of these inputs in agriculture.

The condition for being able to obtain evidence of this sort is, of course, that some past analogous episode can be found, to be used as the basis for econometric estimation. For a number of important economic instruments, no useful analogue can be found. For example, in the case of the introduction of the tax differential in favour of unleaded petrol, there is no past experience of the relevant changes in relative prices, and thus no past basis on which to assess the future consequences of introducing such a differential into motor fuel taxation.

The key assumption in using past statistical relationships to predict the consequences of introducing a new instrument of environmental policy is that individual responses to the environmental policy should be made on the same basis as in the earlier episode. Thus, for example, in using data on the past relationship between energy prices and energy use to infer the consequences of new environmental taxes on energy, it is being assumed that energy users respond to environmental taxes on energy in the same way as they responded to past historical fluctuations in energy prices. Whilst past energy price changes may well be a good guide to general orders of magnitude involved, it is possible to think of some reasons for different responses by energy consumers to market fluctuations in energy prices and to environmental policy measures which increase the price of energy. These may include:

– announcement effects in policy, which may influence the time profile of economic adjustments;
– different expectations regarding the durability of energy price changes; if the fluctuations in energy prices (or the environmental policy) are regarded as temporary, energy users are unlikely to choose to incur the substantial investment costs involved in reducing their energy use;

- differences in the international context; for example, environmental taxes on energy introduced in some countries but not in others could result in some international displacement of energy-intensive industries, which would not have arisen in the case of market fluctuations in the world energy price;

- possible differences in consumer attitudes – for example, higher taxes on energy may be a signal which might encourage greater energy saving by environmentally-aware consumers.

2.3 Ex *post* evidence (evaluation)

The potential gains from the availability of *ex post* evidence on the performance in practice of economic instruments are that such evidence is not subject to the assumptions that are required to make *ex ante* quantifications of the likely consequences of economic instruments.

Thus, in comparison to estimates based on optimising assumptions, *ex post* evidence is able to assess the effects of economic instruments, given the actual responsiveness and motivations in practice of firms and individuals. If, as a result of organisational inefficiency or other considerations not included in the optimising analysis, some firms do not respond to policy in ways which minimise costs, this will be reflected in *ex post* analysis. Similarly, if firms or individuals respond differently to environmental policy measures to the way they respond to market fluctuations in the prices of energy or other inputs, this can be observed and assessed from *ex post* evidence.

As a result, *ex post* analysis of the performance in practice of economic instruments in environmental policy is able to provide more firmly-based evidence about key responses affecting the environmental and economic effectiveness of economic instruments than can be obtained on the basis of considering theoretical argument or *ex ante* forecasts alone.

2.4 Evaluation criteria

An evaluation of any policy instrument must be done with refence to a set of well-defined criteria. These criteria are presented in detail in Chapter 7. However, it is worth repeating them briefly here so they can be used as yardsticks for the evaluation evidence presented in Part II.

Environmental effectiveness relates to the environmental impact and performance of the instrument studied, *i.e.* how much the instrument contributes to the achievement of the policy objective (if defined), or to reductions in emissions (if no specific objective is defined).

Economic efficiency refers to the extent to which the instrument has enabled a more cost-effective achievement of policy objectives, compared to some alternative instrument. In particular, economic theory indicates that the main advantage of economic instruments is their potential for minimising the aggregate pollution-abatement costs across polluters. Whether or not economic instruments provide real cost savings is a key, albeit complex, issue.

Administration and compliance costs relate to the administrative and managerial cost burden imposed on the administrative bodies responsible for applying the instrument, and the economic agents subject to the instrument (*e.g.* the eco-taxpayer). The characteristics and relative complexity of policy instruments surely influence this cost burden.

Revenues: some economic insruments, in particular charges and taxes, provide government revenue. The size and affectation of this revenue is a key feature of the operation of the policy instrument.

Wider economic effects include, *inter alia*, impacts on the price level, technical innovation, income distribution, employment and trade.

Dynamic effects and innovation: economic instruments are generally expected to be more effective than other instruments at stimulating innovation in pollution control technologies.

"Soft effects" refer to various possible effects of economic instruments in terms of *e.g.* changes in attitudes and awareness, capacity building, and the generation and diffusion of information. Although difficult, if not impossible, to quantify, these effects are often quite relevant.

Part II

AVAILABLE EVIDENCE

This part of the report considers existing evaluation evidence on market mechanisms in environmental policy. Data from existing studies on a number of different market mechanisms in OECD Member states are summarised in Chapters 3-6. These consider, firstly, what the existing evaluation evidence shows about the performance of a range of economic instruments, and secondly, what lessons can be learned from these studies about the feasibility and effective design of *ex post* evaluations.

The examples of economic instruments discussed in this report do not attempt to provide a comprehensive coverage of all evaluation evidence on environmental policies using economic instruments in Member states; there are undoubtedly both official and published studies which have been omitted. Nevertheless, they cover most of the major policy initiatives in this area taken by Member states, with a reasonably-broad spread across different instrument types.

They have been chosen principally on the pragmatic basis that data or studies have been found on the *ex post* performance of the instruments employed. In general, this means that the studies are confined to relatively well-established measures, for which enough time has elapsed for experience and data to have been developed on actual performance. The studies, nonetheless, cover a considerable range of instruments, including both tradeable permit and charge/tax measures. A range of environmental problems is also covered, including instruments relating to water pollution (charge and tradeable permit schemes in Europe and the US respectively), air pollution (sulphur and nitrogen oxides taxes in Scandinavia, and emissions trading in the US), the introduction of unleaded petrol (lead trading credits in the US, and the tax differentials in favour of unleaded petrol operated in many European countries), household waste (unit charges for waste collection, and deposit-refund systems for bottles and other polluting goods), and common-property resources (tradeable quotas in fisheries management).

In some instances, the introduction of policy was preceded by explicit *ex ante* study of the consequences of the policy; where appropriate these studies are mentioned as a preliminary to the discussion of *ex post* material, since a key issue addressed in the paper is the extent to which *ex post* analysis can provide more firmly-based information about key aspects of the performance of economic instruments than can *ex ante* analysis or argument.

The principal absence concerns evidence of the performance of the carbon taxes introduced recently in a number of OECD Member states. Although there have been many *ex ante* evaluations of carbon taxes, little new information about the key issues would be provided by *ex post* evaluation of the relatively limited experience with such taxes to date. This experience is unlikely to provide much indication of the economic or environmental effectiveness of such instruments, since the economic adjustments to changes in energy prices are likely to be spread over an adjustment period of as much as fifteen years, whilst the environmental effects of policy measures to combat global warming have to do with very long-term changes to climate patterns. It is therefore really too soon to hope to assemble any meaningful data based on *ex post* evaluation of experience regarding key aspects of the efficiency and effectiveness of carbon tax policies.

Chapter 3

CHARGES AND TAXES: WATER

3.1 Policy background

Water pollution is regulated in most European countries primarily through "command-and-control" forms of regulation. A number of countries operate systems of user charges for water emissions, as mechanisms for raising revenues for water pollution control, alongside the basic framework of command-and-control regulation. The boundary between revenue-raising user charges and incentive mechanisms may be difficult to define in practice with any clarity (Andersen, 1991). In at least three of the European systems with revenue-raising water charges, France, Germany and the Netherlands, the potential for these charge systems also to have some incentive effect has been noted, and subject to considerable analysis (Bower *et al.*, 1981; Bressers, 1988; Bongerts and Kraemer, 1989; Andersen, 1994).

As part of the present OECD work programme three case studies have summarised the operation of these charge systems, and evidence on their effectiveness. A fourth, synthesis, paper has drawn together comparative results from the three evaluations.

3.2 The Netherlands

In the Netherlands the water pollution charges are based on the 1969 Act on Pollution of Surface Water (W*et verontreiniging oppervlaktewater*, WVO). This established both a regulatory system of discharge licences, and a system of water charges to finance the costs of water treatment. Charges for discharges are levied by both the national water authority and the water boards at provincial level.

The charges reflect the number of "pollution equivalents" that are in the particular discharge, where one pollution equivalent is standardised to the amount of effluent that an individual produces. The charges are set so that they finance the costs of pollution control activities, and consequently have risen, as the costs of pollution control investments have risen. Compared to other European countries, the level of charges in the Netherlands is relatively high for both firms and households.

Households pay a flat rate charge equivalent to three pollution equivalents (or one if there is only one person in the household). For firms, the system is applied on a different basis to three categories. First, small companies, with a pollution load below about five pollution equivalents, pay a fixed rate. Second, companies of intermediate size, normally pay the levy according to a schedule which takes into account the number of employees, the type of activity, and consumption of water and raw materials. Third, larger firms, with emissions above 1 000 pollution equivalents, pay charges which are based on measurements of the quantity and concentration of emissions. This system is also available to companies in the intermediate category which wish to opt for direct measurement in place of the schedule-based charge.

Table 3. **Water pollution charges in France, Germany and The Netherlands compared**

	France	Germany	The Netherlands (non-State waters)
Agency operating the charge	Basin Committees (*Comités de bassin*)	State governments (*Länder*)	Water boards for discharges to non-State waters; Ministry of Transport and water for discharges to State waters
Charge rate set by:	Water basin agencies, subject to Ministry of Finance approval	Federal government	Water basin agencies (National government for discharges to State waters)
Geographical variation in rates?	Yes	No	Yes (except for discharges to State waters)
Charges paid by:	Municipalities with more than 400 inhabitants; large firms	Municipalities for household direct discharges, sewage treatment plants, firms	Households, sewage treatment plants discharging to state waters, firms.
Charge revenue (ecu *per capita*)	8.5	2.0	41.1
Change in revenue 1985-92	+56%	−44%	+20%
Revenue earmarked for water pollution abatement policies?	Yes	Yes	Yes

Source: Based on A. De Savornin Lohman, "The Efficiency and Effectiveness of Water Effluent Charges in France, Germany and the Netherlands: a Synthesis of Available Evidence," paper prepared for the OECD Environment Directorate.

As set out by Klok *et al.* (1994) in a comprehensive assessment of the system, there have been three principal evaluation studies of the operation of the system of water emissions charges in the Netherlands, by Bressers (1983), General Accounting Office (1987), and Schuurman (1988). The studies by Bressers and Schuurman both address the question of the effects of the surface water pollution charge, and attempt to assess the extent to which changes in emissions behaviour can be attributed to the operation of the charge; the study by the General Accounting Office, by contrast, was principally designed to identify factors impeding the operation of the water quality policy.

Table 4. **Industrial emissions placing oxygen demands on surface waters, and emissions of heavy metals, 1975-1990**
(1980 = 100)

	1975	1980	1985	1990
Oxygen demand	158	100	61	59
Cadmium	n.a.	100	90	19
Mercury	n.a.	100	44	56
Chromium	n.a.	100	72	15
Copper	n.a.	100	50	45
Lead	n.a.	100	27	19
Nickel	n.a.	100	50	31
Zinc	n.a.	100	34	20

Source: Calculated from data in CBS (1990), *Waterkwaliteitsbeheer, deel* A (Lozing van afvalwater, 1990).

Both studies of the effectiveness of the water charge face the basic problem of distinguishing the effects of the water charges on polluter behaviour from the effects of the system of discharge licensing. Reductions in emissions over the period during which the charge has been in operation have been substantial, but only part of this reduction is likely to be attributable to the operation of the charge; increases in the stringency of licence conditions are also likely to have played a significant role in reducing emissions. (Indeed, once the charges had induced technical changes, these tended to become reflected in more stringent regulations, complicating still further the relationship between charges and regulations.)

This issue was addressed directly in Schuurman's study by asking respondents to identify the most significant reason for the measures they had undertaken to curb discharges. Of the 108 large companies surveyed by Schuurman which had taken measures to curb discharges, and which gave government actions as their main reasons for doing so, 24 per cent identified licence provisions as the main reason for their action, 66 per cent identified the water emissions charges, and 10 per cent gave other reasons. These estimates are not uncontroversial; in a comment on Schuurman's results Bressers (1988) observes that companies might have chosen to give what they perceived as politically-expedient replies which might even have understated the incentive effect of the charges.

An alternative source of evidence which would help to disentangle the effects of the water charge and the licence requirements would be to identify cases which were differentially affected by one or other instrument. Thus, for example, if licence conditions required changes in emissions from one group of firms but not from another, whilst the levy applied to them equally, then differences in the abatement responses are more likely to reflect the effects of the licence conditions, whilst the common element of the response may be more likely to reflect the influence of the instrument affecting both groups. In the case of the Netherlands water charge system, two potential opportunities for disentangling the effects of the charge from those of licence conditions would appear to exist.

First, only the largest firms pay the charge based on direct measurement, whilst smaller firms generally pay on the basis of a schedule of non-measured charges. For the latter group, the incentive effect of the charge is absent; reducing emissions does not reduce charge liability. This would appear to suggest that a comparison of abatement behaviour between the large firms and similar medium-sized firms might be able to identify effects directly attributable to charges; a larger amount of abatement by the larger firms could be evidence of the incentive effect of the charges. The difficulty with this approach, however, is that medium-sized firms have, if they choose, the option of being charged on the basis of measured emissions. This option would be most likely to be exercised by the firms with the largest reduction in emissions compared to the characteristics which determine their liability to the unmeasured charge; if these firms choose to switch to measured charges, this will tend to exaggerate the apparent incentive effect of charging. How serious a problem this is likely to be for this approach may be doubted; the initial fixed cost of continuous measurement of emissions is substantial (perhaps of the order of fl 150 000), which has discouraged extensive uptake of this option.

A second possibility for distinguishing the effects of the charge and licence conditions arises as a result of the local variation in the board charges. The range between the highest and lowest waterboard charges is substantial, and roughly equal to the average level of the charges. There is thus a possibility that significantly greater responses to charge levels might be observed in areas with higher levels of charges, allowing this differential impact to be attributed to the impact of the charge.

Schuurman further seeks to quantify the effect of rises in the charge, and found in some cases a substantial response – a rate increase of 1 per cent yielding a reduction of 0.5 to 1 per cent in the amount of pollution, with the strongest responses observed amongst indirect dischargers and the food industry (cited in Klok *et al.*, page 42).

3.3 France

In France, the programme for water pollution control is run by six Agences De l'Eau (water basin authorities) which are responsible for water quality and resource problems. The basin authorities have levied a "water pollution charge" since 1968 on domestic and non-domestic water discharges.

For non-domestic discharges, the French scheme is based on a system of water quality permits which place constraints upon the expected volume and concentration of effluent; before any firm can start discharging emissions into the water environment they must apply for a permit. The charge applies to private and public sources discharging at least the equivalent of a population of 200; charges are levied for a range of different emissions, including suspended solids, oxidisable matter and nitrate levels. The charge is calculated on the basis of the level of emissions specified in the permit (although end-of-pipe measurement can also be used at the request of either the basin authority or the user).

A 1989 OECD study (OECD, 1989) concluded that the charge rates were too low to act as an incentive mechanism. Charge rates levied by the water basin authorities are however now being sharply increased; over the period 1992-96 charge rates are set to increase by 146 per cent, and the revenues from charges to rise from FF 3.6 billion ($0.7 billion) per year over 1987-91 to an annual average of FF 7.8. billion ($1.6 billion) over 1992-96. These increases in the charge rates may increase the incentive role of the French water charges, which until now has probably been quite small, and secondary to revenue-raising objectives.

3.4 Germany

Water pollution charges in Germany were introduced from 1981 under the Federal Republic's 1976 Wastewater Charges Act (Abwasserabgabengesetz, AbwAG). The charges are levied on direct discharges into rivers, lakes, the sea, and groundwater by both industrial and municipal sources. Indirect discharges, by sources discharging into the treatment systems of municipalities, are not charged. As in the Netherlands, the charging system is based on a formula, under which pollution units are defined, broadly equivalent to the pollution generated by one individual. The charges were introduced gradually, starting in 1981 at a rate of DM 12 ($5.33) per unit, and have then been increased in annual stages, to DM 60 ($36) per unit in 1993. The waste water charge is based on the discharge permit limits agreed for each polluter, rather than on actual emissions. Charges can be reduced in certain circumstances, such as where state-of-the-art abatement technologies are used, or where the polluter constructs or significantly improves a sewage treatment plant; these arrangements for charge reduction, and for offsetting certain pollution-control investment costs against the charge, have substantially reduced the aggregate charge revenues in recent years, despite the steady rise in charge rates.

Box 7. **An example of "soft effects": the "capacity-building" effects of the German water charge**

One interesting aspect of the German water effluent charge system is that it induced a "capacity building" process. In particular, the charge improved administrative competence by:

- providing financial resources for increasing the number and capability of staff engaged in determining and issuing water pollution permits, and in monitoring and modelling activities;
- creating the need for better information and monitoring of effluent discharges; better monitoring strengthened the position of environmental authorities vis a vis polluters;
- introducing into the relationship between authorities and polluters the objective elements of control and enforcement associated with fiscal legislation;
- providing polluters with an incentive to review their discharges, and to consider technological options (awareness effect);
- giving more attention and recognition to issues of municipal sewage treatment;
- signalling the legislators' determination to ensure more effective compliance with existing pollution control requirements.

Source: Drawn from R.A. Kraemer (1995), "The effectiveness and efficiency of water effluent charge systems: case study on Germany" paper prepared for the OECD Environment Directorate.

Also, in order to avoid increasing the overall fiscal burden on direct dischargers, the system allows dischargers to offset the costs of investment in pollution control equipment against charges.

Sprenger *et al.* (1994) evaluate the performance of the *Abwasserabgabengesetz* against the following criteria: ecological efficiency, economic efficiency, distributional effects, budgetary effects, and administrative practicality; their analysis is extensive, and only some of the conclusions in relation to the first two criteria are summarised here. They observe that the information basis for evaluation is limited in some key respects – thus, for example, no systematic official investigation of the outcomes of the system has been undertaken, no data exists on the extent to which use has been made of the opportunities for reductions in the unit charge, on the pattern of revenues according to the particular pollutants, or in the sectoral pattern of source and use of the charge revenues. Also, they argue that there are significant conceptual difficulties in conducting an evaluation of the impact of the Abwasserabgabengesetz (AbwAG) alone, given that it is so closely bound up with the regulatory system, through the use of the regulatory limits determined under the Wasserhaushaltsgesetz (WHG) as the initial basis for charging. Thus, although it is unquestionable that the introduction of the charge has been associated with a significant reduction in emissions of the charged pollutants, it is not possible to attribute this immediately to the effect of the charge, since it could equally reflect the impact of the charges in regulatory limits under the WHG.

Evidence assessed by Sprenger *et al.* (1994) on the ecological efficiency of the charging system – in other words, its effectiveness in reducing environmental damage – related mainly to the early years of the policy, including the period before the charges came into force. Ewringmann, Kibatt and Schaffhausen questioned 92 enterprises and 46 municipalities during the 1974-79 "announcement phase" of the AbwAG, finding that three-quarters of the enterprises and two thirds of the municipalities had increased, accelerated or modified their water pollution abatement measures under the combined pressure of the expected introduction of the measures in the AbwAG and the WHG. For two fifths of the enterprises this anticipatory response could be traced predominantly to the AbwAG. Sprenger and Pupeter (1980), in another early investigation of the effects of the new legislation amongst 54 major industrial direct dischargers, observed an extensive acceleration of abatement measures; they argued that this appeared to be largely the result of the charge, since the increased investment appeared to be much the same for firms which were not required to change their behaviour by the regulatory system under WHG as for those that were.

Further beneficial ecological effects observed by Sprenger *et al.* arise through the incentive that the charge gives for more careful management of abatement facilities, possible beneficial ecological side effects through the reduction of uncharged forms of emission, as a by-product of measures to reduce emissions of charged substances, and various types of "soft effect" in terms of changes in attitudes and awareness of companies, municipalities, and their employees. Less desirable aspects of the system from an ecological perspective included the lack of a systematic ecological rationale for the relative levels of charge applied to different substances, and the lack of regional differentiation in the charge, to reflect differences in the ecological vulnerability of different areas.

As regards economic efficiency, the conclusion of Sprenger *et al.* (1994) is that the system has some significant deficiencies, which restrict the extent to which it achieves the efficiency gains that would in principle be attainable from an economic instrument. First, the close relationship between the charging system and the system of regulatory permits does not allow the cost minimising pattern of abatement to be chosen freely by polluters; instead, much of the abatement measures undertaken are dictated by the pattern required by permit conditions. Second, there is a potential for distortion in competition between direct and indirect dischargers, arising through the fact that only direct dischargers are subject to the charge system. Third, the use of the revenues may not induce much behavioural modification; there may be a substantial "dead-weight" (*Mitnahmeeffekt*), of payments to enterprises which would have undertaken the measures without subsidy. Fourth, the reduction in the charge applicable to enterprises which "overcomply" with the permit requirements reduces the tax burden on residual units of pollution, thus weakening the dynamic incentive function of the charge. The result is that the tax is only really paid by those who resist the official norms, and it has thus become, in effect, an enforcement mechanism for these norms (Sprenger *et al.*, 1994, page 132).

3.5 Conclusions

The well-established systems of water effluent charging in the Netherlands, France and Germany have been extensively discussed in both academic and policy literatures. The broad conclusion of the available evidence appears to be that the Dutch system, which has the highest charge levels, has had a substantial behavioural impact. Behavioural effects from the German system are also documented, especially during the period of its introduction. In the French case, the use of revenues from the system has had major effects, and the recent increase in the rates of the French charges may be likely to lead to a significant incentive effect as well.

The case of water effluent charging exemplifies some of the difficulties which arise in evaluating economic instruments, where economic instruments and command-and-control regulations operate in parallel. In each of the systems, the role played by economic instruments in influencing the level of pollution is secondary to the role of regulatory policies; to a large extent, each of the systems of water effluent charges was introduced initially as a revenue-raising mechanism, and the incentive role of the systems is a by-product of this, or a more recent rationale for the system. Given that emissions levels are primarily governed by license conditions and other regulatory requirements, how can any incentive effect from the effluent charges be distinguished?

The discussion of the structure of the systems, and of some of the available evaluation evidence, suggests a number of ways in which it may be possible to disentangle – at least partly – the separate contribution made by economic instruments. Some examples of situations where a separate effect from the effluent charge could, in principle, be identified include:

- cases where some group of polluters is not subject to the incentive charge system. An example encountered in the case study is the difference in abatement performance between large Dutch firms which must pay the effluent charge on the basis of measured emissions, and smaller firms which pay on the basis of standard coefficients. For this group to act as a control, it has to be assumed that the position of this exempt group would otherwise be the same as that of other polluters which are subject to the charge; this may not always be plausible. Also, the membership of the two groups should not, in general, be a matter of choice for the polluters; this is, of course, the case in the Dutch system, where firms paying on the basis of standard coefficients can opt, if they wish, for measured charging.

- cases where some group is not subject to the regulatory requirements. An example from the German system is the position of firms which already satisfied regulatory requirements at the start of the policy. Any additional abatement by these firms would then be attributable to the effluent charge.

- cases where the level of the charge varies regionally, whilst the regulatory standards do not, or *vice versa*.

Each of these approaches requires disaggregated information about emissions by individual polluters, so that they can be classified into appropriate groups. It is rarely easy to collect this information retrospectively, and effective policy evaluation would thus require advance planning, to ensure that data about emissions is collected from individual sources before and after introduction of the economic instrument.

Chapter 4

CHARGES AND TAXES: AIR

4.1 The nitrogen oxides charge in Sweden

4.1.1 Policy background

A large proportion of the total nitrogen input to waters in Sweden arises as a result of depositions of airborne nitrogen; the airborne contribution is estimated at 30 per cent of the total nitrogen input in the Baltic Sea, for example (Swedish Ministry of Environment, 1991, page 97). There are significant international flows of airborne nitrogen pollution, and only some 20 per cent of nitrogen depositions in Sweden arises from domestic sources (Lövgren, 1993, Table 2).

In 1985, the Swedish Parliament agreed a target for reducing emissions of nitrogen oxides. This requires emissions to be reduced to 30 per cent less than the 1980 level by 1995 (Swedish Ministry of Environment, 1991, page 98). Emissions in 1980 were some 425 000 tonnes, measured in terms of nitrogen dioxide, and the 1995 target therefore is for emissions to fall to some 300 000 tonnes. By 1991, emissions had been reduced to 394 000 tonnes (sem, page 1).

A large part (some 41 per cent) of current emissions of nitrogen oxides in Sweden originates from road transport; industrial machinery and processes account for some 27 per cent, whilst power generation accounts for only some 11 per cent of the total, reflecting the fact that existing power stations are predominantly hydro- and nuclear-powered. The significance of emissions from power generation is, however, likely to increase when new conventionally-fuelled electricity generation capacity has to be built, towards the end of the current decade. The nitrogen oxides charge has been directed at reducing emissions from the power generation sector and large combustion plants in industry, and is thus aimed at a relatively small proportion of total emissions.

The existing regulatory policies affecting this sector took the form of controls on technology and emissions levels (Swedish Ministry of Environment, 199x, page 105). The government's view was that the 30 per cent target could not be achieved on the basis of existing regulatory controls alone (Swedish Ministry of Environment, 1991, page 105). The NO_x charge was intended to accelerate measures to reduce emissions from large combustion plants, and to allow cost-effective implementation of measures to reduce emissions below the levels required under the permit procedure. One source of these extra reductions in emissions was likely to be changes in the procedures for operating boilers, which could lead to significant reductions in NO_x emissions (Swedish Ministry of Environment, 1991, page 105).

4.1.2 Design of the instrument

The instrument is a direct charge levied on measured emissions by a limited group of large emissions sources. The choice of a charge based on measured emissions, rather than a charge based on the characteristics of input fuels (as in the carbon tax case), was governed by the nature of the process by which combustion gives rise to nitrogen oxides emissions. Nitrogen oxides are formed in combustion in two ways, first as a result of a reaction between atmospheric oxygen and the nitrogen contained in the fuel, and second through a reaction between atmospheric nitrogen and oxygen. The significance of the second source of nitrogen oxides depends on the conditions under which combustion takes place, including the precise operating conditions. Direct emissions measurement is thus likely to lead to a much more precisely-focused incentive than charges based on fuel characteristics or other emissions proxies (Swedish Ministry of Environment, 1991, page 106).

The measurement technology is costly; the Committee on Environmental Control Charges in Sweden which considered the initial proposal estimated the annual cost of measurement, including the costs of inspecting and checking the equipment, at SKr 350 000 (approx. ECU 36 800) per plant. As a result, the NO_x charge was confined to a relatively small group of large sources, for whom measurement costs were likely to be low, relative to the potential abatement cost saving. Thus the charge is levied only on large heat and power producers with a capacity in excess of 10 MW, and an annual output of more than 50 GWh. Smaller installations are not charged, and industrial processes involving combustion are also not charged. These criteria limit the charge to a total of some 185 boilers[10] (Lövgren, 1993, page 11), estimated to account for about 40 per cent of total nitrogen oxide emissions from the energy sector (Swedish Ministry of Environment, 1991, page 111).

The charge is levied on nitrogen oxides emissions at a rate of SKr 40 per equivalent kilogram of nitrogen dioxide; this rate has been constant in nominal terms since the introduction of the charge in 1992. This charge is applied to measured emissions, or to presumptive emissions levels of 250 mg/MJ for boilers and 600 mg/MJ for gas turbines. Plant operators are able to choose to pay the charge on the basis of presumptive emissions levels instead of installing measuring equipment, although in general the presumptive emissions levels are substantially higher than actual emissions, so measurement will generally be preferable. The presumptive levels also apply where the measuring equipment is faulty, or does not comply with the specifications required by the Swedish Environmental Protection Agency. To allow time for maintenance and calibration of the measuring equipment, operators may estimate emissions for a maximum of 5 per cent of the monthly operating time, on the basis of measured emissions in similar conditions (Lövgren, 1993, page 11).

To avoid distorting the pattern of competition between the large sources which are subject to the NO_x charge and their smaller competitors (and possibly introducing incentives for inefficient substitution towards uncharged smaller boilers), the system is operated so that almost all of the charge revenues are returned to the participating sources, in proportion to their final energy output.[11] Thus sources with high emissions relative to their energy output are net payers to the scheme, whilst sources with low emissions relative to energy output are net recipients.

4.1.3 Ex ante *assessments and expectations*

The choice of a tax rate of SKr 40 per kg was governed by estimates of the marginal cost of emissions abatement, and broad estimates of the level of charge needed to achieve the required level of abatement. Swedish Ministry of Environment, 1991, (page 112) notes that the marginal cost of abatement varies widely, in a range of some 5 to 60 SKr/kg, depending on the age of the plant, and on the type of abatement measures undertaken. The tax rate chosen was judged to be "an appropriate level for achievement of the desired effects" (Swedish Ministry of Environment, 1991, page 112), reflecting a balance between the need to ensure that the tax was high enough to have a clear incentive effect, and the potential costs to high emitters of an excessive charge level.

It was estimated that, on the basis of initial emissions levels by the plants subject to the charge (some 27 000 tonnes per year), the annual revenue from the charge would amount to at most some SKr 1 100 million. This would be liable to decrease rapidly as emissions were reduced (both as a result of emissions reductions required by the tightening of permit conditions, and as a result of any response to the incentive provided by the charge itself).

As far as the effect of the tax on emissions was concerned, the Ministry's *ex ante* estimates reflected the following reasoning:

Estimates made by the National Environmental Protection Agency and the National Energy Administration of the effects of existing regulatory policies (the permit procedure) was that the tightening of the permit conditions would lead to a reduction in emissions of some 9 000 tonnes annually by 1995. One likely effect of the charge would be to accelerate some of these measures, with significant environmental benefits.

However, in addition to this acceleration effect, the charge would also be likely to induce additional measures, in two ways. First, it would induce modifications to boilers not covered by the tighter guidelines for the permit procedure – probably leading to emissions abatement by some 3 000 to 5 000 tonnes annually by the end of the century. Second, it would be likely to encourage more than the required minimum compliance by some of the boilers subject to tighter permit guidelines. Whilst this additional abatement was difficult to forecast, the Ministry's estimate was that the additional abatement would be likely to be at least some 2 000 tonnes annually. Taking these two sources of abatement together, the Ministry's assessment was that the charge "should lead to reductions in emissions of the order of 5 000 to 7 000 tonnes per year" (Swedish Ministry of Environment, 1991, pages 112-3).

4.1.4 Ex post *evidence on effects*

During autumn 1993, after the system had been in operation for some 20 months, a commission examined its operation. Overall, this study concluded that emissions of nitrogen oxides per unit of input energy from the plants in the system had fallen from some 159 mg/MJ to about 103 mg/MJ. Information covering 163 out of 185 installations covered by the system showed a reduction in aggregate NO_x emissions from some 21 000 tonnes to about 13 500 tonnes (SOU 1993:118, sem, page 2). Two questions concerning this reduction in emissions were addressed: first, the costs of the abatement measures undertaken, and second, the extent to which the abatement observed can be attributed to the NO_x charge.

There were three principal methods by which the reduction in emissions was achieved: combustion measures, SNCR (selective non-catalytic reduction), and SCR (selective catalytic reduction). The costs and use made of these differ widely.

Combustion measures include many ways of reducing emissions at low marginal cost. The cost of reducing emissions through combustion measures was found to vary widely, depending on the choice of fuel, from about SKr 4 per kilogram of NO_x abated to some SKr 52 per kg. The combustion measures used to reduce emissions included low-NO_x burners, flue gas recirculation, air staging, reburning, and "fine tuning" of the combustion system. Changes in operating procedures for a given plant may have a substantial impact on the level of NO_x emissions. Some plants have sought to give employees an incentive to operate the process in the optimal manner by paying bonuses related to the reduction in emissions which is achieved.

SNCR measures, in the form of selective non-catalytic reduction through the injection of urea or ammonia, also proved a cheap way of reducing emissions. Before the introduction of the charge such measures had not been used at all in Swedish plants; it is now used by about 20 plants, and is under consideration by others.

SCR (flue gas cleaning by selective catalytic reduction) is, by contrast, a costly way to reduce NO_x emissions, especially given the relatively small size, by international standards, of the plants concerned. It has, however, proved a cost-effective approach for some larger coal-fired boilers with high initial emissions.

Against the gains from using the economic instrument, it is necessary to set the costs of measurement and administration of the charges. The measurement equipment is costly (some SKr 350 000 per installation), and the cost of measurement per tonne of NO_x abated has been estimated at around SKr 4 000. Nevertheless, some of the plants would already have been required to install measurement equipment to comply with the existing regulatory policies; the additional measurement costs involved in the operation of the charge are therefore rather lower than the gross figure of SKr 4 000 per tonne of NO_x abated (Lövgren, 1993, pages 12, 13).

Administration costs of the Environment Protection Agency have been of the order of SKr 200 per tonne of NO_x abated; part of the administrative burden can be attributed to the processes for refunding the charge revenues (Lövgren, 1993, page 14).

A key issue of policy interest is the effect of the revenue return arrangements on the sources' responses to the charge. Whilst the revenue return has been made on a basis which is, in principle, independent of the level of emissions, and should therefore leave the incentive to reduce emissions unaffected, it is possible that net payers and net recipients would respond differently to the system. Thus, for example, remedial management action might be triggered more rapidly by net payments of the tax than in a firm which was a net recipient, even though there might be scope for reducing emissions in both. Systematic evidence on the pattern of responses of individual net payers and recipients does not appear to be available, and the evidence on the pattern across industry groups is far from conclusive. However, the data in Table 5 on the pattern of payments and receipts across different categories of combustion plant covered by the NO_x charge, and the emissions reductions by each group, show that the largest reductions in emissions have been by waste incineration plants, which have also been the largest net contributors to the system, per unit of energy output. Emissions from the metal industry, on the other hand, which is a substantial net recipient from the system have actually increased marginally over 1992-93.

Table 5. **The pattern of emissions reductions and net payments of the NO_x charge across sectors**

	Number of plants	Net NO_x charge payment (receipt) per GWh of energy produced (Kr/GWh)	Percentage reduction in NO_x emissions, 1992-93
Waste incineration	5	9 763	42
Energy production	53	(878)	23
Chemical industry	23	(94)	17
Pulp and paper industry	39	1 304	13
Metal industry	2	(9 168)	−2
Total	122	176	20

Note: The small net payment shown for the system as a whole reflects the fact that a small proportion of total payments is used to cover administration costs, and some revenue is also retained as a reserve to cover subsequent revisions to the accounts (Lövgren, 1993, Table 3).

Source: Lövgren, 1993, Table 3.

4.2 Sulphur taxes in Sweden

4.2.1 *Policy background*

Soil acidification, forest damage, and fish death have affected large areas of Scandinavia. This has been caused primarily by relatively low critical loads and high levels of exposure to acid rain from sulphur emissions associated to combustion of fossil fuels and some industrial processes. In fact, deposition of sulphur exceeds the critical loads in most parts of Sweden: in the south, depositions need to be reduced by as much as 60-80%.

Transboundary air pollution contributes up to 90 per cent to total sulphur deposition in Sweden. This is due to meteorological patterns which determine the "imports" of acid rain from emitting areas in Britain and the European mainland. At the same time, although energy-intensive industries are present in Sweden, electricity production relies almost exclusively on hydro and nuclear power, with fossil-fuel-fired power stations being used just marginally in periods with excess demand. This explains the comparatively low level of Swedish SO_2 emissions.[12] In 1990, combustion of oil, coal and other fuels in stationary sources accounted for more than 40 per cent of sulphur emissions. Mobile sources (especially shipping) and industrial processes each had a share slightly below 30 per cent. In any case, most coal (generally, the most SO_2 intensive fuel) used in Sweden is not for energy purposes but is applied as a processing input, primarily in the metal industries.

Sweden has traditionally used administrative measures to regulate sulphur emissions. Under guidelines set up by the Environment Protection Act (1969), the National Licensing Board for Environment Protection allocates permits for major stationary sources (emission standards). There are also limits for the sulphur content of various fuels[13] (product standards). The sulphur tax has not replaced those administrative regulations, instead being thought of as complementary to them. In fact, a simultaneous tightening of administrative regulations (emission standards) was introduced in 1993. Thereby, the tax aims at a faster and more cost-effective reduction of Swedish sulphur emissions to comply with the ambitious national targets (reduction of emissions by 80 per cent from 1980 to 2000). Note that the policy options appear to have been quite successful: by the beginning of the 1990s total Swedish emissions had already been cut from 519 000 tonnes of SO_2 in 1980 to around 169 000 (approximately a 70 per cent cut), while during the same period the corresponding European sulphur emissions only decreased by 25 per cent (UN ECE, 1993).

The introduction of the sulphur tax has also been related to the processes of tax reform that have been taking place in Sweden since the beginning of the 1990s. Towards the end of the 1980s, the gradual acceptance of the use of economic instruments in environmental policies coincided with the immediate need to reform the highly distortionary Swedish tax system. The purpose of the reform was to reduce marginal taxes on incomes, introducing transparency and uniform treatment in capital and sales taxes. The parallel reduction in public revenues was supposed to be compensated by the broadening of the tax bases and the introduction of new, mostly environmental, taxes. In 1988 the government had appointed an Environmental Charge Commission (ECC), which suggested a number of environmental taxes, among them the tax on sulphur emissions. As a result of the enquiry, taxes on energy and transport were heavily increased in 1991, and the sulphur tax was introduced on January 1, 1991 (Gov. Bill 1989/90 111, Swedish Code of Statutes). However, the concerns about the induced loss of competitiveness of the Swedish industries led to the appointment of a new Committee on Competition-Neutral Energy Taxation (1991), which recommended that industry should not pay any energy taxes except those that were motivated by local/regional environmental concerns (such as acidification). Most energy taxes were judged to be fiscally motivated and thereby abolished, bringing energy taxation for industry below 1990 levels, although increasing energy taxes for household and transport sectors to avoid large revenue losses. As of September 1994 the sulphur tax is still in place in its original shape.

4.2.2 *Design of the instrument*

The instrument is a tax on the sulphur content of coal, oil (diesel fuel and domestic heating fuel), and peat used for energy generation. Hence, it is a tax levied on the estimated emissions involved with the combustion of the fuels that account for the largest percentage of emissions of sulphur.[14] The tax rate corresponds to SKr (Swedish Kronor) 30 (approx. ECU 3.15) per kilogram of sulphur content of coal and peat fuel, while for oil it amounts to SKr 27 (approx. ECU 2.85) per cubic metre for every 0.1 per cent by weight of the sulphur content in such oil. For practical reasons, fuels containing less than 0.1 per cent of sulphur are not taxed. The rate has been constant in nominal terms since the introduction of the charge.

The sulphur tax is refundable if there is proof that SO_2 emissions to the atmosphere have been reduced through the use of desulphurization devices or other techniques. The National Tax Board must refund (on application, with a minimum request of SKr 1 000 per quarter) the amount of SKr 30 per kg of sulphur in proportion to the reductions achieved. There are deductions for fuels used with other purposes than energy production, or which will be exported to third countries. The revenues obtained with the sulphur tax are not earmarked for environmental purposes, being collected as general revenues in the national budget.

Measurement of the sulphur content of the relevant fuels is necessary for the functioning of the tax. However, this does not present significant problems because according to regulations in force before 1991 (Sulphur-Containing Fuels Ordinance, 1976:1055, and Chemical Products Act, 1985:426), measurement of the fuels was already compulsory. Tax reimbursements are mostly based on continuous monitoring systems, which meet basically the same requirements as for the NOX charge. At the same time, an extra simplification is achieved with the use of the same administrative framework for the sulphur tax and other taxes such as the energy tax and the carbon dioxide tax.

The sulphur content of light fuel oils is also considered in the tax differentiation procedures applied to these products in Sweden since 1991. The system has been designed to favour the introduction of less environmentally damaging fuel oil by compensating the oil companies for the increased production costs. The fuel oil which fulfils the standard requirements is called class III (0.2 per cent sulphur content), while the lower-taxes classes I and II must comply with more stringent conditions, including maximum sulphur content (0.001 per cent and 0.005 per cent respectively) and other environmental characteristics such as level of aromatics, cetane indices, etc.

4.2.3 Ex ante *assessments and expectations*

The tax was intended to reduce the emissions of sulphur through the encouragement of low-sulphur fuels and the adoption of sulphur emission control measures. The rather high rate of the tax was supposed to achieve easily the reductions required to comply with the national targets. The calculation of the rate took into account the estimated sulphur premium on the oil market (around 10-55 SKr per cubic metre for each 0.1 per cent by weight of the sulphur content) and the estimated costs of fuel desulphurization (approximately between 10 and 40 SKr per kg of separated sulphur). The tax on oil was fixed at SKr 27 in order to tax sulphur emissions from the combustion of the considered fuels in an identical manner, thus allowing for a cost-effective reduction of emissions.

The annual estimated revenues were assumed to be around SKr 500 million (ECU 52.6 million) for the sulphur tax levied on oil, and SKr 400 million (ECU 42.1 million) for the tax on coal and peat (Swed. Leg.).

The tax differentiation for light fuel-oils was set to approximate the extra cost for the cleaner fuels. In 1992, the rebates amounted to SKr 0.45 (ECU 0.047) per litre for class I, and SKr 0.25 (ECU 0.026) per litre for class II.

4.2.4 Ex post *evidence on effects*

It is difficult to assess the overall effects of the introduction of the sulphur tax. First, the legislation has been passed just very recently, without leaving enough time to contemplate the outcomes involved with the tax. Also, the structural changes affecting the Swedish economy in recent years (such as devaluation, economic crisis, and tax reform) further complicate the interpretation of the facts. Finally, the existence of parallel regulations (also strengthened during the same period) for the control of sulphur emissions constitutes another drawback in the process of assessment of the particular tax measure. In view of the previous limitations, we provide some general evidence of the impact of the Swedish SO_2 tax.

The sulphur tax seems to have influenced markets quite strongly. Average contents of sulphur in different fuels have been reduced considerably even following the proposal of the tax, and the availability of low-sulphur oils has increased so that heavy and light oils are now available in the market with fairly low sulphur contents and reasonable prices. For instance, the introduction of the sulphur tax has caused a reduction in the average sulphur content of heavy fuel oil down to around 0.4 per cent from a figure around 0.65 per cent (the compulsory standard was actually 0.8 per cent). In most cases, light fuel oil has now a sulphur content under 0.1 per cent, well below the legal limit of 0.2 per cent, and not subject to the sulphur tax, although this has been mainly motivated by the tax differentiation scheme (Lövgren, 1993). Simultaneously, coal has become less competitive due to the introduction of the tax, and low sulphur coals are increasingly being used. The tax has also made it profitable to clean flue gases to a larger degree than before, and the efficiency of sulphur removal has improved in most coal and peat fired facilities.

Official estimates indicate that yearly emissions of sulphur have been reduced by around 6 000 tonnes because of the effects of the sulphur tax. The costs of achieving this reduction (in the form of more expensive raw material and desulphurizing devices) have been estimated to be about SKr 10 000-15 000 (ECU 1 052-1 579) per tonne of abated sulphur (Swedish Environmental Protection Agency, 1993).

Tax revenues for 1993-94 were SKr 217 million (ECU 22.8 million), far less than the expected receipts; proof of the strong incentive effects already introduced by the sulphur tax and previous regulations. In fact, the SO_2 tax has provided only small amounts for the government budget, especially compared to the energy or CO_2 taxes.

Administrative costs are estimated to be less than 1 per cent of the total revenues obtained by the tax (OECD, 1994). This has confirmed the expectations of low expenses, following the decision to share the same administrative framework for the sulphur tax and other existing taxes such as the energy and carbon dioxide ones. With respect to tax refunding, about 65 plants have been reimbursed every year due to sulphur reduction measures (Lövgren, 1993).

Concerning the fuel-oil tax differentiation, the effects on fuel substitution have been quite large since 1991. This differentiation has helped to reduce the sulphur content of some fuels considerably more than expected with the sole application of the sulphur tax. Less than 1 per cent of the light fuel oil sold in 1990 would have fulfilled current requirements for class I or II, but in the first half of 1993 about 15 per cent of them were classified as class I and around 60 per cent as class II.[15] The use of improved fuels has reduced sulphur emissions from diesel vehicles by 75 per cent in average, and up to 95 per cent in the cities. The costs have been estimated at SKr 500 million per year (ECU 52.6 million), and the costs of lower revenues to the government at around SKr 600 million (ECU 63.15 million)[16] (Swedish Environmental Protection Agency, 1993). Some authors have indicated, though, that the tax differentiation seems to have been excessive, favouring class I and II fuels ahead of other more environmentally-friendly options (Sterner, 1994).

4.3 Sulphur tax in Norway

A Sulphur dioxide emissions study conducted by ECON Centre for Economic Analysis, Norway, as part of an inter-departmental evaluation of environmental regulations in Norway, considered the economic efficiency and environmental impact of Norwegian policies to restrict sulphur emissions. The main focus was on local damage from SO_2 emissions; Norway has been able to reduce SO_2 emissions by considerably more than its international obligations require.

The instruments used have included both economic and administrative measures: *individual emissions standards* for industry, either in the form of direct limits on emissions, or indirect limits through technology requirements; *regulations on the permitted sulphur content of fuel oil* (geographically differentiated, with the lowest limits in Oslo and the southern part of the country); *taxes on fuel oil*, including an SO_2 tax on oil products, differentiated according to sulphur content, in operation since 1970.

Impact on emissions

There has been a substantial reduction in emissions from industrial processes, of some 67 per cent between 1973 and 1992. Until the mid-1980s, these reductions were driven largely by the emissions standards for SO_2; more recently, industrial restructuring and a shift to lower-sulphur fuels has reduced emissions below the levels set by the authorities. Emissions from stationary combustion (heating) fell by 86 per cent over 1980-92, due to a mix of factors, with only a limited effect from national environmental policies.

The study argued that the contribution of the SO_2 tax to the changes in SO_2 emissions has been small, because until 1992 the tax was very low (some 1-2 per cent of oil product prices, increased from 1992 to some 15-14 per cent); for most of the period under study, therefore, changes in SO_2 emissions have had causes other than the SO_2 tax. It found that the tax had not led to changes in the relative prices of different oil products, and that it had not led to any significant change in the sulphur content of fuels. The main factors accounting for changes in the sulphur content of fuels were argued to be changes in refinery technology and changes in the supply of low-sulphur oil from the North Sea, combined with the effect of changes in the global oil market.

Cost-effectiveness

The study identified large differences in marginal SO_2 abatement costs for different sources. The SO_2 tax is levied at NKr 17 per kilo; in comparison, marginal costs for reducing the sulphur content of fuel oil and diesel oil were found to be some NKr 29 per kilo, marginal abatement costs in industry were found to range from some NKr 5-15 per kilo in the ferro alloys industry to more than NKr 100 in the aluminium industry. Even allowing that there may be differences in local damage, these marginal abatement cost differences appear to suggest some inefficiency in the pattern of emissions reductions.

The study used estimates for marginal damage costs from the Central Bureau of Statistics which assessed the marginal damage from SO_2 emissions from petrol, diesel and fuel oil at some NKr 23 per kilo in the late 1980s. This largely comprises health costs; the costs of corrosion damage and forest damage are much lower. Since SO_2 emissions are now much lower, the marginal damage costs may now be lower.

Policy options set out in the report to reduce differences in marginal abatement costs were:

- tax all SO_2 emissions on a more uniform basis, eliminating the exemptions currently applying to coal and coke;
- introduce tradeable permits for industrial sources of SO_2 emissions, with the aim of reducing the range of abatement costs;
- abolish the SO_2 tax, and instead impose tighter regulations on those industries with particularly low marginal abatement costs due to the lack of past regulation.

The inter-departmental Committee's assessment of the research findings took issue with some of the conclusions of the SO_2 study. Whilst the conclusion that the SO_2 tax had, to date, played little role was broadly agreed, the argument that differences in marginal abatement costs indicated inefficiency in past policy was disputed, and it was argued that the conclusions reached may understate the importance given to local pollution problems in the design and conduct of past policy.

4.4 Automobile fuels

In 20 OECD countries, a tax differential in favour of unleaded petrol was introduced at the same time as a series of other policy measures to encourage substitution from leaded to unleaded petrol, such as regulations requiring petrol stations to make unleaded petrol available, abolition of certain other types of fuels, regulations (and in some cases, fiscal incentives) requiring new vehicles to meet new, more stringent, emissions standards, and information and awareness campaigns and advertising. For any individual country, it is difficult to isolate the independent contribution of the tax differential, and to disentangle it from the effect of these other policy measures. A rise in the market share of unleaded petrol could, for example, be due to the tax differential, or to other policy measures introduced at the same time, or to a mixture of both measures.

Nevertheless, evaluation studies have attempted to come to judgements about the separate contribution of the tax differential, using a number of different approaches. Some studies have suggested that quite a large proportion of the increase in take-up of unleaded petrol which has followed the introduction of the fiscal differential may in fact reflect the impact of information and awareness campaigns, and regulatory policies requiring supply and changes to vehicle specifications, rather than the incentive effect of the fiscal differential.

Scope for disentangling the separate influence of the tax differential from other parallel measures can be found in a number of ways. The pattern of unleaded petrol take-up across individual motorists may help to indicate the relative significance of the tax differential, for a number of reasons. Some of the parallel measures affect only certain categories of users, for example. Also, the strength of the fiscal incentive varies across users according to the amount of fuel used, whilst the other policy measures may not vary in this way; higher rates of fuel substitution amongst high fuel users may thus be indicative of the impact of the tax differential. Also, cross-country comparison of market shares and policy measures in a number of EU Member states, where both the relative strength and timing of the tax differential and accompanying non-fiscal measures differ, may make it possible to identify the separate contribution of the tax differential.

4.5 Preliminary conclusions

The charge on measured emissions of nitrogen oxides by large sources introduced in Sweden at the start of 1992 is one of the clearest cases of an environmental tax measure introduced for incentive reasons. The revenues from the charge are returned to the firms subject to the charge on a basis unrelated to their emissions level, so that, over the group as a whole, no net revenues are raised.

Assessing the impact of the Swedish NO_x charge is complicated by the existence of parallel regulatory measures, also directed at the reduction of NO_x emissions. Nevertheless, indications of the independent effect of the incentive may be derived from two main sources, the timing of emissions reductions (since the charge was announced and introduced well after the regulatory policies were introduced), and the differences in the pattern of emissions reductions between the large sources subject to the charge, and the smaller producers outside the charging system.

The number of producers subject to the charge is relatively small, and the scope for detailed study of the behaviour of individual plants affected by the charge is correspondingly high. The existing evaluation research on the Swedish NO_x charge draws, relatively informally, on information relating to the pattern of plant responses. There would, however, appear to be scope for more systematic data collection and analysis. Amongst the issues which this might address is the extent of efficiency savings from the system – which plants have responded, and what measures have they taken to reduce their emissions? A second set of issues concerns the return of revenues on a lump-sum (and supposedly non-distortionary) basis to the plants which pay the charge. Does the pattern of revenue return appear to affect the pattern of behavioural responses across plants? Theoretical considerations suggest that it should not, but firms may in practice have various decision rules and management procedures which might trigger more vigorous emissions reductions in enterprises which were net payers than in those which were net recipients. Again, disaggregated data on individual plants would help to shed light on these questions.

With the sulphur tax in Sweden, as with the NO_x tax, there are substantial difficulties in assessing the effect of the tax alone, in isolation from the effects of other parallel measures. Again, disaggregated data on different categories of consumer may help to some degree in distinguishing between effects which are clearly attributable to the fiscal incentive, and those which may have resulted from the simultaneous non-fiscal measures.

Chapter 5

TRADEABLE PERMITS

5.1 Water effluent trading in the US

The various experiments with water emissions trading in the United States have been widely discussed, but these schemes provide, in fact, very limited evidence on the efficiency or effectiveness of economic instruments. Only one of the schemes, that on the Fox River, is yet able to provide *ex post* evidence about the performance in practice of economic instruments. Here, as described below, the experience has been disappointing, with only one trade taking place. Much of the explanation for this, however, would appear to be the extremely restrictive terms on which trades were permitted; as a result, the likelihood that there would be significant efficiency savings from trading was greatly reduced. The system thus provides little indication of how economic instruments would perform in an environment where trading was more freely permitted.

The discussion below of the other systems of water effluent trading in the United States show that they have not, as yet, provided any useful *ex post* evidence, for a different reason. Both the Dillon Reservoir and Tar-Pamlico River permit trading systems were designed so that the incentive for trading would increase over time, as economic growth placed increasing demands on the environmental capacity of the water systems. In practice, in both these cases, economic growth has been lower than planned, and the emissions constraint which would trigger trading has not yet begun to "bite".

5.1.1 *Policy background*

Like most of the OECD countries, the US has regulated surface water quality primarily through the use of traditional "command-and-control" approaches. The basic regulatory framework was set out in the 1972 Federal Water Pollution Control Act, renamed the Clean Water Act in 1977.

By 1983, municipal and industrial point sources were required to meet minimum discharge standards based on "best available technology economically achievable" (Industrial Economics, Inc. 1993, page 2.3, Morton *et al.*, 1993, page 2.1). The National Permit Discharge Elimination System was set up to implement and enforce the effluent standards. This programme requires dischargers to disclose the volume and nature of their effluent discharges, and authorises the US Environmental Protection Agency (EPA), or the delegated State authority, to specify which pollutants may be discharged and the quantity and/or concentration limits imposed on such discharges. Where effluent limits are insufficient to meet state water quality standards based on a waterbody's attainable uses, the permit writer may use these standards to require more stringent effluent limits.

Following the continued tightening of these regulations, the relative importance on nonpoint source pollution has increased until it has become the dominant source of water quality impairment (Apogee Research, 1992 page 1). A large number of waterbodies are unable to attain their water quality goals even if all the relevant point sources were to fully implement controls to meet technology-based discharge requirements. Over 18 000 such cases have been identified (Apogee Research, 1992 page 1).

EPA and the states have sought ways to achieve higher water quality objectives at least cost (Apogee Research, 1992, page 1). Over the past several years the nature and tone of the political debate have evolved rapidly in the direction of market-based approaches (Hahn and Stavins, 1991, page 1). As yet, the Clean Water Act does not explicitly address effluent trading and in comparison with other economic instruments, marketable permits have yet to receive widespread use.

Studies of effluent trading have mostly focused on hypothetical applications although detailed analyses have been made of actual applications on the Fox River, Wisconsin, the Dillon Reservoir, Colorado and the Tar-Pamlico River, North Carolina.

5.1.2 *Fox River, Wisconsin*

In March 1981, regulations were approved by the Wisconsin Department of Natural Resources (WDNR) to allow point sources on the Fox River to transfer permits to discharge wastes that increase biological oxygen demand (BOD). BOD is a measure of the demand for dissolved oxygen imposed on a water body by organic effluents and a key measure of water quality. Existing technological controls on BOD had proved insufficient to assure compliance with applicable water quality standards. The introduction of a trading mechanism was accompanied by more stringent discharge limits for individual sources.

In the Fox River scheme, all trading is external. The initial allocation of rights set a single limit on the waste discharges of an entire facility rather than setting separate limits on the individual pollution sources within the plant. The scheme required all trades to be approved by WDNR. The terms on which trading of permits can take place are restricted in various ways (Apogee Research, 1992, page 22).

First, a facility can only buy rights if it is new, expanding production, or cannot meet the discharge limits in its permit even with the use of the required abatement technology. Trades for which the sole justification is cost savings are prohibited (Apogee Research, 1992, page 22).

Second, trades are effective for a minimum of one year, but for not more than the amount of time remaining on the seller's discharge permit (maximum of five years). They are also required to be effective for at least one waste load allocation season which effectively precludes the trading of rights to accommodate temporary changes in operating conditions.

Third, trading is limited by location to avoid "hot-spots" (geographic concentrations of sources) and trades leading to high concentrations of toxics are not permitted.

Ex ante *assessments*

In September 1981, the water quality and cost effects for the Fox River programme were estimated using a water quality simulation model and a linear programming model (O'Neill, David, Moore and Joeres, 1982).

It was observed that individual abatement costs differed among dischargers by as much as a factor of four (Industrial Economics, Inc., 1993, page 2.3), implying that a fixed central directive was unlikely to be the least-cost approach to maintaining minimum water quality. However, a system allowing one discharger to offset another's pollution had to take into account the possible variations in water flow and temperature such that water quality standards would be maintained under any configuration of permissible discharges.

Although initially the trading of discharge rights was not a priority in the effort to achieve water quality standards for the river, the potential annual cost savings were thought to be substantial. Using industry abatement costs estimated by EPA in 1979, they were estimated at seven million dollars (Hahn and Hester, 1989, 391).

Ex post *evidence on effects*

Since the implementation of a permit trading mechanism in 1981 only one trade has taken place and the actual savings have been insignificant. This single trade was between a paper mill that stopped operating its wastewater treatment plant and a municipal wastewater treatment plant that began taking the mill's wastewater and was given the wasteload allocation previously held by the mill.

Various reasons have been put forward to explain the minimal level of trading activity.

- First, it is conceivable that there could be some uncertainty about the legal viability of the rights being traded. Since the standards set by the WDNR did not conform with the national policy of uniformity established by the Clean Water Act, the standards could be vulnerable to legal challenge (Anderson, Hofmann and Rusin, 1990, page 36).

- Second, trading restrictions severely limit the usefulness of traded rights (Hahn, 1991). They also create difficulties for the point sources in planning and making capital investment decisions (Apogee Research, 1992, page 22).

- Third, the financial incentives for trades were relatively weak, when viewed in the context of other management concerns. Pollution control costs for the paper industry on the Fox River are less than one percent of the cost of the product, and the potential savings from trading are only a small proportion of these costs.

- Fourth, it was unclear how rights to future permit allocations would be allocated; would sellers, in effect, also be giving up their rights to be allocated permits in the future?

- Fifth, administrative requirements add to the transactions costs of trading thus decreasing the incentives to participate (*Apogee Research*, 1992, page 22). For example, the procedures for approval of trades and making the necessary permit revisions could take at least six months, which would have the effect of shortening the life of the traded rights, effectively reducing their value (Hahn and Hester, 1989, page 393).

- Sixth, the characteristics of the industry involved may also have discouraged trades. The industrial dischargers involved, *i.e.* the pulp and paper plants, are in the same industry. It has been suggested (David and Joeres 1983, Hahn, page 14) that due to the oligopolistic structure of this industry the plants may not behave as competitive firms in the permit market. This may partly explain the dischargers' apparent lack of enthusiasm to participate (Hahn, 1991, page 2.6).

5.1.3 *Dillon Reservoir, Colorado*

According to a 1983 EPA study, the Dillon Reservoir would have become eutrophic were the 1982 wasteloads to have been exceeded (Anderson, Hofmann and Rusin, 1990, page 36). In 1984, Colorado approved a plan that allows the trading of rights to discharge phosphorous into the Dillon Reservoir. In addition, the plan requires advanced treatment methods for all point sources and nonpoint sources created after 1984 are required to install control systems to minimise phosphorous discharges. This programme aimed to maintain the 1982 level of water quality, despite the pressures from future economic growth.

The right to discharge wastewater containing specified annual quantities of phosphorous is the commodity for trading (Anderson, Hofmann and Rusin, 1990, page 37). A computer model developed as part of the Clean Lakes Study was used to determine the maximum phosphorous loading that the basin could accommodate and still achieve its water quality goals.

As in the Fox River case, all trading is external. Each point source has a single limit for the entire facility. However, point sources on the Dillon Reservoir are able to increase their discharge levels in excess of their initial allocations (based on 1982 loadings) by acquiring rights from nonpoint sources that were in existence before 1984.

The trading ratio between non-point and point sources is 2:1. This reflects the difficulty of quantifying and identifying nonpoint source discharge and is also hoped to offset the increase from new nonpoint sources. This is not thought to eliminate the potential cost saving from point/nonpoint trading given the very large disparity in costs of phosphorous removal between point and nonpoint sources [$860 and $119 per pound respectively (1983 dollars)].

EPA reviews and approves all trades recommended by the State. Every three years, the state Water Quality Control Commission is required to review and set waste-load allocations. This body also assigns responsibilities for operating, maintaining and monitoring all nonpoint source controls for which credit is received.

Ex ante *assessments*

In this case, few restrictions were placed on trading and the potential annual savings have been estimated at between $773 000 (Hahn and Hester, 1989, page 395) and $1 million (Hahn and Stavins, 1991, page 18).

However, the potential savings were calculated by considering the aggregate discharge limit for all point sources rather than adherence to individual discharge limits. The Dillon programme used the latter approach so estimations based on the former are difficult to interpret. Furthermore, the installation of tertiary treatment was ignored when the projected load levels were calculated. These conditions alter the economic efficiencies underlying the original trading programme.

Ex post *evidence*

Only one point/nonpoint source trade has been completed under the original regulations. A few trades between nonpoint sources have also been proposed. The discharge allocations set in 1984 included point source growth margins to accommodate development through 1990 after which trading activity was expected to greatly increase. In the event, economic development in the area was not as great as had been expected. As a result, permit allocations have continued to exceed discharge levels meaning that there has been no immediate need for dischargers to trade permits between point and nonpoint sources.

In addition, the publicly-owned treatment works in the basin achieved impressive phosphorous load reductions through minor plant alterations and improved efficiency of existing treatment technology (KPA, page 13). These have obviated the need for point source credits to accommodate future growth. Point sources now contribute a small proportion of the total phosphorous loading. This acts a constraint to the volume of existing nonpoint source phosphorous that can be controlled through trading with point sources.

Trading is expected to increase once the waste allocations to point sources are no longer sufficient. There is also a perceived need to offset new nonpoint source discharges of phosphorous with phosphorous removals elsewhere in the watershed (KPA, page 1).

5.1.4 *Tar-Pamlico River, North Carolina*

A nutrient management strategy was devised for the Tar-Pamlico River after it was designated a Nutrient Sensitive Water (NSW) in 1989. This followed increasing eutrophication problems and outbreaks of fish diseases. Water quality standards have been established using chlorophyll as a direct measure of algae growth and an indicator of eutrophication. (Apogee Research, 1992 Section B).

The management strategy consists of two phases. During Phase I (1990-1994) there are provisions for a nutrient-reduction trading programme. In Phase II, beginning in 1995, a long-term nutrient-reduction strategy will be implemented.

The trading programme was designed to allow the wastewater treatment plants in the river basin to fund less expensive nonpoint source controls and to avoid the high compliance costs associated with achieving nutrient-reduction through major facility upgrades.

A coalition of wastewater treatment plants, the Tar-Pamlico Basin Association, is held responsible for achieving an annual nutrient loading allowance for the entire association. Each member must monitor their phosphorous and nutrient loadings and submit a composite annual report. Any nutrient discharges in excess of the total allowable load must be offset by obtaining nutrient reduction credits through monetary contributions to the state Agricultural Cost Share Program for Best Management Practices in the Tar-Pamlico Basin. This programme funds reductions in nonpoint source loadings.

Non-Association members have the option to participate in the trading programme but at a higher cost per nutrient credit than Association members. New dischargers do not have the option to participate and are subject to the most stringent effluent limitations.

Ex ante *assessments*

Under the established rules, it is anticipated that trading will achieve equivalent or better water quality than would have been achieved under originally proposed effluent limits. To ensure the availability of funds for nonpoint source reductions the Association makes a minimum annual payment to the Agricultural Cost Share Program.

Ex post *evidence on effects*

To date the Association has not reached its allowance. It has therefore not been necessary to make an excess loading payment or to allocate allowance among member facilities.

5.2 Air pollution emissions trading in the US

The emissions trading programme within the US system of air pollution control has been the most significant and far-reaching of its kind and has been running for a considerable period of time. As a result, there have been a number of studies relating to the performance in practice of the system. One key feature of the system is that substantial numbers of trades have taken place, and these are indicative of substantial cost savings. There is, however, clearly scope for more extensive *ex post* empirical analysis of the efficiency savings that have resulted from trading based on disaggregated source data. The opportunities for trades are restricted in a number of significant ways. Ex post evaluation studies would need to assess how far these limits on trading, and the behaviour of participants, have resulted in outcomes which achieve or fall short of the optimum cost-minimising pattern of pollution-control costs.

The more recently-legislated system of sulphur emissions trading is still in the early stages of operation, and the environmental outcomes from the system lie in the future. To date, the only experience concerning the operation of the system has to do with the auctions of permits that have taken place. Nevertheless, this evidence is sufficiently important to warrant separate discussion, in Section 5.3, because there has been so little experience to date of the operation of permit markets in circumstances where a reasonably free pattern of trading is permitted.

5.2.1 Policy background

The US Clean Air Act was first passed in 1955 and relies upon a command-and-control approach to environmental protection. Ambient air standards are set to establish the highest allowable concentration of each conventional pollutant in the air. Emission standards are then imposed on specific emission points or sources, such as stacks, vents or storage tanks, subject to considerations about available technology. Technologies yielding larger amounts of control are selected for new emitters and for existing emitters where it is very difficult to meet the ambient standard. The responsibility for defining and enforcing these standards has been shared between the national government and the various state governments.

The EPA's emissions trading programme was designed, introduced during the 1970s and has subsequently been amended with a view to providing industry with increased flexibility whilst continuing the progress towards environmental quality goals.

5.2.2 Design of the instrument

The EPA's emissions trading programme operates nation-wide and covers all significant stationary sources of pollution for five principal air pollutants – hydrocarbons, nitrogen oxides, particulate matter, sulphur oxides and carbon monoxide.

Emission sources continue to be issued with permits to emit certain volumes of specified air pollutants. However, if a source lowers actual emissions below regulatory standards, for example as a result of process change or shut-down, (Foster and Hahn, 1994, page 4) it can trade away its rights in the form of Emissions Reduction Credits (ERCs). The trading of credits typically involves stationary sources although trading with mobile sources is permitted. Subject to certain restrictions, trading can take place internally or externally, in other words involve one or more firms.

The provisions of the Clean Air Act distinguish between new, modified and existing sources. Existing sources are those that existed when emissions were first inventoried in the mid-1970s, those built since then are termed new sources. Modified sources are existing sources which have been altered where this alteration has resulted in significant increases in emissions. These different types of sources have different emissions trading options available to them.

Netting

Netting was introduced in 1974. It allows a modified source to use ERCs from another source within the same plant in order to reduce the net emission increase to a level below that which is considered significant. This component of the trading programme is controlled at state level and has been allowed in both attainment and non-attainment areas.

Offsets

The offset rule was instituted in 1976. Prior to this, no new firms were allowed to enter non-attainment areas, that is areas where ambient standards are not met. The offset policy requires new and modified sources in non-attainment areas to obtain emission credits from sources in the same area to offset their new emissions. Some states have required new or modified sources to offset emissions by a factor greater than one. Under the 1990 Clean Air Act Amendments, higher offset ratios were mandated in ozone non-attainment areas (Hahn and Hester, 1989, pp. 371-373).

Banking

The banking of ERCs for future sale or use was added by the offset provisions of the 1977 Clean Air Act (Carlin, 1992, 5-15). Guidelines were established by EPA but individual states set up and administer the rules governing this practice.

Bubbles

From 1979 onwards, it has been possible to enclose existing multi-source plants in imaginary bubbles. These allow firms to adjust the levels of emission controls applied to the different sources within the bubble, provided that the aggregate limit for that bubble is not exceeded (or is at least 20 per cent lower in some cases). Under these arrangements, trading effectively takes place within a particular plant. Initially, bubbles had to be approved at federal level. In 1981 an amendment allowed New Jersey to give the final approval for bubbles and since then other states have followed suit.

In some areas there are additional regulatory restrictions on trading activity. For example, trades between sources in a certain geographical relation to each other may not be allowed in order to prevent pollutants from concentrating in a particular area. Administrative requirements may differ from state to state but all trades must be approved and this is often a lengthy and costly process.

5.2.3 Ex ante *assessments and expectations*

Quantitative estimates have consistently found air emissions trading has the potential to substantially reduce industry's cost of complying with air pollution control. Cost savings have been estimated to be 50 per cent of traditional command-and-control costs and up to 95 per cent in one study (Carlin, 1992, 5-15; OECD, 1991, p. 5). With the benefit of hindsight it has been suggested that these were unrealistically inflated expectations.

5.2.4 Ex post *evidence on effects*

The performance of trading can be measured in various ways and reveals a mixed outcome (Hahn, 1989, page 101). The level of activity under each of the four programmes varies dramatically. In particular, the cost savings that have been realised have been almost entirely from internal trading and fall far short of the potential savings which could be realised if there were more external trading (Hahn, 1989, page 101).

Hahn and Hester (1986) used data from a variety of sources to estimate the control cost savings yielded by the four programmes from the time when they were each instituted. These estimates varied enormously. Netting has resulted in the greatest cost savings, estimated at between $525 million and $12 billion. The pre-1986 bubbles approved at federal level were estimated to have saved $300 million over conventional control costs while state bubbles resulted in savings estimated at $135 million. Offsets result in no direct emission control cost savings because the use of offsets does not allow a firm to avoid any emission limits. The cost savings from banking were believed to be small, given the number of transactions that have occurred. Most estimates place the accumulated capital savings for all components of the programme at over $10 billion. This does not include the recurring savings in operating cost. (Tietenberg, 1990, page 19).

Table 6. **Hahn and Hester's summary of emissions trading activity**

	Estimated number of internal transactions	Estimated number of external transactions	Estimated cost savings (millions)	Environmental quality impact
Netting	5 000 to 12 000	none	$25 m to $300 m in permitting costs; $500 m to $12 000 m in emission control costs	insignificant in individual cases; probably insignificant in aggregate
Offsets	1 800	200	"not easily estimated... probably hundreds of millions of dollars"	probably insignificant
Bubbles (Federally-approved)	40	2	$300 m	insignificant
Bubbles (State-approved)	89	0	$135 m	insignificant
Banking	under 100	under 20	small	insignificant

Source: R.W. Hahn and G.L. Hester, "Marketable Permits: Lessons for Theory and Practice", *Ecology Law Quarterly*, Vol. 18, 1989.

It is virtually impossible to determine how much, if any, of the improvements in air quality can be attributed directly to the emissions trading programme. In general it is thought to have had a neutral effect although the level of compliance with the Clean Air Act has increased since its implementation.

In a detailed study of the performance of emissions trading, Foster and Hahn (1994) used data from Los Angeles to analyse the pattern of trades that have taken place. The data was obtained from AER*X, the principal broker in the Los Angeles Market, and the South Coast Air Quality Management District (SCAQMD), the regulatory body for the Los Angeles basin.

Los Angeles is characterised by the greatest level of trading activity under the emissions trading programme. From the early 1980s until 1991, the netting program involved between 200 and 500 transactions annually. Offsetting activity did not begin until 1985. Although the annual number of trades under the offsetting programme is small compared to netting, the total volume of pollutants exchanged under each of the two programmes is in the order of 10 000 tons/year. By 1990, 66 ERCs had been deposited in the bank, amounting to credits for about 8 100 tons/year. Of these, 28 had been used in subsequent trades, amounting to about 2 600 tons/year. Banked trades represent 15 per cent of the total number of trades carried out over this period (Foster and Hahn, 1994, page 11).

Foster and Hahn argue that emissions trading activity has been heavily affected by the frequent amendments to the detailed regulations governing the market. For example, their evidence suggests that the price dispersion of ROG credits increased after 1990 as a result of the geographical segmentation of the market, as a result of which, the basin was divided into 38 distinct zones and firms were only allowed to sell ERCs to downwind trading partners (Foster and Hahn, 1994, page 15). Between 1990 and 1991 there was a threefold increase in the difference between the maximum and minimum price. They conclude that this was at least partly due to the new geographical trading restrictions which created a large number of segmented markets with differing demand and supply conditions and converted an already thin market into a set of thinner markets.

In addition, Foster and Hahn found that a key factor limiting the efficiency of the ERC markets has been the relatively high level of transactions costs associated with trading. Once a trading partner has been identified firms must obtain bureaucratic approval from the SCAQMD which takes between five and twelve months. The financial costs involved include administrative fees to the regulatory body, the cost of preparing substantial supporting documentation for each trade and additional fees for certifying ERCs, banking them and reissuing them in smaller units. The transaction cost of trades frequently exceeded the market value of credits themselves (Foster and Hahn, 1994, page 23).

There is also considerable uncertainty surrounding the trading process. In the first instance, firms encounter difficulties in identifying a suitable trading partner. This has resulted in firms concentrating on trading internally, using the SCAQMD to identify a suitable partner or approaching intermediaries. This inevitably increases the financial costs involved. Some firms have exchanged "multi-pollutant clusters" of credits which avoids the need to find a number of different trading partners, one for each of the pollutants concerned. Furthermore, only about 20 per cent of trades which reach the approval stage are approved as proposed; about 40 per cent are rejected out of hand. Foster and Hahn argue that this uncertainty seems likely to have acted as a significant impediment to trading.

5.3 Sulphur emissions trading in the United States

5.3.1 *Policy background*

In June 1989, reacting to the internal and international pressures to adopt a solution to the growing problems of acid deposition, the US administration proposed a 10 million ton annual reduction in SO_2 emissions by the year 2000 (9.07 million tonnes, nearly a 40 percent reduction from the previously stated 1980 levels), with the establishment of a permanent national cap beginning in the year 2000. A two million ton reduction in NO_x emissions (1.8 million tonnes) was also proposed. A key part of the package of measures to achieve the reductions in SO_2 emissions was a market system to trade sulphur dioxide allowances. By the end of 1990, the previous schemes and national reduction targets had been included as an Amendment to the Clean Air Act (Title IV) by the US Congress, within a wider legislative package that explicitly acknowledged the role of economic incentives for environmental policies.

5.3.2 *Design of the instrument*

The Acid Rain Program is an allowance trading programme with a national emissions cap.

The programme affects existing utility units[17] with an output capacity of 25 megawatts or greater, and all new utility units (including those under 25 megawatts) that use fossil fuels with a sulphur content greater than 0.05 per cent. It focuses on all utility plants except the smallest boilers and turbines because they cover the largest percentage of SO_2 emissions in the US, and trade distortions are likely to be small as long as electric power generation is an activity difficult to export.[18] In particular, the programme avoided the complexities that would be associated with the inclusion of other types of sources such as industrial facilities, motor vehicles, etc.

The Amendment seeks to achieve the SO_2 emissions reductions progressively, regulating affected sources in different stages. Phase I began in January 1995 and required emissions reductions from 110 mostly coal-burning plants located in the eastern and midwestern states.[19] Phase II becomes effective on January 2000, tightens the annual emissions limits imposed on the previous phase, and extends the programme to the whole continental US (around 2 050 plants). This phase of the programme implements the permanent emissions cap, which takes effect fully in 2010. In order to generate the 9.07 million tonne reduction in sulphur dioxide emissions by the year 2000, electric utility[20] emissions are limited to a maximum of 8.07 million tonnes per year, a reduction of 7.7 million tonnes below the 1980 level. The remaining 1.37 million tonnes of sulphur emission reductions are required to come from non-utility sources, and, according to the EPA, have almost been achieved already for industrial sources (one million tonnes).

Electric utilities are allocated a number of allowances, each of which authorises the emission of one ton (0.907 tonnes) of SO_2 in a year. Allowances are generally issued in perpetuity, and are allocated ("grandfathered") based on a formula reflecting historical emissions. In Phase I plants receive allowances on a formula of 2.5 lbs (1.12 kg) of sulphur dioxide emissions per million Btu,[21] while in Phase II utilities receive allowances with a formula of 1.2 lbs/m.Btu (0.54 kg), exactly the current NSPS for sulphur dioxide emissions. To avoid unfair treatment of facilities that have previously taken measures against sulphur emissions, the figure is obtained on the basis of the source's past levels of production rather than emissions. New sources of emissions, however, will be allocated allowances based on a formula of 0.3 lbs/mm.Btu (0.13 kg). Utilities established after the year 2000 will not receive an allocation of allowances, and will have to purchase them on the market from existing utilities' allocations. Allowances are specifically excluded from being defined as property rights, may be traded to any party anywhere within continental US, and may be "banked" for use in subsequent years.

Once the baselines and the allocation of the emission credits to the sources have been set, subsequent trading among the participants is allowed without excessive regulatory intrusions. In fact, the Agency does not approve trades on the basis of whether or not they are environmentally or economically beneficial, it simply records transactions among the parties involved, a clear improvement in comparison with previous emissions trading systems.

Measurements of sulphur emissions are obtained through the use of continuous emissions monitoring systems, with quarterly electronic reporting to the EPA of hourly discharges. Thereby, all phase I and II units must be equipped with continuous emissions monitors. The total number of tons of SO_2 emitted by each source is then subtracted from the allowances of the source, with any excess allowances carried forward to the next year. If SO_2 emissions exceed the number of allowances held, statutory penalties[22] and an automatic deduction of one allowance per excess ton are immediately imposed.

The legislation provides for an annual auction of about 2.8 per cent of the total allowance allocation, starting in 1993. This is designed to deliver signals on allowance prices in the early stages of the programme, and to ensure that allowances are available to independent and new power producers. Proceeds of the auction are returned to existing utilities (from whom the auctioned allowances have been taken).

5.3.3 Ex ante *assessments and expectations*

It is believed that because of the wide variety of plant types, ages, and fuel mixes, the US electric utility industry shows fairly large variations in costs per tonne of SO_2 reductions, with considerable opportunities for cost-savings through the emission trading scheme (Rico, 1993). This is clearly supported by the current EPA simulations of the cost savings obtained with a sulphur emissions trading system (see table below). Note that the estimates are probably fairly conservative because cost minimisation was only considered through selection of some established control technologies, without allowing for blending strategies or other special opportunities for emission reductions.

Table 7. **Estimated annual costs of the regulations affecting sulphur dioxide emissions on the electric generating sector**
(billions of 1990 US dollars)

	Costs of traditional approach low/high	Costs of the trading system low/high	Savings low/high
1995	1.0-1.5	0.6-0.9	0.4-0.6
2000	3.2-4.9	1.1-2.1	2.1-2.8
2010	2.3-5.1	1.0-3.7	1.3-1.4

Source: US EPA (1992).

Savings involved with the introduction of the emission trading system, though large in absolute terms, are not very significant when compared to the approximately $200 billion US annual costs of generating electricity. Hence, the impact of the trading system on average costs of electricity generation and prices to consumers are assumed to be fairly limited (see Table 8). At the same time, given that utilities are structured as regulated monopolies, the effects of small price changes are not likely to affect their financial situation. It is also expected that consumers' responses to limited price modifications will be unimportant.

When the system was designed, one fundamental issue was to outline whether the emission reductions in SO_2 were large enough to protect sensitive ecosystems. Since there is a concentration of sulphur emissions and depositions in the Midwest and in the north-eastern areas of the country, some analysts thought that a single market could encourage undesirable trades between East and West. Thereby, in the initial drafts of the programme, two trading regions were established to deter western utilities from selling their allowances to the East. However, some factors resulted in the elimination of the subnational trading regions: allowances could not be effectively constrained from flowing across borders because several utilities operated in both trading regions, electricity generation could be shifted outside any trading region (avoiding the regional emissions cap), and a single market would still result in major reductions in emissions from the Midwest because that region has the lower control costs.[23]

The system generally operates without regard to the spatial distribution of emissions, although some features seem to prevent the presence of localised environmental problems or "hot spots". First, the allowance system does not affect other air pollution regulations that limit SO_2 emissions at local and regional levels. Second, after modelling the introduction of emission reductions and trading, the studies available from the NAPAP show the possibilities for a wide variation of final emissions without a proliferation of "hot spots".

Table 8. **Savings in average electricity costs with the introduction of a trading system**
(per cent)

	Low scenario	High scenario
1995	0.2	0.3
2000	0.8	1.1
2005	0.4	0.5
2010	0.5	0.4

Source: U.S. EPA (1992).

5.3.4 Ex post *evidence on effects*

A substantial volume of transactions in sulphur allowances has taken place since the system began. Some 36 million allowance trades have been recorded, two thirds of them external trades between companies. Internal trades, occurring within companies, do not have to be reported, and their volume is believed to exceed the volume of recorded, external, trades.

The main focus of interest in evaluating the performance of the sulphur allowance trading regime has been the arrangements for allowance auctions, which commenced in 1993. There are two separate auctions: a "spot market" auction of 100 000-150 000 allowances usable in the year of the auction, and an "advance" auction of 100 000 allowances usable seven years later. The auctions are conducted by Chicago Board of Trade on behalf of EPA.

Prices in the allowance auctions have been unexpectedly low. Whilst the EPA's 1990 estimate was $750 per allowance, the market clearing price in the 1993 spot auction was $131 (EPA, 1993), and subsequent prices have been even lower, declining to $66 (Korb, 1996). As Burtraw (1996) discusses, explanations of the lower-than-expected prices have been put forward which have involved both institutional factors, and factors relating to market fundamentals.

In the former category, some of the features of the auction system, including the requirements that successful bidders pay the amount they bid, and the lack of a price floor in the auction, may have provided incentives for strategic underbidding by participants, which may have led to low auction prices (Rico, 1993). These aspects of the auction arrangements might also account for lower prices in the auctions than the prices for bilateral trades between individual utilities. A number of other institutional factors might lead the market to perform below its potential.

First, highly regulated electric utilities would be the major players in this market, with two likely outcomes: they might have little incentives to buy and sell allowances, since the state public utility commissions could prevent investors from keeping any of the resulting profits; and a conservative policy on allowances may arise because they are generally obliged to serve all the demand (Hausker, 1992). Second, substantial regulatory uncertainty could loom over the market[24] firms from engaging in allowance transactions. Third, regulatory requirements (*e.g.* in the form of compliance plans to be submitted to the EPA for approval or the complicated issues involved in Phase I) could be impediments to trading. Finally, it has been indicated that the auction design might lack adequate mechanisms for proper performance, such a special treatment to long-term buyers, or possibilities for sale of streams of allowances. In fact, all these reasons could encourage utilities to hoard their allowances, forcing up their prices, thereby making compliance more expensive, and thwarting the expansion of other producers.

Whatever the strength of these various possible institutional explanations, other commentators have also noted major changes in the market fundamentals which are likely to have changed the likely demands for allowances. In particular, Burtraw (1996) and Ellerman and Montero (1996) point to major changes in the coal market due to sharp reductions in rail freight charges which have made low-sulphur western coal a viable option for utility plants in the Midwest. As a result, the much lower-cost options are now available for compliance with the sulphur emissions cap, and the marginal value of each sulphur allowance has fallen sharply compared to initial expectations.

5.4 Inter-refinery lead trading in the United States

Lead trading in the US provides the opportunity to observe an application of a tradeable permit-type mechanism of finite and predictable duration; some of the problems of uncertainty which have been problematic for other permit trading schemes do not arise here, since the scheme was, from the start, conceived as a transition mechanism, designed to reduce the costs of adjustment to lower lead levels in motor fuels.

The evidence from the lead trading scheme about the performance of economic instruments is in general highly favourable; substantial numbers of trades took place, in a market environment which appeared broadly efficient. The trades have been estimated to be associated with substantial economic savings, but the basis of these estimates – and, in particular, the extent to which they rely on genuine *ex post* data rather than simply an extrapolation from *ex ante* assessments – is unclear.

5.4.1 *Policy background*

Lead added to petrol raises its octane and improves engine performance. However, lead is acutely toxic and its widespread use has prompted concerns over adverse health effects from airborne lead. In response, the US Environmental Protection Agency (EPA) required that unleaded petrol be made available by July 1974 and restricted the lead content of leaded petrol to 1.7 grams per gallon after January 1, 1975 (Carlin, 1992, 5-7).

Following phased reductions in limits for the lead content of leaded petrol, EPA required that after January 1, 1979, the average lead content for individual refiners across leaded and unleaded petrol was to be 0.5 grams per gallon. Similar requirements applied to motor fuel importers (Carlin, 1992, 5-7).

However, the demand for leaded petrol declined during the early 1980s. This meant that limits on the average lead content of petrol became increasingly less restrictive of the lead content of leaded petrol. In view of this, EPA imposed new limits on the lead content of leaded petrol – 1.1 grams per gallon from November 1982, 0.5 grams per gallon from July 1985 and 0.1 grams per gallon from January 1986 (Anderson, Hofmann and Rusin, 1989, page 23). Slightly less stringent standards applied to small refiners (with an output under 5 000 barrels per day) for the first half of 1982.

Partly in response to concerns that small refiners in particular would experience difficulties in complying with the rapid application of these stricter standards, lead trading was instituted from July 1983, to operate during the transition period to the new lower limit of 0.1 grams per gallon.

5.4.2 *Design of the instrument*

Lead trading, formally known as "inter-refinery averaging" allowed refiners and importers to trade lead reduction credits in order to meet limits for the lead content of petrol. Trading could be internal or external – a firm could use lead rights itself by adding more lead to its petrol at some point during the quarter than would otherwise be allowed, or it could sell its rights to another firm (Hahn and Hester, 1989, page 382).

Transactions were reported to the EPA and each refiner was required to have a net balance of lead rights greater than or equal to zero for the quarter. The quantity of rights to which a firm was entitled was determined by the amount of leaded petrol produced by the firm and the current EPA standard required (Hahn and Hester, 1989, page 381).

Smaller refiners, when subject to less stringent standards than larger refiners, could not sell lead rights to larger refiners. After July 1, 1983 all refiners were subject to the same lead content standards with the exception of Californian refiners. Petrol lead content standards in California were more stringent than EPA's and refiners here were not allowed to trade rights in order to exceed the state limits.

Initially, rights simply expired if they were not used or sold during the quarter in which they were created. However, in all four quarters of 1985, refiners were able to "bank" rights for their own future use through to the end of 1987, or for sale to other refiners until the termination of the lead trading programme at the end of 1986.

Refiners and importers were required to complete reporting forms on a quarterly basis. These detailed all trades, banking deposits, withdrawals and balances, along with data on petrol volumes produced and traded. Since each individual transaction was to be reported by both the buyer and the seller, the authorities had information allowing them to match individual purchases and sales of lead credits. Enforcement was largely operated through paper audit of the reported transaction statements, to identify discrepancies and inconsistencies. Enforcement through direct measurement of the lead content of samples of petrol from individual refineries was, given the structure of the scheme, of little use; the limits applied to the average lead content over an entire quarter, and thus spot checks of lead content at a particular point in time were not able to indicate whether refiners were in compliance with their declared lead rights.

5.4.3 Ex ante *assessments and expectations*

Trading was instituted to allow refiners some flexibility in achieving lower limits for the average lead content of petrol. In particular, it was expected that smaller refiners would purchase lead rights from larger refiners allowing the former to adjust more gradually. Without trading in lead credits it was thought that either the phase down would take longer or it that it would lead to a short-term contraction in the supply of petrol and possibly supply disruptions in some areas (Carlin, 1992, pages 5-8).

The EPA estimated that about 9.1 billion grams of lead would be banked and that banking alone would save refiners $226 million (Carlin, 1992, pages 5-9). EPA estimates from 1985, reported by Hahn and Stavins (1991, page 17), were that the savings from the lead trading programme were approximately 20 per cent over alternatives without lead trading.

5.4.4 Ex post *evidence on effects*

Several hundred refiners, constituting over half the total number, participated in the reduction credit market. The market was very active and trading activity generally increased throughout the life of the programme. In particular there was extensive use of banking. Interestingly, the proportion of large refiners engaged in trading was greater than that of small refiners in almost all quarters suggesting that the former were more likely to take advantage of the flexibility offered by the programme. In addition, roughly equal proportions of small traders bought and sold rights indicating that they were not uniformly hard-pressed to meet the new lead standards (Hahn and Hester, 1989, page 384).

However, there is some evidence that small traders found it more difficult to meet the new standards. During the first six quarters of the trading programme small refiners consistently exceeded the EPA limit for lead added to petrol. They were able to do so by purchasing credits from large refiners who added lead to petrol at levels slightly below the EPA limit.

In 1985, firms of all sizes anticipated the further lowering of lead limits due in July of that year by adding less lead to petrol than allowed during the first two quarters and using the opportunity to bank

◆ Figure 1. **Percentage of refineries and importers making trading and banking transactions under the Lead Trading Programme**

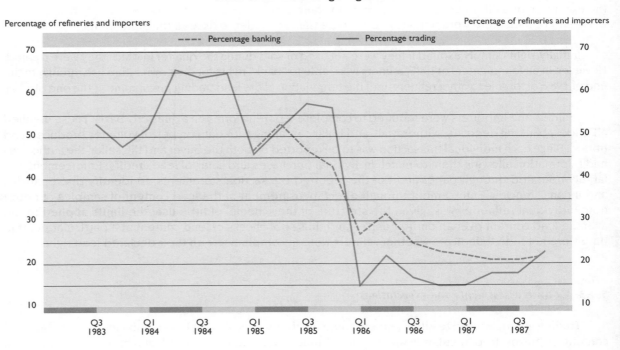

Source: EPA data from Quarterly Reports on Lead in Gasoline, taken from Anderson, Hofmann and Rusin, 1989, Table II.3.

◆   Figure 2.   ***Quantities of lead rights banking transactions under the Lead Trading Programme***

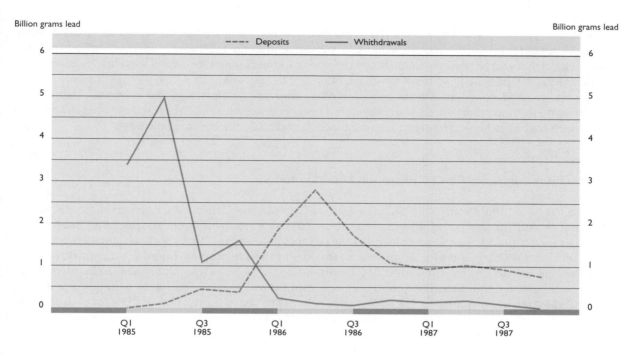

Billion grams lead   Billion grams lead

Source: EPA data from Quarterly Reports on Lead in Gasoline, taken from Anderson, Hofmann and Rusin, 1989, Table II.3.

rights. However, whilst most large firms were able to do this only about a third of small firms did so. After July, large refiners continued with this practice but small refiners exceeded the new lead limits by withdrawing banked rights and buying them from large refiners (Hahn and Hester, 1989, page 384).

In 1986, rights could no longer be banked unless they were purchased from another firm; few firms did this. When a lower limit on lead came into effect it was exceeded by refiners of all sizes who withdrew rights banked previously. Until 1987 small refiners continued to add more lead to petrol than did large refiners.

The prices at which trades were made were not required to be reported to EPA, and systematic data on prices is not available. Anderson, Hofmann and Rusin (1989, page 26) report, on the basis of anecdotal evidence, that lead rights may have traded at a range of prices between 0.75 and 4 cents per gram. Other estimates are that prior to the institution of banking, prices were consistently below one cent per gram after which they fluctuated between two and five cents.

The large volume of rights traded and banked imply that savings have been substantial. The actual amount banked turned out to be some 10 billion grams, very close to the *ex ante* EPA estimate, for an average saving of 2.5 cents per gram banked (Carlin, 1992, pages 5-9).

The environmental effects of the trading programme cannot be calculated exactly, and depend crucially, of course, on what lead content standards are assumed would otherwise have applied. If it is assumed that the same time profile of standards would have operated, without any provision for trading, then the effect of trading on environmental outcomes may have been negligible; however, if it is assumed that trading permitted a more aggressive time profile of reductions than would otherwise have been feasible, then lead trading may have accelerated the reduction in lead emissions from motor vehicles.

The general consensus of the studies reporting and evaluating the experience of the lead trading programme is that the scheme worked much better than most other practical applications of tradeable permit mechanisms. There has been some discussion of possible reasons for this. Amongst the features of the situation which, it is suggested, account for the good performance of lead trading are that the time-scale of the exercise was clearly set out in advance (although, in practice, subsequently adjusted through the introduction of banking provisions), rights and obligations were clearly defined, and the commodity traded was clearly defined and homogeneous. A further positive factor may have been that the personnel at different refineries were already accustomed to conducting transactions with each other (for refinery feedstocks and products). Hahn (1991) also observed that the programme was implemented after agreement had been reached about environmental goals, which may have helped to overcome resistance to trading on the part of participants.

5.5 Market mechanisms for CFC phase-out in the United States

The 1987 Montreal Protocol on Substances that Deplete the Ozone Layer agreed drastic action to phase out production and use of chlorofluorocarbons (CFCs), a group of chemicals which had been widely used in a range of products and industrial processes – including uses in refrigerators, as aerosol propellants, in the production of expanded polystyrene packaging, in the electronics industry, etc. For developed countries, the Protocol initially required CFC consumption (in all but a few minor uses) to be phased out by the year 2000, a deadline subsequently brought forward to 1996. In compliance with this agreement, the United States has required its chemical manufacturers to cease production of CFCs for consumption in the US by the start of 1996. The process of attainment of this target has been supported by a series of policy measures, designed to promote efficient adjustment in the chemical industry, and to stimulate the development of replacement technologies for CFCs. Specifically, these measures included:

- national and local legislation, regulating and banning certain CFC uses;
- a tradeable permit regime, covering CFC manufacturers and importers;
- an excise tax on ozone-depleting chemicals;
- "entrepreneurial" approaches, sponsored by the Environment Protection Agency (EPA), to catalyse the development of alternatives to CFCs for a range of applications; these included a "Golden Carrot" prize for the development of a CFC-free refrigerator, and a government/industry working group to devise methods of recycling CFCs from car air conditioners at automobile service stations;
- changes to defence procurement rules, to ensure that procurement standards could be met by non-CFC products and manufacturing processes; where necessary, these were backed up by collaborative actions to identify or develop adequate replacement technologies.

Prior to the phase-out, it was anticipated that eliminating all CFCs in the short time-scale permitted by the agreement would entail significant costs and disruption in CFC-user industries. Industry, in particular, had maintained that there were no viable alternatives to many CFC applications, and that the envisaged phase-out would be costly.

An evaluation of the policy measures adopted in the US to implement the CFC phase-out has been conducted by the World Resources Institute and a group of collaborating institutions (see the summary by Cook, 1996). It argues that, in practice, the difficulty of the phase-out was less than had been anticipated. Whilst, in 1988, the EPA had estimated that the average cost to halve CFC use would be $3.50 per kilogram, within two years its cost estimate had been revised sharply downwards, as it became clear that acceptable alternatives to CFCs would be more easily found than originally anticipated. In 1990 the EPA estimated a cost of $2.20 per kilogram for a more stringent policy, the elimination of all CFC uses by 2000. Even when the target date for ending CFC use was brought forward to 1996, the estimated cost per kilogram remained at much this level, rising to only some $2.45 per kilogram.

In practice, the phase-out of CFC uses proceeded significantly more rapidly than the legislated consumption cap required, with consumption falling to two-thirds of the cap in 1990, and half the cap in 1993. Between 1990 and 1994, US CFC consumption fell by more than three-quarters; nearly all of this reduction occurred ahead of the legally-mandated timetable.

Given the variety of policy instruments employed to secure the CFC phase-out in the US, identifying the contribution made by particular components of the policy package is difficult, as the WRI study recognises. "Without question", however, the study argues that the main impetus for CFC users to find alternatives to CFCs came from the deadline set by the international community to eliminate CFC use; in anticipation of the deadline, CFC users began the search for viable alternatives, and once these had been found, were often prepared to adopt the CFC-free technologies, even before this became mandatory. Consumer pressure also appears to have played a role in encouraging the quick phase-out in some fields, for example, in finding alternatives to the use of CFCs in fast-food packaging. Also, the various working groups sponsored by EPA, including those concerned with military procurement, played an identifiable role in facilitating the reduction of CFC use in certain applications. Nevertheless, the study also concluded that a non-trivial part in achieving a relatively smooth transition, without excessive cost, was played by the two main market instruments in the package, the tradeable permits and ozone-depleting chemical tax. These "created an efficient, responsive and flexible policy framework", with low administrative costs for EPA, and even lower record-keeping costs for business; the flexibility which they provided to CFC users was particularly valuable in this case, given the diversity of CFC uses, and the considerable *ex ante* uncertainty about the costs and feasibility of abatement in each individual use.

The marketable permits system allocated CFC allowances to existing importers and producers of CFCs and halons; based on each firm's market share in 1986. Since the market was dominated by a small number of firms, the initial allocation of allowances involved less than thirty firms. Firms could trade permits amongst themselves on a basis which took account of the relative ozone-depleting potential of the different CFC compounds; the system thus capped the aggregate use of CFCs, expressed in CFC-11 equivalent terms. A Provision was made for 1 per cent of the CFC allocation traded to be withdrawn when a trade was made, which in practice would appear to be only a very small impediment to cost-reducing trades.

Cook (1996) reports that the administrative costs of the system for both the EPA and the firms were low; the system was operated by a staff of four at the EPA, and was estimated to cost industry only some $2.4 million in the first year for reporting and record-keeping. Cook argues that these administration costs were substantially lower than if the reduction in CFC use had instead been regulated by detailed command-and-control regulation of individual sectors using CFCs; for this the EPA would have needed some additional 33 staff, and would have incurred extra costs of some $23 million annually, whilst industry would have faced costs of some $300 million for reporting and record-keeping.

Cook (1996) also reports some efficiency gains to the companies using CFCs, arising because of the flexibility that the system provided. As the market for CFCs declined, the system allowed firms to rationalise production between different production facilities according to the least-cost pattern of supply. It also gave CFC users the scope to switch between different CFC compounds, within the overall limit in terms of their aggregate ozone-depleting potential. This allowed firms to benefit from their rapid elimination of certain uses of CFCs, by permitting a correspondingly slower time profile of adjustment in other applications.

The "ozone-depleter tax" was introduced in 1990. It was levied on CFCs and halons at an initial rate of $1.37 per pound of CFC-11. Different CFC compounds were taxed at rates which reflected their relative ozone-depleting potential, expressed in terms of amounts of CFC-11. The rate was subsequently increased, to $5.35 in 1995, and the scope of the tax was broadened to include additional compounds. The tax raised on average some $0.6 billion annually in revenue during the first five years of its operation.

The impact of the tax on CFC prices was substantial. Cook (1996) reports that after the 1995 increase in the tax rate, CFC-11 and CFC-12, the two most common CFCs, were selling at more than three times their pre-tax price. She also argues that the price signals created by the tax had a powerful impact on CFC consumption, and are the reason for aggregate CFC use to have fallen well below the consumption cap set by the CFC permit allocations during the period 1990-93.

5.6 Individual transferable quotas in fisheries management

In contrast to the other cases reviewed in this report, which concern environmental policies directed, in the main, at pollution externalities, the systems of fisheries quota trading concern the management of a natural resource. There are some important differences between this case and the pollution cases in the objectives of policy and hence in the criteria relevant for evaluation.

The case of fisheries regulation is one where the aggregate value of quota has a clear interpretation – it provides a measure of the fishery rent generated by efficiently controlling access to the fishery, and hence the gain compared to a system of open access, or compared to inefficient regulatory policies, such as the operation of "Total Allowable Catch" (TAC) limits, which dissipate the potential value of the fishery. Much of the discussion on the empirical studies in the New Zealand case has concerned the extent to which the prices of traded quota in practice provide an accurate measure of this rent.

It will be observed that the economic gain from the efficient regulation of the fishery system comprises two elements, only one of which corresponds to the cost-efficiency sought from economic instruments in the environmental policy field. Much of the economic waste from operation of TAC limits could be eliminated by the introduction of non-tradeable individual quota; this would, however, as in the pollution case, be liable to be economically inefficient. Trading of quota allows the quota to pass to operators able to make the most profitable use of quota; this gain, which corresponds to the efficiency gain from using economic instruments in pollution control, is only one of the two elements in the economic rent measured by the aggregate value of quota.

Despite these differences, the fishery quotas case study has been included in this paper because of the evidence it provides on the operation of the permit market. The efficiency of the permit market is one of the key uncertainties in the performance in practice of tradeable permits, but is critical to the attainment of any efficiency gains from using tradeable permits in environmental policy applications. The fisheries case studies, like the Fox River tradeable permits experience discussed in Section 5.1, include cases of markets for quota which have not turned out to be perfectly competitive, and there is a certain amount of evidence of inefficient pricing. Nevertheless, the broad indication from the *ex post* evidence on the operation of fisheries quota systems is a positive one, despite the complex restrictions on the terms of trading in some of the countries.

5.6.1 *Policy background*

Fisheries management faces a classic common property resource problem. Without some form of restriction on the behaviour of individual fishing operators, the fish stock will be exploited for current profits, and insufficient fish will be left to maintain the level of fish stocks in future periods. In an unregulated "open access" fishery, each operator will decide on a level of fishing activity which will maximise private profitability; there will be no incentive for any of the operators to take account of the externality to the industry as a whole which is caused by overfishing, since the impact that an individual operator's restraint would have on the operator's own profitability is negligible. Some form of concerted action to limit short-run over-exploitation is required in order to maximise the long-run profitability of the industry.

Whilst the risks of over-exploitation of fisheries have long been recognised, major initiatives to deal with the consequences of over-exploitation have really only begun during the past three decades. Initially, these have taken one of two main forms: first, regulations on access to particular fisheries, limiting fishing to existing participants, and imposing limits on the size of boats, the type of gear that may be employed, etc., and, second, "Total allowable catch" (TAC) limits on the aggregate amount of fish that may be taken in any season. Neither of these approaches is wholly satisfactory as a solution to the problem of unprofitability in an open access fishery. Access restrictions attempt to maintain profitability by restricting entry to the industry, but still leave the underlying source of long-term deteriorating profitability in place – the incentive for individual participants to fish at levels higher than the long-run profit-maximising level. TAC limits are, on the other hand, effective at limiting exploitation of the fish stock, but do so in a way which dissipates most of the potential profitability of the industry, by setting up a "race for fish" in which individual participants devote excessive resources to maximising their catch early in the season, before the TAC limit has been reached, and then sit idle for the reminder of the season. Excessive resources are thus devoted to the fishery, as fishing operators engage in a destructive race to maximise their share of the TAC.

Given the difficulties of regulating fisheries using these methods, a number of countries have employed economic instruments to discourage overfishing. These have taken the form of individual transferable quotas (ITQs), which give individual fishing operators an entitlement to a particular level of catch in a given period; this fixed entitlement eliminates the early-season race for fish, allowing the operator to choose the most efficient pattern of fishing activity over the season as a whole. The aggregate level of quotas issued restricts the aggregate catch taken, whilst the provision for trading allows rationalisation to take place, where this would promote efficiency.

ITQ systems have been employed extensively in New Zealand, and, on a more limited scale or in a more restricted form in Australia, Canada and Iceland. This case study discusses in detail the available evidence on the performance of the New Zealand system, and provides a shorter discussion of evidence relating to the operation of the systems in the other three countries.

5.6.2 *Design of ITQs in New Zealand*

The New Zealand ITQ system was established following New Zealand's assertion of a 200 mile exclusive economic zone (EEZ) in 1978, which brought under national control significant deep-sea fisheries previously exploited by foreign operators. An ITQ system was initially introduced for the management of seven principal deep-sea fish species in 1982. In 1986, the initial ten-year quotas granted in 1982 were transformed into permanent quotas, and the ITQ system was extended to include 21 species in the inshore fishery. There were some further more limited extensions in 1987 and 1989, and the ITQ system now covers all of the commercially significant fisheries, except for tuna fishing (Clark, Major and Mollett, 1988; Campbell, 1991).

The ITQs are transferable property rights allocated to fishers in the form of a right to harvest any amount up to the limit equal to the quota over the course of a specified fishing period. The basic unit of quota is 1 tonne of a given species in a given area annually in perpetuity (or for 25 years in the case of rock lobster). The measurement is standardised in terms of "greenweight", the units used by fisheries managers for stock control; this allows appropriate account to be taken of the various different degrees of processing which may have been undertaken by the time the fish is landed (Campbell, 1991, pages 5, 9).

Changes have been made over time to the definition of the "property right" which the quota establishes (Campbell, 1991, page 7). In the 1986 system, quota were initially set in terms of tonnages, and the TAC was adjusted by open-market operations, which repurchased the required amount of quota. However, it became necessary to make drastic reductions in some quota in 1989/90, which would have required substantial government expenditure. To avoid the public expenditure cost of large-scale buy-back, the system was amended to change over to a proportional quota system, in which each unit of quota establishes an entitlement to a given proportion of the TAC, rather than a given tonnage.

Initially, when quota were allocated for the first seven species in 1982, the allocation was based on the level of catching and processing capacity and throughput. In the subsequent extension of the system in 1986, quota were allocated on the basis of historical catch – specifically, at the average catch achieved in the two best of the previous three years.

Given this provisional allocation of quota, reductions were then made in the aggregate level of quotas, in order to reduce Total Allowable Catch below previous levels for heavily-exploited species. The reductions in aggregate quota were achieved partly through repurchasing initial quota allocations from fishing operators willing to dispose of their quota allocation, and partly, where repurchasing proved inadequate, by making equal percentage reductions in the value of the remaining quotas to bring TAC down to the required level (Clark, Major and Mollett, 1988, page 327).

The range of trades permitted is extensive. Fishers may trade in perpetuity, by lease, by sublease and with any desired conditions of contract attached. Unrestricted forward trading is permitted, and retrospective trading is also allowed, although only within the current fishing period. The only significant limit on trading (except for the requirement that quota ownership is restricted to New Zealand nationals) is that new entrants to a particular fishery must purchase a minimum quota of 5 tonnes.

A quota trading exchange was established to facilitate trades. This includes a videotex system, fish quota brokers and a full quota trading information network. Membership is open to any individual or company and requires the payment of an initial application fee, an annual subscription and transaction fees of 1 per cent of the transaction value (Clark, Major and Mollett, 1988, page 333).

Enforcement is based on the scope for cross-checking provided by documentary records kept at three stages in the process – a Catch Landing Log, completed by the skipper as soon as the catch is landed, a Quota Management Report, supplied by the quota holder (this gives details of the quantity of fish caught for each species in each area for which quota is owned or leased; supporting documentation must also be held for at least 3 years), and a Licensed Fish Receivers Return, detailing transactions by individuals licensed to purchase fish from commercial fishermen (Clark, Major and Mollett, 1988, pages 329-30).

Provisions have been made for dealing with the unpredictable species mix which is caught by trawlers and other net fishing operations. Fishing operators may have difficulty matching catch with quota at the end of each month, even given the scope for trading. The ITQ system thus permits operators with a catch exceeding quota by more than 10 per cent at the end of the month either to surrender the excess catch to the authorities, or to trade the excess off against quota in another species at a given rate (the "Catch-Quota Trade-oFF System").

When the ITQ programme was established, the government stated that it intended, over time, to appropriate a substantial part of the rent generated by the programme. Resource rentals are payable for quota, regardless of whether the quota are used in any given period. The amount varies by species and area, and the rental level is doubled if the fish are caught by a foreign vessel. Initially, low rental levels were set on quota for most species, with provisions to increase these by up to 20 per cent annually (Campbell, 1991, page 5).

5.6.3 *Effectiveness of ITQs in New Zealand*

Clark, Major and Mollett (1989) discuss the operation of the ITQ system in the first two years of operation. They observe that the implementation of ITQs was relatively free of problems, although a large number of objections were made initially concerning the allocation of quota. The system of monitoring and reporting quota has proved effective. Quota owners have tended to hold and use their quota, although among larger quota holders there are slightly more holders than owners suggesting that some specialisation in investment has taken place.

The system led to some changes in the structure of the fishing industry; an expansion in deepwater fishing has required increased catching capacity and the growth in investment has also led to increases in employment.

Practical problems in the operation of the ITQ system discussed by Clark Major and Mollett (1989) include the operation of procedures for by-catch (fish species caught as a by-product of fishing for other species), the arrangements for dealing with cases of overfishing, the difficulties of using tonnage quotas (subsequently dealt with, as noted above, by the introduction of quota defined as proportions of the TAC), and issues connected with Maori fishing rights.

Two aspects of the operation of the ITQ system have attracted particular attention, the efficiency of price determination in the quota market, and the measurement of the aggregate economic benefit from the operation of the regulated fishery. The two issues are related, in the sense that in an efficiently-operating quota market, the price of quota may be used to infer the level of fishery rent generated by the system.

Lindner (1990) presents evidence showing substantial variation in prices for quota in individual species. In some months, the maximum quota prices recorded were more than ten times the level of the lowest quota prices recorded, and in most months the range of prices was substantial – generally at least as large as the average quota price. A number of reasons may be considered to account for this observed price dispersion.

First, there is reason to believe that some quota trading markets may not be perfectly competitive as existing participants may keep the prices paid for quota artificially high to deter new entry. For example, three-quarters of total quota in hoki and orange roughly and three fifths of total quota in squid were held in 1986/87 by the six largest quota holders (Lindner, Campbell and Bevin, 1991).

A second reason for quota price dispersion is that some market participants could be very poorly informed about the going price levels in the market. This is unlikely to be an explanation that can account for much of the variation, except in some markets, such as that for Snapper which involve smaller operators. In the major markets, where the large companies are involved, quota transactions are made by fishing quota market managers. In addition, the videotex system, and other aspects of the trading arrangements should have tended to ensure that most market participants have the opportunity to become reasonable well-informed before trading.

Other possible explanations are that the price dispersion may reflect false reporting of prices, which could arise for a number of possible reasons, heterogeneity in the precise terms of quota trades (some of the very high prices may have included ships or equipment as well as quota), or transfer pricing problems in non-arms-length transactions.

The wide range of observed prices complicates estimation of the aggregate fishery rent generated by the system. As Campbell (1990) describes, three possible approaches may be taken to the measurement of fishery rent, based on data on prices of perpetual quota, annual lease quota, and industry profitability data.

The reported trading value for perpetual quota would value the total quota issued in the New Zealand fishery at $550 millions in 1986/7 and $765 millions in 1987/8 (Lindner, Campbell and Bevin, 1989). Since the government's costs of operating the management scheme were broadly balanced by the level of resource rental charged to the fishery operators at that time, these figures for the aggregate perpetual value of quota may indicate the long-run expected net contribution of the industry to the economy. It is, however, difficult to infer anything from these estimates about the level of resource rents currently being earned, since they may reflect expectations about long-run changes in costs, fishing prospects, and fish prices.

Traded values for annual lease quota, based on data for the same years, (adjusted for some price observations believed to be anomalous) would measure the annual fishery rent at $59 million in 1986/7 and $75 million in 1987/8. This data, however, raises some puzzles. In particular, as Lindner and Campbell (1989) observe, some of the lease quota transactions appear to take place at prices close to or in excess of the landed price for the corresponding catch. Some of these high figures may reflect the sources of data error discussed earlier. However, there are good reasons to believe that in the initial period of operation of an ITQ system, quota could be traded at prices well above the long-run value. As Campbell (1990) observes, the price of annual lease quota may reflect "a quasi rent arising from temporary artificial scarcity of quota relative to catching power"; until the level of capacity engaged in the industry has adjusted, operators may be willing to purchase quota at prices that give a return over variable costs only, rather than over total costs. In these circumstances annual lease quota prices could overstate fishery rents.[25]

Industry profitability data gives a very different picture to that derived from annual lease quota values. Lindner, Campbell and Bevin (1989) estimate that in 1987/8 the industry incurred an aggregate economic loss of some $54 millions. This can, of course, be reconciled with the lease quota picture, to the extent that it reflects the disequilibrium in the market, as capacity adjusts to the new system of regulation.

5.6.4 ITQs *in fisheries management in Australia, Iceland and Canada*

Australia

Australia introduced an ITQ system for one part of the fishing industry - blue fin tuna fishing – in 1984, following a marked deterioration in the economic position of the industry in the early 1980s. Other ITQs now operate for the south east trawl fisheries, and for the abalone fisheries (the latter under the control of the state governments rather than the federal authorities). The majority of the fishing industry, however, remains regulated through entry limits and input controls.

Scott (1992) describes the operation of the ITQ system for blue fin tuna. Individual quota allocations are based on shares of the TAC, and are tradeable, with few restrictions; they may be sold, leased, and used as collateral for loans.

As Scott's account shows, introduction of the ITQ system for blue fin tuna led to a very rapid process of restructuring of the industry. Between 1983 and 1987, the fleet based in Western Australia contracted by 80 per cent, and the New South Wales fleet virtually disappeared; the South Australia fleet came to control some 91 per cent of quota, compared to its initial allocation of 66 per cent.

As theory would predict, there was an appreciable reduction in the level of capital employed in the industry. The number of vessels operating fell by 70 per cent. Simulations by the Australian Bureau of Agricultural and Resource Economics (ABARE), quoted by Scott (1992), compared the fishery under ITQs with alternative management regimes along the lines of those previously employed. The conclusions of this comparison were that aggregate capital employed under ITQs was some A$10-12 million lower than it would have been under the earlier regimes, whilst the system generated approximately four times the economic rent (some A$6.5 million per annum) that would have been achieved under the earlier system.

In comparison with the resource rents generated by the ITQ regime, the costs of managing the fishery are relatively low – some A$600 000, of which roughly half is currently paid by the operators, and the rest borne by the taxpayer. One feature of the system which helps to keep management costs low is the relative ease with which the blue fin tuna quotas can be enforced; the major markets for the output are abroad, and the Australian home market would be unable to absorb a substantial diversion of illicit catch.

Iceland

In Iceland, ITQs were introduced in 1984 to the large demersal fisheries, fishing for groundfish species, principally cod. This followed an earlier scheme applied to the herring industry from the latter part of the 1970s. However, participation in the demersal ITQ system remained voluntary until 1990 for many operators, who could instead opt to remain subject to the earlier quotas which restricted fishing effort. Even with the extension of the ITQ system to cover all participants in the demersal fishery in 1990, the system also retains other elements of regulation, including both capacity restrictions, and a ban on new entry.

Quotas, taking the form of shares in the TAC, were allocated to existing participants on a historic basis – the allocations made in the 1990 extension of the scheme were based formally on the previous year's catch, but that, in turn, was determined by catch levels limited under previous quota regimes. Quota are permanent, divisible, and tradeable subject to relatively few restrictions. The principal restriction on trades is designed to prevent short-term inter-regional employment fluctuations in the industry; this takes the form of certain limits on transfer of annual quotas between geographical areas. A small annual charge, of less than 0.2 per cent of catch value, is levied on quota holders to cover costs of administration and enforcement.

Arnason (1992) presents evidence that indicates a substantial improvement in the condition of the demersal fishing industry, compared to what would have been expected under continuation of the previous management regime. Using a simple model to predict trends in the industry in the absence of the ITQ system, he concludes that resources employed into demersal fishing in 1990 were only some 57 per cent of what they would have been under the earlier system. Annual capital growth had fallen from some 6 per cent per annum before ITQs to 3 per cent since the system came into operation.

In addition to this counterfactual evidence, indications of the economic value of the ITQ regime can also be obtained from analysis of the aggregate value of outstanding quota. Substantial proportions of the aggregate quota are traded (between 20 and 30 per cent of the outstanding quota stock for demersal fisheries in recent years), so that quota prices are likely to be determined in a broadly competitive market. Arnason estimates the total value of outstanding quota to be some $46 million in 1984 and $166 million in 1988. These figures are unlikely to be a perfect measure of the true value of the fishery for two, partly offsetting reasons: on the one hand, Arnason suggests that they may understate the true value of the fishery, since they ignore the parts regulated in ways other than ITQs; on the other hand, during the adjustment to an ITQ regime, before the capital stock has fully adjusted, short-term quota prices may overstate long-run values.

Overall, Arnason concludes, the ITQ system has been of considerable benefit. Despite the limitations which arise due to its coexistence with other forms of regulation, Arnason estimates that the system achieved some 50 per cent or more of the maximum attainable economic rent from the demersal fishery.

Canada

In Canada, there has been a gradual introduction of individual quotas (Enterprise Allocations, or EAs) in a number of fisheries zones during the 1980s. However, the Canadian system remains far from a pure ITQ system, since not all of the quotas are tradeable and the system of fisheries management contains many other elements of regulation, including both input and output controls.

EAs began experimentally with the four largest offshore groundfish companies in 1982, and the programme was made permanent in 1989. EAs were extended to a number of other fisheries during 1984 to 1986. Crowley (1992) discusses the performance of some of the EA systems.

In the offshore groundfish fisheries, the previous system of open-access TACs had led to substantial diversion of fishing effort into an early-season race for fish. The 1981 offshore quota for northern cod had been caught in the first seven weeks of the year. EAs in this fishery date from 1982. The result of the system of EAs, according to Crowley, is that fishing activity has become more evenly-spread throughout the year, whilst the capital used has probably fallen (the number of vessels active in this fishery has fallen from 142 in 1979 to 114 in 1989).

In the offshore groundfish system, sale of quota is not permitted, but barter arrangements (in the form of exchanges of one species for another) are allowed. Lack of quota tradeability does not, of course, diminish the effectiveness of quota systems in restraining the race for fish; individual, non-tradeable quotas can also accomplish this, although at potentially greater cost in terms of inefficiency. In any case, Crowley argues, "Canadian experience is that if trading of quota is not permitted, participants will find ways to achieve the same ends, notwithstanding legal discouragement" (Crowley, 1992, page 52). Thus, for example, certain take-overs in the industry may have been partly motivated by quota ownership considerations.

The system of quotas for herring, also introduced in 1982, permitted trading, and is thus a more conventional ITQ system. Nevertheless, certain restrictions are placed on trading; in particular, a seller of quota must leave the industry entirely. The price of quota has been substantial; the price for 1 per cent of the aggregate quota ranged from $76 000 to $96 000 over the period since the system was introduced; under the 1988 quota allocation this 1 per cent quota would have represented some 1 300 tonnes of herring plus 26 tonnes of bait. In contrast to the offshore groundfish industry, Crowley notes that there have been some difficulties with enforcement of herring quota, since the many possible landing sites for herring cannot all be subject to effective monitoring.

The ITQ system operating in Lake Erie is the only fully transferable and divisible system operating in Canada. Crowley reports evidence that it has led both to appreciable restructuring (crew numbers fell from 915 to 714), and a marked increase in profitability (average incomes rose from $25 000 to $40 000 per annum).

Chapter 6

OTHER MARKET MECHANISMS (WASTE)

6.1 "Pay-per-bag" for domestic refuse collection

The case of unit charging ("pay-per-bag") for household refuse shows the extensive experience which is accumulating as a result of the schemes operated at municipal level in the US and elsewhere. With some exceptions, the evidence of the studies described in this section is that unit charging reduces the level of household waste, although at the cost, in some cases, of undesired side-effects such as increased illegal disposal. The scale of the reduction in waste has varied between areas, partly because of differences in the accompanying measures taken, such as the provision of improved recycling opportunities.

The studies also show a number of ways in which it may be possible to distinguish the effect of unit charging from the effects of other policy measures often implemented in parallel with unit charging, such as the introduction of kerbside recycling facilities. In particular, cross-section analyses of municipalities which have introduced unit charging, with different charge levels, or in different patterns of combination with supporting policy measures, provide scope for the separate contribution of unit charging to be identified.

The studies of "pay-per-bag" for domestic refuse collection illustrate which particular aspects of the costs and benefits of economic instruments can be better assessed using *ex post* evidence than on the basis of *ex ante* information. Thus, the most significant addition to knowledge about the costs and benefits of unit charging contributed by *ex post* experience relates to the quantitative response to the charging system, a key parameter which cannot easily be quantified on the basis of *ex ante* considerations alone. *Ex post* evidence, on the other hand contributes little new to the translation of these behavioural responses into waste disposal cost savings, over and above what can be assessed *ex ante*. An intermediate case is that of evidence on the distributional impact of unit charging. *Ex ante* estimates of the likely distributional impact can be produced *ex ante*, on the basis of data on the pattern of waste by income group, which provides a "first-round" estimate of the probable distributional incidence of the unit charge. However, *ex post*, it is possible to assess how far the behavioural responses differ between income groups, thus providing additional information relevant to issue of distributional impact, not available from the *ex ante* standpoint.

6.1.1 *Policy background*

Increasing affluence has led to increasing levels of household solid waste in most OECD countries; in the OECD area as a whole, the amount of municipal waste grew by some 9 per cent (by weight) over the period 1980-85. In most OECD countries, the predominant method of disposal of household solid wastes is by landfilling, although in some countries, including Japan, France and Sweden, a substantial proportion is disposed of through incineration (OECD, 1989*b*). Where landfilling is used, many countries are experiencing rapidly-rising costs of disposal, as landfill sites become scarce, and more costly.

The United States exemplifies many of the problems facing OECD countries in the management of solid waste. Between 1960 and 1988 the volume of municipal solid waste more than doubled; the upward trend is forecast to continue. Although about half the waste consists of materials which could be recycled straightforwardly, the overall rate of recycling is only some 13 per cent. About three-quarters of waste is landfilled. Landfill costs have risen dramatically in recent years partly under pressure from environmental policy measures requiring more stringent standards to be maintained in landfill management, and partly because public opposition to the siting of landfills has greatly increased (up to $10 million) the costs of finding and obtaining approval for a new landfill. As a result, the number of new landfills established had fallen by the mid-1980s to less than 20 per cent of the 1970 level. Many existing landfills are reaching capacity; EPA figures show that about 80 per cent will reach capacity in the next 20 years, whilst ten states have less than five years' landfill capacity remaining (Repetto *et al.*, 1992, page 15).

In the past, household refuse collections have been typically financed through municipal taxes (such as residential property taxes) or flat-rate user charges (paid either to the municipality or to a private refuse collector). Such financing mechanisms have the drawback that household payments are unrelated to the amount of refuse collected; as a result they do not give households any incentive to reduce waste levels. One response to the rising cost of disposing of domestic refuse, taken in a considerable number of cities and towns in the US, and also adopted in a number of other parts of the OECD area, has been to seek to reduce the levels of household refuse generated through the use of pricing mechanisms, charging for household refuse collection according to volume or weight. The recent OECD survey of economic instruments in Member states found charges for municipal waste based on actual measurement employed in at least some areas in nine OECD Member states (OECD, 1994a, page 62).

6.1.2 Design of the instrument

The systems of charging for household refuse based on the amount collected vary in different areas in terms of the detail of the charging base, the level of charges, and the extent to which the charging systems have been supported by accompanying measures. Typically, the form of the charge is related to the amount of refuse collected in a relatively rough-and-ready way, rather than through precise measurement. Thus, many unit-based pricing programmes require households to pay for the number of bags or bins of refuse collected; the relationship to waste volumes or weights arises either because they require households to use containers of a standard size or format, or because limits are placed on the amount of waste which each may contain (Fullerton and Kinnaman, 1994, page 1). The charge may be levied through billing for a chosen number of bags or bins per week, through the sale of bags, or through the sale of stickers which households are required to place on each bag of waste put out for collection. A more restricted variant on this arrangement is where households continue to face a fixed monthly fee or pay for solid waste disposal through their annual property tax but face a surcharge on "excess" quantities. Under this approach, households face a marginal cost of zero for waste, up until the trigger volume for the surcharge is reached (Anderson, Hofmann and Rusin, 1990).

6.1.3 Ex ante *assessments and expectations*

Before the initial applications of unit charging, there was little basis on which to make *ex ante* predictions of the likely impact on household refuse volumes of the introduction of pay-per-bag charging schemes for household waste. There are no analogous activities which were likely to indicate the strength of the household response to the introduction of a non-zero charge per unit for waste. Thus, the key parameter in assessing the likely costs and benefits of unit charging was not quantifiable.

This situation has now changed considerably. Since household waste collection tends to be organised at the municipal level, it is possible for a considerable amount of policy experimentation to take place. Municipalities which are now considering the introduction of unit charging for household waste have the experience of more than 100 municipalities in the US, and others elsewhere in the OECD area, on which to draw.

Aside from the key question of the scale of the behavioural response to unit charging, other aspects of the costs and benefits could, in principle, be more readily assessed in advance of any experience with charging systems. Thus, for example, the translation of the financial savings to the waste operator can be straightforwardly obtained from data on landfill or incinerations or costs or – in the case of privately-operated landfill – the charges levied by landfill or incinerator operators. There are likely, of course, also to be various external costs and benefits associated with different disposal options, such as the disamenity to local residents who live near a landfill or incinerator. These could, potentially, be assessed *ex ante* in various ways, using the conventional techniques employed for environmental cost-benefit analysis, such as using hedonic pricing models to assess the impact of such facilities on the value of neighbouring residential property or through contingent valuation approaches, based on individuals' stated valuation of the costs they bear (see, for example, Brisson and Pearce, 1994). Given that in the US systems of unit charging have been introduced through the initiative of individual, generally small, municipalities, the extent to which such costly and sophisticated *ex ante* appraisal techniques have been employed has been limited. Generally, the *ex ante* analysis has been limited to informal assessments of the likely costs and benefits.

Nevertheless, *ex ante* discussion of the likely consequences of unit charging identified some key issues. Thus, for example, critics feared that unit charging systems may induce the largest behavioural changes from the poor, since they are least able to absorb the added cost. There were also concerns about the feasibility of effective enforcement and that unit charges might create the incentive to illegally dispose of waste (EPA, page 13).

6.1.4 Ex post *evidence on effects*

The key variable which *ex post* evidence can help to quantify is the size of the impact of unit charging systems such as pay-per-bag on the amount of household waste. In principle, this effect can be estimated in a number of ways, including comparisons of waste levels before and after introduction of unit charging, and comparisons of waste levels in areas with and without unit charging.

The most straightforward source of evidence on the impact of unit charging is data on the aggregate quantity of waste collected by the relevant municipality or agency, over the period when unit charging was introduced. Data of this sort is available for a number of areas which have introduced unit charging systems, and generally indicates a substantial effect of unit charging in reducing household waste levels.

In High Bridge, New Jersey, for example, the level of household waste was reduced by 25 per cent (from an average of 8.5 to 6.3 tons per day), following the implementation of the pay-per-bag scheme. In Perkasie, Pennsylvania, the volume of solid waste collected dropped by more than half in the first year following the switch to a pay-per-bag system. Most of this reduction was attributed to the separation and recycling of aluminium cans, paper and glass. As a result of the reduction in waste levels the cost of waste disposal fell by 30-40 per cent (Anderson, Hofmann and Rusin, 1990, page 30). In Vancouver Island, unit charging reduced household waste in the core municipalities involved in the scheme by 18 per cent in 1992, according to Resource Futures International (1993, page 3), and by the autumn of 1993 it was estimated that the region as a whole was diverting approximately 22 per cent of its waste.

The effect in Seattle has been more complex. Between 1970 and 1988 the amount of solid waste generated per household fell by about 5 per cent (from about 1 800 pounds to 1 700 pounds). Although this reduction is small, the appropriate basis for assessing the impact of unit charging is of course a comparison with what would have happened otherwise; in areas in the US with uncharged disposal of marginal waste, household waste levels rose substantially over this period. From January 1989, Seattle's programme was bolstered with improved enforcement monitoring and the introduction of active recycling programmes for newspaper, glass, plastics and metals. Monthly collections in that year fell by about 30 per cent relative to 1988 levels (Anderson, Hofmann and Rusin, 1990, page 30).

A lower effect was encountered in Woodstock, Illinois, where participation in the unit charging programme was voluntary. By 1989 participation in Woodstock's programme had reached 88 per cent, but the reduction in waste levels was only some 4-8 per cent in 1988. Anderson, Hofmann and Rusin (1990, page 31) suggest that this comparatively low rate may be attributable to the relatively low pay-per-bag fee, which is less than half that faced by Seattle or High Bridge residents.

The above discussion suggests two difficulties in relying on data on the change in the aggregate level of household waste in a single authority to estimate the impact of waste charging. One is that, whilst it may be relatively easy to attribute changes in waste levels achieved over a short period, such as in the year after introduction, to the impact of the charge, it may be more difficult to derive a good estimate of how much of this effect lasts beyond the initial year, and hence of the impact of pay-per-bag over a longer period of time. Another is that observation of a single authority is unlikely to be able to provide evidence about how far the level of the charge affects the scale of the response. Whilst it is suggested that the lower impact of charging in Woodstock, Illinois was due to the lower charge, there may be other possible explanations for the differences between Woodstock and the other areas, and the role of the level of the charge is not convincingly demonstrated.

A methodology which may help to provide more firmly-based evidence on the long-run impact of charging on levels of household waste, and which can indicate the relationship between charge levels and the quantitative impact on waste levels is used in a study by Repetto *et al.* (1992). This study comprises an econometric investigation of the effect of household waste unit charges on the tonnage of waste collected and landfilled in a sample of fourteen US municipalities, ten of which had introduced some form of unit charging scheme between 1980 and 1989, and four of which financed waste collection through charges unrelated to the level of household waste.

The study estimates the effects of unit charges on the volume of household waste, in a monthly panel covering the fourteen municipalities, taking into account community-specific differences (fixed effects), the possible interactive effect of the existence of kerbside recycling schemes, and other possible influences on the level of refuse, including population density, average household size, income, climatic factors, and the price paid for recycled newspaper. The results show a large and statistically-significant effect of the unit charge on household waste volumes, which can be summarised in the following terms. Implemented on its own, without a parallel system of kerbside recycling, the effect of unit charging at a level of $1.50 per 32 gallon bag would be to reduce waste levels by some 18 per cent (0.42 pounds/capita/day) compared to the level of waste generated without unit charges. Implemented together with kerbside recycling, unit charging would further reduce waste volumes, on average by more than 30 per cent compared to the no-charge case.

These effects summarise the average responses actually obtained across the sample of municipalities. The use of cross-section data for a number of municipalities potentially allows an assessment of the long-run impact of charging, as opposed to the initial effects which may be measured in simple comparisons of "before and after" waste levels.

Repetto *et al.* (1992) then translate the estimates of the volume effect of unit charging into figures for the likely cost savings that would arise from general adoption of pay-per-bag schemes in areas of the US with high and medium waste disposal costs. In a high-cost region, they estimate that the market costs of disposal of household refuse are of the order of $120 per ton, comprising $45 per ton collection costs, $65 tipping costs, and a $10 cost reflecting the incremental depletion of low-cost tipping sites. Non-market disposal costs are reckoned, in line with estimates for Massachusetts by Stone and Ashford (1991) to be about $75 per ton, giving a total economic cost per ton of waste of $195. In "moderate-cost" states, the corresponding figure might be some $110 per ton. Translating these figures into disposal costs per bag (32 gallons, assumed equal to 21 pounds), gives figures of $1.83 per bag for disposal in high cost states and $1.03 per bag in medium cost states. Charges set at these levels would, on the basis of the model Repetto et al present, generate reductions in waste levels of 20 per cent and 11 per cent respectively. If all areas with high and medium waste disposal costs were to levy such charges, the net economic savings would be of the order of $650 millions, whilst the unit charges would raise revenues of some $7.5 billion (Repetto *et al.*, 1992, page 25).

A number of studies have estimated the impact of unit charging using data for individual households. In comparison with the cross-section methodology employed by Repetto *et al.* (1992), this may have the advantage that it is better able to separate residential and non-residential waste; also, since there is much more variation in household characteristics with household data than with data for area groupings, it may be possible to estimate the relationship between household characteristics and waste behaviour more precisely. Recent studies using data for individual households have included Hong, Adams and Love (1993) and Fullerton and Kinnaman (1994).

Hong, Adams and Love (1993) use data from a 1990 survey of households in Portland Oregon metropolitan area to estimate the effects of unit charges and household characteristics on the quantity of non-recyclable waste generated by households, and the frequency of households' participation in curbside recycling. About 2 300 households were included in the estimation; for each household there was a single observation of the variables. The variation in unit charge levels necessary to be able to estimate the price effect arose because the 25 waste collection firms providing services in the area set different charging tariffs, with different marginal charge rates per unit.[26]

Hong, Adams and Love found that the marginal effect of a higher unit charge for waste disposal is to increase the probability that households will participate frequently in recycling. However, their analysis found no statistically-significant impact of the charge on the level of household waste generated.

Fullerton and Kinnaman (1994) estimate household response to the implementation in July 1992 of unit-pricing for garbage disposal in Charlottesville, Virginia, using before-and-after data collected for the study from a sample of 75 households. During late May/early June and September (*i.e.* before and after the implementation of the programme) the bags or cans of garbage and recyclable materials of the households were counted and weighed daily for four weeks.

Equations were independently estimated for per capita weight, volume and density of garbage and weight of recycling. The effect of the unit charge on both weight and volume of garbage was estimated to be negative and statistically significant. It was found that individuals responded to the volume-based pricing programme by reducing the volume of garbage in greater proportions than they reduced the weight of garbage; the effect of the eighty-cent-per-bag sticker scheme in Charlottesville was to reduce the volume of garbage by, on average, some 37 per cent, and the weight of garbage by 14 per cent. This presumably reflects the operation of the "Seattle stomp" – compacting garbage into a smaller number of bags to reduce the number of charged bags. Using the estimated coefficients, the price elasticity of demand for the collection of garbage, measured in pounds, at mean levels of price and weight is equal to –0.075 and at mean levels of price and volume is –0.227.

Households were also found to respond to a price for garbage by increasing their recycling, on average by some 16 per cent – the implied cross elasticity was 0.074 at mean levels. This is compared to US EPA estimates (based simply on aggregate before and after figures for each community) of the same cross-price elasticity for Perkasie, PA (0.40), Illion, NY (0.48), and Seattle (0.06 in 1985-86 and 0.10 in 1986-87) (Fullerton and Kinnaman, 1994, page 15; EPA, 1990).

Distributional effects of unit pricing

A number of the studies can provide evidence on the distributional impact of unit pricing for household solid waste. There is concern that unit charging may prove to be highly regressive, if the income of elasticity for household waste lies well below zero. In most cases the evidence provided on this score is essentially of a form which can be obtained *ex ante*, through studies of the pattern of household waste across income groups. Experience of actual unit pricing is not needed to derive an initial estimate of the likely regressivity, although studies of household responses to charging could potentially investigate whether the response to charging varies across income groups. Fullerton and Kinnaman (1994) cite a range of studies in addition to their own income elasticity estimate of 0.049: these all lie well below 1.0, ranging from 0.2 to 0.4.

Further evaluation issues

Further issues concern the extent to which unit charge schemes for household waste encourage socially-undesirable responses, which may be worse than the cost of uncharged waste. There is anecdotal evidence cited by a number of studies that unit-pricing programmes may have encouraged individuals to divert waste to uncharged areas, to dump waste in the countryside, in city litter bins, in charity donation bins or at recycling points, or to incinerate waste illegally. Fullerton and Kinnaman suggest that about one in twenty of their households may have reacted to unit charging by some form of illegal dumping, whilst, on the other hand, in a sample of 1 400 households in Tompkins County, New York, Reschovsky and Stone (1994) found no evidence that unit charging had been responsible for the pattern of illegal burning of household waste.

6.2 Deposit-refund systems for drinks containers

Evaluations of deposit-refund systems for drinks containers highlight in a particularly clear way a difficulty which in principle arises in all *ex post* evaluation studies. This is the problem of how to define an appropriate "counterfactual", showing what would have happened otherwise, against which the effects of the system can be judged. In many countries in Europe, deposit-refund systems have been introduced to prevent changes taking place in the relative use of returnable and disposable bottles, and, especially, to prevent the growth in the market share of disposables observed in countries without any form of regulation on their use. The criterion for success in this situation is that the policy should lead to no appreciable change from the starting position; analysing the effects of the policy on the basis of changes over time, without explicit construction of the counterfactual scenario thus would miss the point of the policy.

Estimating the counterfactual is, however, problematic. Probably the most realistic basis for assessing the long-run market share of disposable and returnable containers in the absence of a deposit-refund system is to observe market shares in countries without such systems, such as the UK. Nevertheless, the adjustment period in consumer responses to the presence or absence of a deposit-refund system may be long, since there may be specific cultural factors and specific conditions which would prevent immediate adjustment to the pattern of behaviour observed in a country without any history of control. As a result, using patterns observed elsewhere to estimate the counterfactual can only be taken as the long-run position, and cannot be easily used to analyse shorter-run costs and benefits.

6.2.1 *Policy background*

OECD countries generate approximately 140 million tons of packaging waste annually. Various measures to reduce the amount and toxicity of packaging and to encourage its recycling have been proposed including bans on certain packaging materials and negotiated agreements with industry to reduce packaging. One measure implemented in all or parts of 11 or more OECD countries is a system of mandatory deposit-refund requirements for beverage containers. Policy measures of this kind have been responsible for the most widely documented successes in the field of waste minimisation and reuse (OECD, 1992, page 7).

In the US there has been a significant amount of activity at state and local level. Since 1971, at least 10 states with a combined population of around 74 million people have established mandatory refund values for beer and soft drinks containers (OECD, 1992, page 49). In 1977, the State of South Australia (which includes about 8 per cent of the country's 17 million people) enacted a compulsory deposit-refund scheme (OECD, 1992, page 19).

In Austria, the 1990 Federal Management Law established a deposit system for refillable plastic bottles, based on a 4 schilling deposit. Here, unlike elsewhere, the market share of refillable containers had not markedly declined, largely due to consumer pressure (OECD, 1992 page 24).

Four of Canada's twelve provinces and territories require deposit-refund systems for beer and soft drinks containers and several others have considered introducing similar measures following the adoption of the National Packaging Protocol in March 1990. In 1989 it was estimated that packaging comprised a third of Canadian municipal solid waste by weight (OECD, 1992 page 25).

Norway and Finland both use taxes and deposit requirements to reduce packaging. Under statutory orders that took effect in 1977 and 1982, Denmark has, until recently, prohibited the sale of beer and soft drinks in anything but refillable packages, which carry a deposit. In Germany and the Netherlands a system of glass refillable bottles carrying deposits for most beer and soft drinks has been maintained.

6.2.2 *Michigan*: ex ante *analysis*

Michigan's "bottle bill" was introduced in December 1978. It requires that redeemable deposits are put on containers of packaged beer and carbonated soft drinks. By law, all beverage retailers are also required to act as container receiver centres.

Prior to the introduction of mandatory deposits in the state of Michigan, Porter (1978) analysed the social costs and benefits of the proposals. The study sought to quantify five principal sources of changes in social benefits and costs: litter (both eyesore and pick-up costs), solid waste, containers, consumer convenience and production and distribution. Other potential effects, such as those which could, in principle, operate through changes in the average price of beverages, and changes in market structure in the industry were not quantified, or argued to be of negligible importance.[27]

The extent to which consumer demands would shift as a result of the increase in the prices of beverages delivered in "one-way" containers relative to the prices in refillable bottles was assessed on the basis of experience in Oregon, where, within a year or two of mandatory deposits, more than 90 per cent of all beer and soft drink containers were refillable (Gudger and Bailes, 1974, pages 18-23). Porter assumed that mandatory deposits would induce a 100 per cent refillable bottle system in Michigan since the deposit was to be set at 10 cents per container rather than the 2-5 cents set in Oregon.

Litter costs

Beverage containers make up roughly 60 per cent of all litter by volume but only about 20 per cent by number. It has been estimated that 4-11 per cent of beverage fillings result in a littered container (on roads alone) but that refillable bottles are only 15-38 per cent as likely to be littered as the average container. It is therefore clear that a significant reduction in beverage container litter and hence litter in general can be expected from a switch to an all-refillable delivery system [Estimates from Porter (1978) p. 356 and Rao (1975) p. 23].

Porter estimated that in Michigan, a complete conversion to refillable bottles would be accompanied by a 62-85 per cent decline in beverage container litter (Porter, 1978, page 357). Eyesore and pick-up costs for beverage container litter are influenced by its weight, volume, number and sharpness. Cost of pick-up and disposal is estimated at between one and four cents; litter pick-up cost per container filling would be between 0.04 and 0.26 cents (Porter, 1978 page 357). Porter used Californian experience of "litter-injuries" to estimate their social cost at 0.06-0.09 cents per filling; the costs of farm equipment damage from litter were put at 0.06-0.08 cents per filling. Eyesore costs are extremely difficult to quantify, and Porter's analysis uses a range of possible estimates, to find critical ranges for eyesore costs.

Overall, the net benefit of mandatory deposits from the viewpoint of litter was estimated to be (0.23x + 0.15) cents per filling (where x is the mean willingness-to-pay by residents for a 62-85% reduction in beverage container litter).

Solid Waste

Porter estimated that the number of beverage containers disposed of as solid waste would decline by between 91 and 96 per cent, depending on the litter rate assumption employed, and that total municipal waste would then fall by some 2.1 per cent (Porter, 1978, table 1 p. 356). In 1974, the average cost for collection and disposal of municipal solid waste in Michigan was roughly $22 per ton. Assuming that the average and marginal costs of collection and disposal of solid waste are identical in the long run and that the cost per ton is the same for beverage containers as for other solid waste, Porter estimated the savings in solid waste costs to be 0.07 cents per filling.

Containers

Refillable bottles cost about twice as much as one-way containers, but the price per filling for refillable bottles depends on how many times they are reused. Porter assumes that the average trippage of refillable bottles would remain at 15 under mandatory deposits and that the mandatory deposit system would induce a complete switch to refillables. The saving in container cost following the introduction of mandatory deposits would then be 3.08 cents per filling.

Production and Distribution

Refillable bottles are likely to result in increased costs of production and distribution. Porter estimates the extra labour, storage and investment costs which retailers are likely to incur under a mandatory deposit scheme to be of the order of 0.76 cents per filling, and the increased production and distribution costs for soft drinks manufacturers and brewers at 1.32 cents per filling and 2.71 cents per filling respectively.

The overall weighted increase in production and distribution costs across all types of container is then 2.77 cents per filling, which is less than the estimate for the decrease in container costs implying that the money price of beverages will decline in an all-refillable delivery system (Porter, 1978, pages 362-365).

Consumer Convenience

Porter argues that the principal convenience cost is the time taken in returning bottles under a deposit-refund system. Given the difficulties in estimating this, Porter considers a frequency of possible values, which can be used to calculate critical values. The time-of-return cost of a refillable container is estimated to be (0.68y) cents per filling, where y is the mean time value assumed.

The social benefit-cost evaluation

Summing the five cost components gives a net social cost saving from the mandatory deposit-refund system of $(+0.53 + 0.23x - 0.68y)$. Given this formula, the critical values of eyesore and time-of-return costs can be calculated that result in social indifference between the mandatory deposit-refund system and the status quo. If the time-of-return costs are as low as 0.78 cents per returned container, then the system of mandatory deposits would be preferred in an efficiency sense even if there were no willingness-to-pay for reduced container litter. If the latter were as high as $27.12 per resident per year then mandatory deposits would be preferred no matter how high the time-of-return cost. Porter argues that either of these extremes is unlikely, and that the social desirability of a system of mandatory deposit system in terms of the costs and benefits considered under this analysis remains debatable, and dependent on the unknown values of x and y.

Porter notes that the net cost saving is relatively insensitive to the estimated cost of litter pick-up or the solid waste savings. However the impact of different estimates of production and distribution costs is more critical – if the estimates used are adjusted by 25 per cent in either direction then Porter argues it can significantly alter the overall balance between costs and benefits.

6.2.3 Michigan: ex post *evidence on effects*

In 1982, Porter reassessed his benefit-cost analysis of mandatory deposits in the light of Michigan's experience (Porter, 1982). As he had expected, beverage-related litter had fallen dramatically by some 85 per cent and the rate at which consumers returned empty containers was high, estimated at around 95 per cent. However, the effect of mandatory deposits on container mix had been less than the 100 per cent switch to refillables that had been assumed in the earlier study (Porter, 1978). Given that the benefit-cost results are very sensitive to this mix Porter (1982) recalculates them on the basis of a mix of beverage containers of 50 per cent refillable bottles and 50 per cent aluminium cans.

Following the switch toward refillable bottles, the prices at the brewer/bottler level did not decrease. Given that container cost savings were not being passed on to distributors and retailers there was nothing to offset cost increases at the distributor and retail level. The final result was an estimated real price increase due to mandatory deposits of 2-3 c per filling for soft drinks and 3-5 c per filling for beer. Thus, not only did beverage delivery in cans remain significant following the introduction of mandatory deposits but it also involved higher costs and higher prices.

Porter noted that if beverage price increases fully reflected cost increases, then the annual aesthetic or eyesore value of the litter reduction must have been worth as much as $14 to $24 per resident for mandatory deposits to have been economically efficient. However, if the net beverage cost increases had been zero, then the aesthetic value of litter reduction need only have been between $1 and $4 to have passed the economic efficiency test (Porter, 1983).

In terms of quantity sold, bottled and canned beer sales declined from 6.47 million barrels in each of 1977 and 1978 to 6.03 million barrels in 1979, but this has also been influenced by factors other than mandatory deposits, including an increase in Michigan's minimum drinking age from 18 to 21 and a decline in real personal income per capita. Overall, Porter estimated that the decline in beer and soft drink consumption due to mandatory deposits amounted to 170 million fillings per year and 106 million fillings per year respectively.

Porter estimated the loss in consumer surplus due to mandatory deposits to be $7-12 million and the price increase losses to continuing consumers to amount to $120-180 million. Whether these should be balanced in part by gains to producers arising from the container cost savings depends on whether the absence of a price reduction by brewers and manufacturers reflected other sources of higher cost, or their possession of some monopoly power.

Porter's earlier analysis had argued that return rates for empty bottles would be likely to be high in Michigan because of the high deposits. However, Michigan's return rate appeared to be equally high for the 5 c as the 10 c deposit containers. The adjustment period in Michigan was short, probably due to the number, knowledge and convenience of container return centres (Porter, 1983).

6.2.4 *The Netherlands*

A system of obligatory deposits on beer and soft drinks in glass bottles has been in use in the Netherlands for a considerable time. It is based on a Decree issued by the Association for the Industry of and Wholesale Trade in Carbonated Soft Drinks and the Wholesale Trade in Beer (SK, page 124). Deposits vary from 0.125 ECU to 2.15 ECU depending on the size of bottle. In the vast majority of cases products can be returned to the same place where they were bought.

Various evaluative studies have been carried out for the deposit/return system adopted in the Netherlands. Ernst found that the readiness of consumers to return products covered by deposits depends largely on the effort that needs to be spent on doing so, while the moment at which the products can be returned is of far less influence. The extent to which consumers "switch" products to avoid deposits seems in practice to be partly determined by the "consumer friendliness" of the return system. This in turn is determined by the ease of returning the products (SK page 127).

The study by Kip concludes that similar high return percentages (*i.e.* approximately 90 per cent) are realised in all countries employing deposit systems in spite of considerable differences in the price level of the deposit money between the various countries. Nevertheless, financial compensation per se is a key factor determining the response rate – for systems without any financial compensation the response rate is much lower, even if there are a great many collection points.

Part III

AN EVALUATION FRAMEWORK

Despite wide ranging and increasing experience with the use of economic instruments, evidence concerning their performance and effects is still limited. The evidence summarized in Part II of this report clearly indicates that whilst *ex post* evaluations have been done, they remain largely ad hoc and non systematic. There are many reasons for this, in particular the lack of data, the existing programme management "culture" and a common unwillingness to perform such evaluations. Yet the use of economic instruments is often challenged. For instance, environmental taxes face strong opposition from industry, on the ground that their theoretical virtues are not borne out in reality.

During the course of this project, it was quickly realised that unless specific frameworks and procedures could be set up, the evaluation of policy in general, and of economic instruments in particular, would remain anecdotal and uncertain. In other words, specific arrangements must be installed to ensure *e.g.* the generation of suitable data and a consistent evaluation process.

The purpose of Part III is to propose a general framework for achieving this aim. This framework was elaborated in stages, during various consultations and workshops. It does not aim at constructing a prescriptive, detailed and generally applicable set of guidelines or "cook book". The main objective is to discuss key issues in the evaluation process in a systematic manner and raise awareness about the advantages and technicalities of policy evaluation and the need for adequate and timely data collection.

Chapter 7

EVALUATION CRITERIA FOR ENVIRONMENTAL POLICY INSTRUMENTS

An evaluation of a particular policy measure seeks to describe the effects that the measure has had, and may then seek to compare these effects against the initial objectives of policy, or to weigh them up in a more general assessment of costs and benefits. Relevant effects include indicators of effectivenesss relating to the target variables which policy seeks to influence; in the case of environmental policy instruments these will presumably include indicators of environmental impact, although other targets perhaps relating to economic variables, may also be relevant. In addition, however, the evaluation will need to assess the costs and possible side-effects of the use of the policy measure. Thus, for example, the principal argument for using economic instruments in environmental policy is not that "command-and-control" regulations are ineffective (though, in particular applications, they may be), but that they achieve their environmental objectives at a higher economic cost than would instruments based on market incentives. Costs, and side-effects, are thus central to the evaluation of different environmental policy instruments.

This chapter sets out the range of costs and benefits which may be relevant in evaluating environmental policy instruments. Whilst many of the criteria will be relevant to most economic instruments, the key criteria will vary depending on the instrument employed. Boxes 8-10 highlight the issues of key significance evaluating three types of economic instrument – emissions taxes and user charges, tradeable permits, and deposit-refund systems.

7.1 Environmental effectiveness

A central issue in evaluating the effects of environmental market mechanisms is their environmental impact – how far, and in what way, they achieve the required reduction in emissions or environmental damage which is the objective of policy.

Environmental effectiveness is a key issue in evaluating all environmental policy measures, but is of particular importance in assessing the relative costs and benefits of measures such as emissions taxes or charges, where the environmental effectiveness depends on polluters' responses to a market signal. Regulatory policies, by contrast, may deliver environmental effects with greater certainty by imposing rigid quantity limits on polluting emissions (although this clearly depends on effective enforcement).

The environmental effectiveness of economic instruments may be considered at a number of levels:

1) the impact on polluting emissions, measured in physical units (for example, a reduction of so many tonnes of pollutant emitted);
2) the impact of reduced emissions on environmental damage, again measured in physical units (for example, a reduction in the concentration of pollutants in neighbouring waterways, or in the atmosphere);
3) the economic value of reduced damage to the environment, measured in monetary terms.

Ideally, the third of these is the yardstick of effectiveness which should be considered by policy-makers. However, it may be easier to obtain quantitative information on more straightforward magnitudes such as polluting emissions than to quantify the impact of policy on environmental damage. Data on emissions is less likely than data on environmental quality to be affected by factors other than policy. Also, data on pollution quantities does not require difficult and imprecise judgements about the value of environmental damage – an assessment based on pollution quantities confines the analysis to measurable, easily-defined, magnitudes.

Ex post evaluation of the environmental effects of economic instruments will need to take account of changes in circumstances, and any relevant special factors which may have reduced pollution below what would have been expected, or increased it above what would have been expected from the policy. As noted above, a key distinction between certain market-based policies such as emissions taxes, where the policy works by fixing the price of pollution, and other policies where the policy works by fixing the quantity of pollution, is the impact of uncertainty on emissions. With market instruments, therefore, outcomes may well differ significantly from what would reasonably have been expected when the policy was formulated. Evaluations of environmental effectiveness should take account of the difference in information available *ex ante* (*i.e.* before the policy was implemented) and *ex post* (*i.e.* in the light of experience), and should avoid unreasonable criticism based solely on the wisdom of hindsight.

Two further complications in assessing the environmental effects of policy may arise in some cases.

First, the environmental effects may not be limited to those for which the instrument was designed. There may be "secondary" environmental effects in some cases. An example would be where sulphur dioxide emissions were reduced as a by-product of greenhouse gas abatement policies.

Second, discounting issues will arise where costs and/or benefits take place over time. How should benefits in the future be evaluated, in relation to current benefits, or in relation to initial costs? In cases where some or all of the benefits of policy are expected well in the future, it will be particularly important to pay careful attention to the treatment of risk and uncertainty in the evaluation.

In addition, a problem which pervades the whole subject of assessment of economic instruments should perhaps be stressed here. Economic instruments have in practice almost always been implemented in parallel with other environmental policy measures, such as technology or emissions regulations. In these circumstances, assessing the environmental effects of policy will face the problem of disentangling the environmental effects attributable to the economic instruments from the environmental effects arising from the other parallel policy measures (see the more extensive discussion of this issue in Chapter 10).

7.2 Economic efficiency

The case for using economic instruments in preference to "command-and-control"[28] regulation in environmental policy rests heavily on the lower level of economic costs that should be incurred in achieving a given level of pollution abatement with economic instruments. Assessing the extent to which economic instruments have, in practice, achieved a cost-minimising pattern of pollution abatement should therefore be central to an assessment of the relative costs and benefits of these environmental policy instruments.

The costs concerned may be described as the direct economic costs of achieving the changes in polluter behaviour that policy seeks. These direct economic costs consist of the (broadly-defined) abatement costs incurred by both businesses and households/individuals.

Box 8. **Key issues in evaluating emissions taxes and user charges**

- **Quantitative effect on pollution or emissions**. The primary area of uncertainty with price-based environmental market mechanisms such as emissions taxes and user charges is their impact on emissions levels. How far do such measures induce changes in polluter behaviour in response to the incentive provided by the charge? Which polluters, in particular, appear to respond, and which do not modify their behaviour. What evidence is there that the pattern of behavioural responses results in significant savings in abatement costs – is it the high-abatement-cost polluters who respond most?

- **Revenues, use of revenues.** The aggregate revenues raised from environmental taxes and charges will depend, in part, on the scale of the behavioural response; since the tax or charge is levied on the remaining units of pollution, the greater the behavioural response, the smaller are likely to be the revenues raised.

- **Costs of administration and enforcement.** The relevant costs would include both costs to the public enforcement agencies, and the "compliance" costs borne by the private sector subjects of the policy.

- In *the case of businesses*, the direct economic costs could include:

  - the costs of abatement equipment;
  - the costs of operating more costly, but less polluting, production techniques.

In principle, these costs will be directly measurable expenditures by the businesses concerned (on capital equipment, raw materials and intermediate inputs, other factors of production, etc.), although there may of course be considerable practical difficulties in definition and measurement. There may also be difficulties in comparing business costs with different abatement technologies if there are differences in the quality of outputs; less-polluting technologies may lead to the production of goods and services which are not identical to those produced using more-polluting processes.

- In *the case of households*, the direct economic costs may include measurable expenditures, but may also include the costs of changes in consumption patterns towards less-polluting products or activities.

In this case, the abatement costs take the form of the loss in consumer or household utility resulting from changes in consumption patterns. An example would be the loss in individual utility that would result when higher petrol taxes discourage private motoring. Unlike the direct costs incurred by business, these costs are not directly observable, but require an assessment of the impact of observable changes in household consumption patterns on utility. Estimating these costs will be less straightforward, more sensitive to the methodology chosen, and hence potentially more unreliable than the measurable direct costs to business.

The literature contains a number of *ex ante* studies of how marginal abatement costs differ across polluters. These suggest the potential for considerable gains through market mechanisms, which allow polluters with the lowest marginal costs of abatement to undertake more of the total quantity of abatement, and which reduce the amount of abatement required from high-abatement-cost sources.

Ex post evidence on direct costs would require an assessment of the extent to which abatement has shifted towards sources with lower abatement costs than would have been the case with regulatory policies based on, for example, uniform abatement requirements across all polluters. In most cases, this will require data on the relative abatement costs of different sources, and on the pattern of abatement achieved across these sources.

In the case of *tradeable permits*, however, it may be possible to use the volume of trades as a simple (and readily-observable) indicator of the scale of likely abatement cost savings. Where the initial distribution of permits is based on existing abatement requirements, trading will generally reflect shifts in abatement between lower-cost and higher-cost sources. Observing a high volume of permit trades would tend to suggest a large redistribution of abatement, towards a lower-cost pattern. Permit systems in which little trading activity takes place are, by contrast, unlikely to be achieving any significant reduction in abatement costs compared to what would be achieved by regulation.

7.3 Administration and compliance costs

The administration and compliance costs of market-based and regulatory environmental policy instruments will be an important consideration in evaluating the relative merits of different policy approaches. From the point of view of the economy as a whole, such costs are a dead-weight cost of the system, in the sense that they absorb potentially-productive resources; other things being equal, environmental policy measures with lower administration and compliance costs are to be preferred.

- Administration costs should be defined widely to include those administrative costs incurred by the public sector (government departments and regulatory agencies) in operating regulatory and market-based systems, including measurement, monitoring and other information costs, the costs of collecting charges or taxes, and costs of enforcement activities.

- Compliance costs are the administrative and managerial costs incurred by the taxpayer in complying with the environmental policy measures.

In some systems, a substantial part of the administrative burden of environmental policies may be borne by the regulated subjects rather than by government. This shift in costs may be achieved through, for example, requirements for self-reporting of emissions, backed up by occasional audit by government regulators. Whilst this may change the balance of costs between government and the private sector, compared with a system in which government agencies are responsible for continuous supervision and monitoring of emissions from each source, the overall dead-weight cost to the economy may be unchanged.

Important issues to be considered in assessing the administrative and compliance costs of different approaches to environmental policy will be the extent to which the various information and monitoring procedures needed can be combined with other activities; "piggy-backing" of the administrative requirements of environmental policy may reduce the additional costs attributable to the environmental policy measure. Thus, environmental policy administration may be combined with other government functions, such as taxation. There may also be scope for compliance cost savings, too, if some of the monitoring and record-keeping which is required for environmental policy purposes would have been undertaken in any case for purely commercial reasons, or if it provides information of at least some value to the enterprise.

7.4 Revenues

Some environmental market mechanisms, including user charges, environmental taxes, and certain types of tradeable permits, may generate government revenue. In some cases, the revenue generated may be the primary purpose of introducing the measure (as in the case of some of the water pollution charges in European countries, which are designed to generate revenues for environmental improvements). In the case of market mechanisms which are designed to have an incentive effect, the revenues raised through the market mechanism may constitute a second source of benefits from their use, over and above their environmental impact.

In the context of "green tax reforms" the revenues raised from environmental taxes would be needed to offset reductions in other tax revenues, arising due to the reduction or abolition of existing distortionary taxes.

The scale of the revenues from environmental measures is, to a certain extent, likely to be inversely related to their environmental effectiveness. Where the incentive effect of an environmental tax or charge on a particular polluting activity or product is high, this will reduce the tax base, and hence reduce the revenues achieved.

In most cases the primary focus of interest is likely to be the revenues derived directly from the environmental tax or charge. In some cases, however, the revenue implications of using a particular instrument may extend beyond the revenue directly obtained from the instrument itself. These wider revenue effects may arise if the environmental tax is levied in addition to other existing taxes on a particular product, or if there are significant "second round" tax consequences of changes in private sector behaviour induced by the instrument. For example, a carbon tax levied on petrol would be levied on a base which is already highly taxed; if it reduces petrol consumption, it will also tend to reduce revenues from existing petrol excises. At the same time, there may be wider, and more indirect, revenue effects, for example, through higher tax revenues collected from public transport, if higher petrol taxes induce greater use of public transport. In most cases, the second round effects may be sufficiently small to be ignored, although there may be some cases, such as the carbon tax example discussed here, where they would not be negligible.

The use made of the revenues raised from environmental taxes, charges and permits may have a significant impact on their overall effects. The revenues may for example be allocated to the general public budget, or may be "earmarked" to a specific environmental fund, or may be returned to taxpayers in some way, for example, in the form of reductions in other, existing, taxes such as those on labour and capital incomes. It is necessary to specify clearly which of these uses has been made of the revenues in evaluating the effects of economic instruments. This may not always be straightforward; "what would have happened otherwise" to the pattern of public revenues and public spending cannot be observed, and may be difficult to determine.

7.5 Wider economic effects

Under the heading of "wider economic effects" may be included the range of economic costs and benefits associated with different environmental instruments apart from the direct abatement costs, administration and compliance costs, and the costs (and value) of changes in tax revenues. They thus include potential effects on:

- the price level, and possibly the rate of inflation;
- competitiveness;
- trade patterns;
- employment;
- income distribution;
- economic growth;
- the rate of innovation.

These costs include some which are likely to be predominantly short-term costs of adjustment, and others which may be more durable, or experienced over a longer time horizon. The time frame over which these costs are assessed should be carefully specified. It will, of course, rarely be possible to obtain *ex post* evidence on the long-term effects of instrument choice. Most economic instruments have been implemented relatively recently, and it will be some years before the longer term effects can be observed. Also, the longer the lapse of time, the harder it will be to separate the influence of instrument choice from other, unrelated influences on economic variables.

Economic models will generally be required to assess some of the wider economic costs of the choice of environmental policy instruments. The type of model used will tend to determine the range of wider effects that can be assessed, and, particularly, the time frame over which the assessment can be made. Macroeconomic models will generally be well-suited to looking at the level and time profile of economic

---

Box 9. **Key issues in evaluation of tradeable permit mechanisms**

Volume of trades. The number of permits traded gives an indication of two important aspects of the system – the extent to which the system appears to have led to efficiency gains, and the efficiency of the permit market. Where few permit trades take place, there will be a suspicion that the system has not succeeded in reallocating the pattern of pollution abatement towards lower-abatement-cost sources. Also, where few permits take place, there may be concerns about the competitiveness of the permit market itself; if this market is too "thin", with insufficient numbers of permit buyers and sellers willing to trade, buyers or sellers may be able to exploit market power, reducing the extent to which potential efficiency-improving trades take place. The volume of trade probably also reflects the complexity of trading rules: in some US systems the complexity of the rules governing permitted trades may have increased transaction costs and inhibited some trades.

Permit prices. The average price at which permits trade gives an indication of the economic cost of achieving the given level of pollution abatement. With permits, or other quantity-based pollution control measure, the maximum marginal abatement cost which will be incurred in cutting back pollution to the required level is uncertain; this uncertainty about costs is, in effect, the counterpart to the certainty which permits can provide on emissions levels. Evidence on the distribution of permit prices may also be an indicator of whether the permit market functions efficiently; a wide dispersion of prices may be a sign of inefficiency in the permit market.

Geographical redistribution of emissions through trading. Permit systems guarantee an upper limit to total emissions, without specifying the distribution of emissions between sources. Trading will tend to redistribute emissions between sources, and whilst this may give rise to efficiency gains, it may also lead to costs, if, for example, the geographical location of emissions is not a matter of complete indifference.

Impact on new entry. Systems where permits are distributed free ("grandfathered") to existing firms in an industry, or on some other basis than competitive auction, may have the effect of discouraging new entry to the industry. New entrants have to buy permits from existing firms, incurring high costs, and possibly, in thin permit markets, facing strategic behaviour by existing firms, trying to prevent the arrival of new competitors. Thus, where permits systems involve grandfathering, the impact of permit allocation practices on new entry will be an important issue in judging its overall performance. However, at the same time, it will be extremely difficult to assess in practice. Although the extent of new entry can be observed, it will be difficult, if not impossible, to assess how much new entry *would have taken place* if the permit trading system had not been in operation.

Enforcement procedures and cost. How is compliance by individual firms monitored in a system of tradeable permits, at what cost in terms of enforcement resources, and with what degree of compliance?

---

effects in the relatively short-term. Computable general equilibrium models would be more suited to assessing longer term effects (although the observations made above on the difficulty of *ex post* assessment of long-term effects clearly apply).

It may also be noted that some of the wider economic effects listed above may lead to policy changes which may in turn affect the effectiveness of economic instruments. For example, trade effects and effects on income distribution could lead policy-makers to reduce tax or charge levels, either selectively for certain sectors or across-the-board.

7.6 "Soft" effects

Under the heading of "soft" effects of economic instruments may be grouped various possible effects of such instruments working through changes in attitudes and awareness. Thus, for example, a small environmental tax imposed on a particular commodity may have the effect of signalling the environmental costs of the commodity to environmentally-aware consumers, and may achieve an effect on behaviour through this route, over and above any direct incentive effect. It has, for example, been suggested that the rapid take-up of unleaded petrol in many OECD countries can be attributed as much to the effect of the tax differential in raising consumer awareness of the environmental issues surrounding lead in petrol, as to the financial saving which motorists could make by choosing unleaded fuel.

Box 10. **Key issues in evaluating deposit-refund systems**

Participation rate. Participation of all groups concerned is of great importance for an effective and efficient operation. This includes the producers, packers, distributors, wholesale and retail traders, and the consumers.

Rate of return. The rate of return of products (empty containers, used batteries, etc.) in the system should be sufficiently high. If too low, the system could turn out to be ineffective and inefficient.

Costs and benefits. The desirability of deposit-refund systems will largely depend on the long-term balance of: *i)* the initial and running costs (including non-material costs such as extra inconvenience to consumers) and *ii)* of the savings on disposal and litter management, plus positive environmental benefits (which may be difficult to value). The timing of the profiles of costs and benefits may be relevant; initial costs may be a barrier to implementation, and this may then require financial assistance to be provided for a short transition period.

Handling costs. Retailers incur various collection and storage costs in operating a deposit-refund system. Does experience suggest that a handling fee paid to retailers – possibly by introducing a small difference between deposit and refund – helps to ensure smooth functioning of deposit-refund arrangements?

Perverse effects. Monopolistic producers may use a new deposit-refund system as a justification for price increases which are not justified by factor prices. In border regions, consumers might travel abroad and buy similar products which are not under a deposit-refund system.

Trade barriers. Mandatory deposit-refund systems could cause trade barriers for foreign producers which can be seen as an unacceptable distortion.

"Soft" effects are difficult to quantify, and difficult to evaluate, although there may be some scope for understanding the role played by attitudinal and other factors through opinion surveys of industry, non-governmental organisations and other environmental actors. It will often be the case that their impact is inseparable from the direct financial impact of the market instrument.

7.7 Dynamic effects, and innovation

Economic instruments are, in principle, likely to be more effective at stimulating innovation in pollution-abatement technologies than regulations which merely require a given level of compliance. Measuring this innovation effect is likely to be difficult for three reasons:

First, the relevant time horizon is likely to be long, and, as with long-term macroeconomic effects, there are clear practical difficulties in assessing effects over long time periods.

Second, the pace of innovation in pollution abatement technologies is unlikely to be determined by the policies in force in one country alone. In the open world trading system, abatement technologies developed in one country may be marketed elsewhere, and the rate of innovation is thus likely to be determined as much by the extent to which economic instruments are in use or in prospect world-wide, as by their use in a particular country.

Third, many different and complex factors influence technical change, and environmental policy is only one of them.

For these reasons, *ex post* evidence on this aspect of the use of economic instruments is likely to be very difficult, although some light may be shed by surveying the views of the relevant decision-makers in industry.

7.8 Some methodological issues

7.8.1 Scope and timescale

Ideally, an evaluation of the effectiveness of economic instruments should include a comprehensive assessment of the full range of effects set out in Sections 7.1-7.7. In practice, it will rarely be possible to do this. Both data constraints and resource constraints may limit the scope of analysis to those aspects of the use of economic instruments which can be readily observed, measured, or quantified.

The limitations which are placed on the scope of evaluation studies by resources and the availability of information need to be borne in mind in interpreting the results. There is an obvious danger of bias in concentrating solely on those aspects which can be measured, and ignoring considerations which are not readily amenable to evaluation. Some of the aspects of the effects of particular instruments may be inherently difficult to measure or quantify. As already noted, for example, it is unlikely that evaluation studies will be able to provide robust *ex post* evidence of the effect of the dynamic efficiency incentive from economic instruments. The difficulty of obtaining evidence on these dynamic effects of using economic instruments does not, however, mean that these effects are negligible, or that they can be ignored in comparing the relative merits of different instruments.

An initial decision has to be made in any evaluation study concerning the timescale over which the effects of different policies are to be assessed. The maximum time period over which effects can be assessed *ex post* is the length of time between the start of the policy and the evaluation study. Frequently, policy considerations will call for evaluations to be undertaken soon after a policy is initiated, so as to produce results and conclusions which can help in the modification and adjustment of the policy. An early evaluation will only be able to reflect the short-run effects of policy, and cannot provide evidence on longer-run consequences.

This means that evidence will more often be available concerning effects such as the short-run effects on static costs, initial environmental effects, and initial wider economic consequences; fewer evaluations are likely to provide good evidence about longer-run environmental effects, macroeconomic adjustments, and long-run technology decisions.

The timing of the evaluation may also be relevant in affecting the accuracy of the data available for the evaluation. Evaluation too long after the introduction of a particular measure is likely to mean that some of the relevant economic actors are no longer available to survey or interview (firms go out of business, managers retire or move jobs, etc.). Also, over the longer run, the effects on levels of pollution and environmental damage of a particular economic instrument may be much more difficult to distinguish from the effects of other factors also affecting pollution and environmental damage.

It is necessary to take account of the possibility that the behavioural response to an economic instrument may partly anticipate its introduction. Polluters may respond to the advance announcement of measures, and may make long-term investment decisions, or decisions about the retirement or replacement of existing capital stock in the light of future policy requirements (or even based on their assessment of possible future policy developments). Deciding an appropriate starting date for evaluating effects may be difficult; if anticipation effects are likely to arise, the date of introduction of the measure will be too late to include all of the relevant effects.

7.8.2 Disentangling policy packages

A frequent difficulty in assessing the effects of an economic instrument in environmental policy is that economic instruments are in practice rarely used in isolation, but are combined in a "package" of policy measures. Often, the effects of new economic instruments are reinforced by regulatory measures, or other measures, taken at the same time.

Thus, for example, in many European countries, the introduction of a tax differential in favour of unleaded petrol was accompanied by regulatory measures requiring certain existing types of petrol to be withdrawn from sale, advertising and publicity campaigns encouraging take-up of unleaded petrol, etc. Isolating the impact of the tax incentive alone is in principle difficult because of the existence of these parallel measures.

In many cases, it will simply be impossible to separate the individual contribution of policy measures implemented as part of a package; the evaluation will have to be content with evidence on the joint effect of all the elements of the package taken together. Sometimes there may be some scope for international comparisons to indicate the extent to which particular components of policy packages are responsible for outcomes, if the packages implemented in different countries combine different measures, or the same measures in different proportions, allowing the separate contribution of each component to be separated. However, such opportunities will be rare, and the evidence derived from such cross-country comparisons will depend critically on the assumption that the countries are otherwise equivalent in terms of the responses expected from the implementation of particular policies.

7.8.3 *Defining the counter-factual: "What would have happened otherwise?"*

It is unlikely to be the case that all effects on pollution levels after introduction of an economic instrument can be attributed to the effects of that economic instrument; some of the changes might have occurred in any case, regardless whether policy had changed or not. The effects of a policy change do not include all changes that took place subsequent to the policy change, but only those that have been caused by the policy change. What would have happened in the absence of the policy change must therefore be assessed as the baseline against which the effectiveness of a particular policy instrument is to be judged.

Box 11. **Methods for constructing a baseline against which the impact of policy can be assessed**

Various different methods are available to construct a baseline scenario. These include:

- *trend extrapolation.* A simple approach to constructing a policy baseline is to assume that trends visible prior to the policy change would have continued unchanged if the policy measure had not been implemented.

- *econometric methods.* Econometric models may be estimated which, for example, link pollution levels of various economic variables (*e.g.* the level of gross national product), and which include a "dummy variable" for the date of introduction of the policy measure. The model can then be used to make a "counterfactual" prediction of what would have happened to pollution levels if everything else had remained unchanged, except that the policy had not been introduced.

- *linear programming techniques* can be used to indicate how the decisions of firms might change in response to different constraints and incentives; the problem with these measures is that they assume some form of optimal decision-making, which may in practice be unrealistic.

- often it will be better to use *"judgemental" methods* than any of the other techniques to describe the baseline in the absence of policy. However, one problem with definitions of the baseline scenario constructed purely on the basis of judgement is that the outcome of the evaluation study will depend critically on the judgements made; there may easily be scope for doubts about the realism of such a baseline.

What can be done depends partly on the availability of suitable data. In turn, data availability depends partly on the institutional setting of the evaluation. Issues of commercial confidentiality may obstruct access to some of the key data needed.

7.8.4 *Multi-media effects*

Assessing effectiveness of policy instruments in terms of environmental quality should allow for side-effects in other environmental media. Imposing incentives on one residual, *e.g.* SO_2, may simply result in transferring problems to another environmental medium. Thus, in imposing economic instruments on activities to *e.g.* reduce discharges of SO_2, one result is likely to be the production of a slurry, which in turn requires a sedimentation step which eventually produces a solid residual for disposal. Economic instruments which induce removal of some undesired material from a liquid waste stream result in a semi-solid sludge which requires handling or disposal. If the material removed is considered hazardous, then special handling is required. Therefore the possible transfers of pollutants from one medium to another must be considered explicitly when contemplating use of economic instruments (or any incentive).

7.8.5 *Transboundary effects*

Side-effects of economic instruments have already been briefly touched upon. Environmental effectiveness may be affected unfavourably by certain applications of economic instruments, if foreign substitutes of domestically-charged products are ignored. A more general observation is that environmental policy instruments do not operate in a national vacuum. As much as domestic instruments may not lead to intended effects as a consequence of foreign influences, national instruments may have international effects, for example in case of induced international transfer of economic activities. Foreign or international environmental policy is one of the many possible, influential factors relevant in evaluating national policy instruments.

Chapter 8

THE INSTITUTIONAL CONTEXT OF EVALUATION STUDIES

Institutions matter for the operation of economic instruments. Neglecting the role played by different institutions and actors when evaluating the operation and outcomes of existing economic instruments may provide a misleading picture of their potential. The research design for an evaluation study thus needs to include appropriate scope for considering the impact of institutional factors on the design of economic instruments and on their effects.

Institutions also matter for the design and conduct of evaluation studies on the performance of economic instruments. How far evaluation is feasible, and how far the results of evaluation studies are likely to influence the course of future policy will depend on the institutional context within which the evaluation is conducted, and its results considered. Who should do evaluations, and for whom, may have an important bearing on the feasibility and policy impact of the study.

This section considers these influences of institutional factors on the agenda which evaluation studies should address, and on the conduct of evaluation.

8.1 Institutions and the effects of environmental policies

8.1.1 *Institutions and interest groups*

To understand the way in which market instruments perform in practice, and to be able to assess how prospective economic instruments might perform if implemented, we need to know how they interact with both interests and institutions in the economy. Does a particular instrument harmonise with the interests of the key actors in the policy process, and is it compatible with the institutional framework within which it operates?

Two papers written as part of the OECD work programme on evaluation of economic instruments have discussed the role of institutional factors in the performance of economic instruments. One, "The importance of institutions in the design and implementation of economic instruments in environmental policy", written by Skou Andersen provides a predominantly conceptual discussion of the influences of institutions. The second, "The role of actors and institutions in the design and implementation of economic instruments in environmental policy: the case of the Netherlands," written by Schuddeboom provides a review of the conceptual issues, and an illustration of their application to evaluations of five economic instruments in the Netherlands.

The institutional network, which comprises the whole range of institutions involved in policy-making and implementation, and the relations between them, may encompass both formal and informal institutions. The former comprise political institutions, (broadly conceived to include the rules reflected in constitutions and legislation, as well as the political structures such as parliaments, local councils, etc.), administrative institutions (the civil service, environmental agencies, etc.), and economic institutions (such as the framework of property rights, and the distribution of economic power). The latter, the informal institutions, include traditions, beliefs and culture. Thus, for example, differences in national policy styles, or in the expectations of the "targets" of environmental regulation (*i.e.* polluters) about the way in which policy will be applied and enforced, may lead the same instrument to have different outcomes in different countries.

Institutions provide a vehicle by which interest groups can influence the design or operation of environmental policies; as Skou Andersen observes, such groups can establish procedures, norms or organisations that will strengthen their bargaining power. Thus, for example, groups with a vested interest in the continuation of existing policies may be able to use their position or influence within institutions to impede policy reform. Also, groups with an interest in reform articulate this interest through the network of formal and informal institutions. However, institutions do not only provide a route through which interests can bring pressure on policy decisions and implementation. They may also impose constraints of various sorts on the way in which policy is designed and operated, reflecting the rules, traditions, procedures, expectations and cultures which exist within institutions. Past practice, in particular, can exert a major influence over the shape of future policy and operation.

Schuddeboom makes a distinction between the influence of institutional factors on two distinct aspects of the practical application of economic instruments – policy-making, and implementation. Both phases may be subject to a wide range of institutional influences, reflecting the pressure which particular interests can exert, and the impact of existing practices and expectations.

8.1.2 *Institutional factors and policy-making*

In the policy-making phase, institutional factors may affect the feasibility and acceptability of particular options for policy.

Feasibility is partly a function of the likely effectiveness of the proposed policy measures; to the extent that policy-makers propose measures in good faith, the capacity of the measures to achieve the goals of policy will be one consideration governing the probability of their adoption. In this way, knowledge and expectations about similar policies in practice may improve policy-making, and evaluation evidence from similar measures in other countries may have a role to play in spreading good practice, and ensuring that the instruments adopted have the potential to function as intended.

However, feasibility in the policy-making process will also depend on the impact of proposals on the interests of those who may have influence over the policy-making process. This could include the interests of public officials (for example, in maintaining an influential role for certain agencies), and interests of the target group (*i.e.* of polluters).

In addition, the feasibility of particular policy measures will also be influenced by less objective considerations, including factors of ideology and continuity. In the case of policy proposals for economic instruments, for example, the probability of adoption may have been limited in some countries by the prevalence of "ideological" views, or attitudes, that such instruments are in some way suspect, since they explicitly allow pollution to take place legally, and therefore appear to condone pollution by those with the ability to pay. In other cases, however, the use of economic instruments may have been promoted by policy cultures or ideologies, in countries where economic instruments appear to "chime in" with the dominant overall ideology of policy (the "meta-policy" as Schuddeboom calls it). The overall policy culture of deregulation which underlies many areas of policy in countries such as the UK and the USA may have helped to create a policy-making climate which is receptive to the idea of economic instruments in environmental policy.

Continuity with the legal framework, administrative culture and pattern of institutions is also likely to increase the probability that particular policy measures will be adopted. This may be partly

---

Box 12. **The institutional context of policy instruments**

Formal institutions

- Centralised vs. decentralised institutions and their respective power and role.
- Existence of special districts or jurisdictions designed for environmental management (*e.g.* river basin agencies).
- Nature of management agency (*e.g.* decentralised office of central ministry, municipal, regional, interstate).
- Existence of private institutions and organisations.
- Distribution of tasks and responsibilities between institutions, public and private.

Informal institutions

- Bureaucratic cultures (*e.g.* existing "corps" of engineers, inspectorates...).
- National policy styles (co-operative or conflicting relations, reliance on flexible or fixed procedures, detailed requirements or general guidelines, etc.).
- Perception of environmental problems (perceived as health hazard, quality of life, or natural resources issue).

Allocation of tasks between institutions

- Institutions respectively responsible for design, implementation, enforcement and evaluation of policy instruments.

Role of private institutions

- Private organisations may be involved in the implementation or operation of environmental policies, *e.g.* where voluntary agreements are implemented.

Source: Based on M. Skou Andersen "The importance of institutions in the design and implementation of economic instruments in environmental policy," paper prepared for the OECD Environment Directorate.

---

a matter of psychological resistance – officials who have been accustomed to operate in a particular way may be sceptical that better effects could be achieved through different instruments. It is also a matter of self-interest, or group interest, amongst those with a stake in the current way of doing things; agencies which would be rendered redundant by a policy reform may be unlikely to lobby for the reform to be adopted. The importance of continuity may mean that incremental policy reform often has a greater chance of success than wholesale reform; the starting-point of existing policies may thus tend to govern the reforms that would be feasible. For example, it has often been suggested that the reason that the US has adopted tradeable permit instruments more readily than other countries is that existing US command-and-control policies were based on quantitative emission limits for individual sources, from which the move to tradeability was a small step. In countries where regulatory policies take a different form, adopting tradeable permits would require a more fundamental reorientation of the system, to introduce procedures for establishing and monitoring emission limits for individual sources, as the precondition for making the property rights in emissions a tradeable commodity.

8.1.3 Institutional factors and implementation

The role of institutional factors in the implementation phase of environmental policy measures centres around two aspects, firstly the impact of institutional ideology (the "style of government") and "commitment" on the way in which policy is applied, and secondly the resources and information available for implementation.

Style of government and commitment

As far as the role of the style of government and commitment is concerned, many of the reasons for these to affect policy-making also affect implementation. It may take time for the culture and expectations of institutions to adapt to changes in the nature of the tasks which they have been given; individuals whose careers have been based on one set of principles and rules may find it difficult to adapt to the requirements of a new type of policy. However, changes in the general climate of policy – the "meta policy" – towards greater deregulation in a range of fields of government policy, for example, may make it easier for agencies and individuals to adapt to market instruments than in a situation where no such general shift in attitudes was taking place.

Likewise, the attitudes of target groups towards the individuals and agencies running environmental policies could affect the level of success which they achieve. An administrative style based on confrontation may in some circumstances achieve less than one which seeks to build an atmosphere of co-operation between environmental policy-makers and target groups. Thus, for example, there may sometimes be advantages to implementing policy in a climate of goodwill and tolerance, in which temporary violations of emissions standards are not immediately met with the threat of prosecution, but instead lead to a co-operative approach between the polluter and the regulatory agency to try to identify procedures and methods to prevent such violations recurring. Economic instruments could help to stimulate such an approach – by, for example, giving polluters a clear financial interest in avoiding accidental violations – or they could instead make firms more suspicious of reporting problems, for fear that this would increase the charges they would face. In which direction the effect runs cannot be determined except through evaluation of experience with actual policies. In addition, however, as discussed below, the nature of the relationship between agency and target group may have important effects on the information available for policy implementation, which may be critical in determining its effectiveness.

The resources available to the institutions involved in the process of implementation will affect their ability to measure, monitor and control the way in which a given policy is applied. The staFF and financial means available for enforcement of regulations or of the terms of economic instruments will be a key determinant of their relative performance.

Availability of information

In addition, however, a second important aspect of resources is the information at the disposal of the public agencies implementing policy. All policies require information for their efficient operation, and much of this information cannot simply be "purchased" through an adequate level of staffing (although this will always be relevant), but has to be obtained from the subjects of regulation themselves. The information required for environmental regulation can be obtained in various ways, both through co-operative routes (voluntary disclosures and reporting of emissions and practices) and through non-co-operative procedures (for example by taking measurements of ambient environmental standards in the vicinity of pollution sources, or by compulsory installation of emissions measurement devices).

Different instruments will require different amounts and types of information. Thus, for example, one of the advantages of economic instruments is that an efficient allocation between polluters can be achieved without knowledge of the costs and possibilities for abatement by each individual source; to achieve the same outcome through direct "command-and-control" regulation would require considerable information about the circumstances and costs of individual polluters, which they may be unwilling to provide.

The relationship between the environmental policy agencies and the targets of the policy will influence the extent to which the agency has access to information of various sorts. Thus, for example, an institutional atmosphere of co-operation between agency and target groups may increase the amount of information the agency has available for policy operation, and for the design and modification of future policies.

Regulatory capture

At the same time, however, co-operation between agency and target groups may run the risk of subverting the design and operation of environmental policy instruments to meet other goals. Thus, for example, if industrial interest groups are involved in the design of environmental policies, the measures which result may reflect other interests of the groups involved in the process – environmental policies may then have the effect of protecting domestic production against imports, or may reflect the interests of large firms to the detriment of smaller firms less able to articulate their interests in the lobbying process. Similarly, if environmental agencies have to co-operate with the target groups in order to obtain the information necessary for implementation of policy, the way that they operate policy may tend, unavoidably, to come to reflect the objectives of the target groups as well as – or instead of – those of the agency.

This process of "regulatory capture", which is widely recognised as a problem in many areas of government regulation, arises because of the asymmetry of information between the regulator and the subject of regulation; because the subject can control the flow of information to the regulator, it is also able to control, at least, in part, the regulatory decisions to which it is subject.

It is possible that the use of economic instruments may be less vulnerable to subversion through regulatory capture than certain other types of policy. In particular, instruments applied on a more discretionary basis, based on the circumstances of each individual case, may be severely prone to capture by the individual subjects of the regulation, since a large amount of information relating to individual circumstances is required to operate discretionary policies; much of this will necessarily have to come from the regulated subject. By contrast, economic instruments are more rule-based (or "parametric") in their application, and situations where the subject can influence implementation are less likely, and may be easier to identify and remedy.

8.1.4 Institutional factors and performance

So far, we have discussed the impact of political institutions on the *design and implementation* of economic instruments mainly in terms of the way in which institutional arrangements channel and focus the pressures from groups with various interests at stake. How far, for example, does the organisation and culture of government affect the likelihood that environmental taxes or other economic instruments might be adopted, and how does it affect the way in which measures, once agreed, are actually implemented in practice.

There are, however, further ways in which institutional factors will affect environmental policies which take the form of economic instruments. These have to do with the effects of the institutional "environment" or "context" on the *performance* of economic instruments. Two aspects of this may be of particular relevance in determining whether economic instruments actually achieve the effects that they could achieve in ideal conditions.

– "Policy failures" in other areas of government policy may create an adverse starting point for economic instruments, which may prevent them attaining their full potential. Such "policy failures" are far from rare. For example, tax breaks for commuter costs may work against policies which try to use vehicle or fuel taxes to discourage unnecessary vehicle use. Similarly, agricultural price support schemes may offset the incentives and effectiveness of a system of fertiliser taxes.

– Broader institutional "rigidities" may affect the outcomes achieved from the use of economic instruments. These may include the market failures due to poor information (which may inhibit adequate investments in energy efficiency, for example, in response to higher energy prices). They may also include various legal provisions which inhibit responses which might be desirable from the environmental policy point of view. Thus, for example, legislation in Denmark which prohibits landlords charging tenants on the basis of metered water consumption, requiring water costs to be covered in the rent, was introduced to protect tenants. However it may have the side effect of reducing the potential effectiveness of correct water resource pricing.

8.1.5 Studying the effects of institutional factors

The influence of institutional factors over the design and outcomes of policy instruments requires particular techniques for evaluation. Given the complexity and qualitative nature of the effects of institutional factors, it will normally be necessary, as Skou Andersen argues, to draw on case study techniques to understand the role played by various institutional relationships and procedures in the effects of market instruments. In these case studies, which may, for example, compare the performance of a similar instrument across a number of different countries, it will be necessary to combine hard quantitative data with more qualitative data on contextual and institutional variables. An example of a study of this sort is given by the work of Skou Andersen on water pollution charges (Skou Andersen, 1994), and a cross-country comparison of water charges also formed the basis for one of the case studies undertaken as part of the OECD work programme on evaluation which is the subject of this report.

Properly assessing the role of institutional factors undoubtedly makes evaluation difficult, in view of the range and subtlety of the potential effects which institutions may have on the design and implementation of policy. There is, however, a more fundamental problem for evaluation which is introduced when institutional factors exert a significant impact on the design and probability of implementation of particular policy instruments. If institutional factors affect the probability of implementation of economic instruments, those economic instruments which are observed in operation are no longer a random sample of applications. Instead, they will tend to be applications where the institutional barriers to implementation have, for one reason or another, been overcome. This could happen, for example, by "buying off" the opposition which would otherwise exist to a particular instrument on the part of targets or actors within government agencies. Sometimes, this process may, in turn, affect the potential of the instrument to achieve the effects which a "purer" instrument could achieve. Thus, for example, an environmental agency's concern to maintain a pivotal role for itself in the implementation of policy could limit the scope for a system of tradeable permits to achieve an efficient reallocation of emissions between sources, if the agency were to maintain its role by insisting on a lengthy and bureaucratic procedure to approve trades before they could take place.

This observation suggests that whilst evaluations of practical experience of economic instruments may be of value in assessing their strengths and weaknesses, the cases of economic instruments which are observed should not necessarily be taken as indicative of the consequences of a more general application of such instruments. The applications observed may include some cases unusually suited to the introduction of economic instruments, where they have been easy to introduce because some of the usual sources of opposition may have been absent. They may also include cases where implementation has only been possible by changing the instrument to make it acceptable to the various actors involved; this may result in an instrument which is a long way in practice from the ideal.

8.2 Evaluation studies within the policy process

The institutional context within which evaluation studies are conducted will also have an important influence on the success of the evaluation, and on its policy impact. There are a number of reasons for this.

First, evaluation studies cannot be conducted in a vacuum, without any contact or engagement with the institutions and actors involved in the operation of policy. At the very least, evaluation studies will be dependent on the institutions responsible for the operation of policy for factual information and data. Frequently, it may be appropriate for the interaction between evaluators and institutions to be more extensive than this, and for the evaluation to draw on the judgements of institutional players about various aspects of the performance of particular policy measures.

This will mean that evaluations conducted from within the organisation responsible for the operation of policy may often have much better access to data, and may thus be much better informed, than evaluations conducted from outside the organisation, for example by independent consultants. One reason for inside evaluators to be better informed is that it may be difficult to give outsiders access to commercially-sensitive information obtained in the course of the operation of policy.

Evaluations may also need to obtain the co-operation of the subjects of the policy – the polluters whose emissions it seeks to regulate. Some of the data needed for evaluation may not have been routinely collected for other purposes. The evaluator may have to approach polluters to provide data on such subjects as, for example, pollution levels, technology options and costs, monitoring and compliance costs, the reasons for particular choices, etc. It will be difficult to do this in a way which can ensure that the information provided is not slanted so as to influence the outcome of the evaluation to suit the interests of the polluter. Thus, for example, polluters concerned that an existing policy might be replaced by an alternative policy which would impose higher costs on them may be inclined to give answers which they think will show the existing policy in a favourable light. The evaluator will need to assess the extent to which the information provided is therefore liable to be compromised and unreliable.

It will be noted that this problem of evaluation of economic instruments goes to the heart of the case for using economic instruments in the first place. If it were possible to obtain reliable information on the circumstances of individual polluters, it would be possible to design an efficient regulatory policy based on direct "command-and-control" regulation; it is precisely because the authorities cannot obtain such information that economic instruments may be able to achieve a more efficient outcome than command-and-control. Evaluating the efficiency of economic instruments in environmental policy requires the evaluation researcher to obtain data which, if it could be routinely available to environmental policy agencies, could be used to implement an efficient policy through command-and-control. In this sense, it might appear that an evaluation of the efficiency of economic instruments is only possible in policy situations where the use of economic instruments is unnecessary, because command-and-control policies could be efficiently designed using the information available to the evaluation researcher. There is, however, one important difference between evaluation and day-to-day policy implementation, and this concerns the scale of the task. Useful evaluation results can be obtained by studying a limited (but representative) sample of actual cases, and it may be possible to devote considerably more effort to obtaining data about these cases than would be feasible for day-to-day implementation of a command-and-control policy.

Second, the relationship between the evaluator and the institutions with responsibility for the policy may affect the actual or perceived objectivity of the work. Whilst insider evaluators may be better informed, they may be perceived as biased in favour of conclusions which put their current operations in a good light. This perception may be reinforced by policies of, for example, publishing the results of evaluations on a selective basis, so that only favourable conclusions reach the public domain, or of restricting access by other researchers or interested parties to the data and methods used for the evaluation.

Third, translating evaluation findings into future policy requires that the institutions responsible for policy formulation and implementation accept the findings of the evaluation. Their acceptance of the findings may be assisted, if they perceive themselves as having some form of "ownership" or commitment to the evaluation, and if they cannot criticise the evaluation for ignorance of key "insider" detail.

Box 13. **Inter-department evaluation of environmental regulations in Norway**

At the end of 1992, an inter-departmental committee, headed by the Ministry of the Environment, began evaluating the performance of environmental regulations in Norway. The Committee was appointed with a mandate "to review the administrative instruments currently used to reduce environmental problems, with a view to making these instruments more effective". In particular, the Committee was instructed to describe the administrative instruments in use, the changes in emissions and the environment which have been achieved by applying these instruments, and the associated administrative and economic consequences. It was to analyse the effect of the instruments in relation to goal-achievement, cost-effectiveness, distributional effects, ability to motivate technological development, and other positive and negative effects.

The terms of reference for the study were therefore wide-ranging, and the work constituted a major attempt at evaluation and reappraisal of the design and effectiveness of environmental policy interventions in a country which has a high level of environmental consciousness, and has applied high environmental standards in policy over the past two decades. The initial impetus for the study came from the Ministry of Finance, as part of its overall brief to ensure the efficient functioning of the economic system, but the Committee operated under the auspices of the Ministry of Environment, with participation from the Ministry of Finance and four other relevant ministries, and research groups in economics and law. The study was announced publicly, and there was a commitment to publish the findings.

The focus of the study, as set out in the Committee's mandate, was principally on regulatory policies ("administrative instruments"), although in a number of fields which the group examined, Norway also has economic instruments, of various forms, as an element of policy. Thus, in the case of sulphur emissions control, policy has included both sulphur regulations and a sulphur tax; the control of lead pollution has been achieved partly through a tax differential in favour of unleaded petrol; the control of waste oil pollution has made use of a deposit-refund system to ensure that waste oil is recovered and disposed in an environmentally acceptable manner; and, in policy towards emissions of CFCs, the threat of a tax was used as a means to ensure that industry implemented adequate measures to curtail CFC use on a voluntary basis.

The interdepartmental group commissioned analytical studies to inform its work from an economics consultancy, ECON. The studies examined environmental regulations in Norway from three different angles, based on geographic area, industry, and type of emissions, respectively.

Geographic area. One of the commissioned studies involved a cost-benefit analysis of the entire complex of environmental policies, as they have affected one particular geographical area. The location selected for this study was Greenland, one of the most industrialised areas in Northern Europe.

Industry. A second study examined environmental regulation in the pulp and paper industry, which has been highly-regulated since the early 1970s, primarily on the basis of emissions standards.

Emissions. A third study evaluated the efficiency and effectiveness of environmental policies relating to five different types of emissions – sulphur dioxide, CFCs, waste oil, lead emissions and mercury pollution.

The commissioned studies were undertaken quickly, over a period of eight months, in order to meet the timetable of the interdepartmental group. They formed virtually the only external analytical material available to support the group's work; no other existing studies were available in this field. The group itself, however, undertook some additional analytical work, supported by data supplied by the State Pollution Control Authority (SFT).

The studies considered six key questions:

- changes over the period in *environmental damage*;
- *factors causing emissions reductions*, including both policy effects and external factors;
- the *effects and practicability of policy instruments*, including the basis on which emissions standards were set for individual firms, and their impact on firms' behaviour;
- *cost-effectiveness and cost-benefits* of the policy, especially the extent to which policy led to large differences in marginal abatement costs causing the same environmental damage;
- *institutional relations*, including the co-ordination of multiple policies;
- *recommendations* for future policy, including possible reforms, and use of alternative policy instruments.

(see next page)

(continued)

The assessment of the effects of policy intervention was largely judgmental, and the definition of the baseline against which the effects of policy were to be assessed proved complex. How far had the emissions reduction been due to policy, rather than to autonomous changes in technology, which had led to lower emissions as an automatic consequence of new investment?

Econometric or other formal techniques were not employed in the studies to construct a no-policy baseline against which the effects of policy could be judged, partly because of the difficulty of constructing a model to predict the baseline over a long historical period. One way, however, in which the studies attempted to assess the impact of policy was through process evidence – observing whether firms' decisions directly followed from the imposition of policy requirements. Outcome evidence was also seen as relevant – the drop in emissions was correlated with the start of stringent environmental policy requirements.

A key focus of the studies was the issue of cost effectiveness, by considering how different the marginal abatement costs of different polluters; in practice, except in the case of the SO_2 study, none of the research studies was able to obtain much detailed quantitative evidence on this question.

It proved difficult to obtain cost data, especially cost data relating to past investments in abatement measures. Many of the firms concerned no longer had such data available – the relevant documentation was not kept for periods as long as the timespan of the inquiry, and many of the personnel involved had moved to other posts, other firms, or had retired. Relatively little use could be made of cost data from technology suppliers, except in the case of the SO_2 study.

The studies encountered some difficulties in attributing abatement costs where investments in clean technologies had taken place over the period. How much of the investment cost in introducing a new plant, based on cleaner production processes, should be attributed to the pollution-control requirements of policy.

The general views of industry about the system of environmental regulation were that the system appeared to work reasonably well (although there may have been a risk that this answer reflected a concern that the study might be used to advocate environmental taxes). Firms were asked, amongst other things, whether the authorities had demanded pollution control investments which were clearly cost-inefficient, and it was generally felt that they had not; only one reasonably clear-cut example of wholly-inefficient investment was found. There were, however, some concerns about control activities. Control is largely based on self-declaration, backed up with spot checks. There was concern that the spot checks focused too much on the details of compliance, and did not pay enough attention to the systems and procedures for pollution control, appraisal of staff competence, etc. The spot checks were thus felt to impose compliance costs on firms, whilst having relatively little significant control function. The absence of rigorous control was seen as benefiting non-compliant competitors in the industry, at the expense of firms which complied with the regulatory requirements.

The Committee encountered difficulties in reaching generally-agreed conclusions about the costs and benefits of policy, partly because of the lack of robust data and evidence on both sides of the equation. Because the costs of past environmental measures had not been recorded at the time, retrospective evaluation proved difficult, and assessments of the costs of policy measures were disputed in the groups's discussions. Similarly, on the benefits side, the study was able to find good data demonstrating the substantial achievements of environmental policy in Norway taken as a whole, but found it harder to prove a causal link between particular environmental policy instruments and the environmental outcomes.

The Committee was established in a government system which had not, in the past, routinely conducted evaluations of the outcomes and effectiveness of policy. Its significance was thus twofold. First, the findings of the Committee's work provided new information on the workings of environmental policy in Norway. Second, and in the long run perhaps equally significant, the study established a pattern and procedures for more systematic feedback and evaluation about current environmental policies. The report stated: "The Committee is of the opinion that, in addition to undertaking comprehensive evaluations of relevant alternatives before new instruments are introduced, it is necessary to carry out subsequent evaluations when the instruments have been in use for some time. The establishment of systems of outcome assessment should be an integrated part of the use of instruments in any area. Such follow-up processes will enable the authorities to both correct the course if necessary, and also accumulate experience regarding the properties of the different environmental policy instruments, both in respect of environmental impacts and of costs."

The issues set out here concerning the institutional context of evaluation do not point to a single clear conclusion. It is likely that, in some circumstances and for some purposes, evaluations will be most effective if they are conducted by insiders with good access to information; in other circumstances it may be more appropriate for evaluation to be undertaken by an independent outsider. The trade-off between information and objectivity will, however, often involve difficult decisions. There are, however, a number of ways of reducing its severity. Thus, for example, where evaluations are conducted by "insiders", it may be possible to enhance the objectivity – and, perhaps more important, the perception of objectivity – of the evaluation by such measures as:

 – establishing a steering group to oversee the evaluation, including outside members;
 – making data and research methods open to peer review and scrutiny;
 – making a prior commitment to publication, regardless of the evaluation findings.

Likewise, institutional structures and procedures may play an important role in ensuring that evaluations feed through into subsequent policy adjustments and reforms. This is often a matter where forward planning may be helpful. Thus, for example:

Early planning of evaluation can ensure that the necessary data is collected in the course of operating the policy; it may be much less costly to collect data as a routine by-product of administration than in a special evaluation exercise. For this reason, an *"in-built" approach* to evaluation would be desirable, in which an early commitment is made to evaluation, and the necessary data for later evaluation is collected at all stages.

Announcing in advance that an evaluation will be conducted may help to smooth some of the difficulties in advance; it is less likely to be perceived by the subjects as a threat than where proposals for evaluation are brought forward with little warning, and perhaps in the context of existing controversy over the performance of a policy or agency.

"Ownership" of the research findings is important in ensuring that they feed through effectively into policy. Participation of all relevant parties in the supervision and discussion of evaluations, for example through an inter-departmental steering group, will help to create a climate in which findings affect future policy, rather than simply being dismissed as irrelevant, ill-informed or inaccurate.

Chapter 9

AN IN-BUILT EVALUATION FRAMEWORK

This chapter outlines an approach to evaluation of environmental policy instruments which aims to incorporate evaluation, and planning for evaluation, into the policy development and implementation process at an early stage. We refer to it as an "in-built" approach to evaluation.

9.1 The approach

The main reason for proposing an in-built evaluation framework is to try to overcome (some of the) problems of finding appropriate data for evaluation. Such problems are clearly shown in the survey of evaluation studies in Chapters 3-6. Many of these problems can be traced back to a number of circumstances.[29]

- insufficient *ex ante* analysis in terms of missing data or weak evaluation model;
- non-predicted instrument impact;
- unforeseen developments in the policy and implementation context;
- adapted instrument design;
- unforeseen additional policy measures or instruments.

Establishing a closer link between *ex ante* and *ex post* analysis and between policy evaluation and the design and implementation process could help to solve some of the problems.

Policy evaluation sets out from various angles. The common distinction between *ex ante* and *ex post* evaluation marks two different approaches. Ex *ante* evaluation generally is more restricted than *ex post* evaluation. Ex *ante* evaluation attempts to forecast the impact of intended policies by creating experimental models of the policy and societal context and evaluating the effects against predetermined criteria. Ex *post* evaluation seeks to trace back revealed changes in variables under evaluation to instruments that were meant to bring about these changes, and checks such changes against selected criteria derived from the policy objectives. However, both approaches should have in common the necessity to either build (*ex ante*) or rebuild (*ex post*) the institutional and societal context of the policies under evaluation. Ex *post* evaluation requires a baseline inventory which could be part of an *ex ante* assessment.

Box 14 illustrates the advantages of on-going data collection, as a device to bridge the gap between *ex ante* and *post* evaluation.

9.1.1 Why an "in-built" evaluation process?

The approach described in this chapter is an *ex post* evaluation approach, but, in order to do justice to the dynamics of policy design and implementation, it attempts to "in-build" the policy and societal context, not in retrospect, but during the evolution of policy and societal variables, in a longitudinal way. Such an

---

Box 14. Energy Policy and CO_2 taxes in Denmark

Since the energy crises in the 70s, Denmark has a rather strict planning of the supply and consumption of energy. In order to be able to efficiently and effectively conduct this energy policy, the Danish Energy Agency has a tradition of collecting data on energy aspects in a detailed manner. This data collection also has a relevance for environmental policy, *e.g.* with regard to CO_2.

CO_2 taxes became an issue in environmental policy when targets for reducing CO_2 were agreed in international gremia. In Denmark, the CO_2 tax was designed in such a way as to reduce negative economic impact to a minimum. Different tax rates apply for different forms of energy use. Various designs of the tax system were tested by modelling and calculated the impact of the taxes on economic variables, such as employment rates.

Due to the tradition of extensive collecting data on energy, data for *ex ante* evaluation of the impact of CO_2 taxes were readily available, which contributed to reliability of the evaluation results.

---

approach may overcome some of the problems listed above as its offers the possibility of keeping track of the changes occurring through time, that have an impact on the outcome of the instrument in operation.

A main problem of *ex post* evaluation is assessing the impact of the reviewed instrument on realisation of the policy objectives. Policy instruments are operational in a complicated, sometimes chaotic context. Design, implementation and enforcement of policy instruments are subject to many forces, executed by many actors in the policy arena. The policy process consists of many steps, and can meet a great number of obstacles that may stagnate or change its course. The instrument actually in force can deviate a great deal from the instrument originally intended. External factors that were accounted for at the time of the definitive design of the policy instruments may have changed completely at the time of execution of the instrument.

An "in-built" evaluation framework approach should be capable of keeping track of the many internal and external factors and the changes therein, that influence the outcome of the reviewed policy instrument. Such an approach guides the data gathering through the process and its changes, facilitating immediate monitoring. *This implies that the evaluation procedure should start together with the conceptualisation and design of the instrument under evaluation, and should continue during all the stages of discussion, adaptation, implementation and enforcement of the instrument.*

9.1.2 *The time dimension*

The above already suggests that the time dimension is extremely important in evaluation procedures. There are several aspects, including the different moments of evaluation, the maturation time of instruments and the dynamic context of policy instruments.

Proper evaluation procedures require *ex ante* as well as *ex post* assessment of the policy impact of the reviewed instrument. Since *ex ante* evaluation is prospective analysis, the used "model" is necessarily restricted in its capacity to reflect reality. As time evolves, circumstances will change, which may render the results of *ex ante* evaluation less reliable. Ex *post* evaluation may use the assumptions made in the *ex ante* model, as a reference for assessing the impact of changed circumstances on the outcome of the reviewed instrument.

Instruments need time to grow to maturity. After implementation, a minimal period of time must elapse before *ex post* evaluation can be carried out. The appropriate length of time depends on many factors. A sufficiently long and careful preparation of instrument implementation may result in early reactions, facilitating timely evaluation. Full *ex post* evaluation is also dependant of possible phasing-in of the instruments under review. Strong instruments in the context of harsh problems may need more time to overcome objections and dragging, before a stable situation has evolved.

The more time elapses between implementation and *ex post* evaluation, however, the more internal and external factors are subject to changes, in other words, the more dynamic the policy context may be. Influential factors include factor prices, technological innovation, other economic conditions, other policy instruments. Evaluation could be relatively easy if most of the influential factors can be held constant. More variables exponentially complicate the evaluation model.

9.2 The framework

9.2.1 An "in-built" evaluation framework

In an "in-built" evaluation framework, the evaluation procedure is tied up with the policy design and implementation process (policy process[30]). To describe the links between both processes, the policy process and the evaluation procedure must be broken down into separate stages.

However, although in the discussion below we describe the policy and evaluation processes as a restricted set of successive stages, this does not imply that these processes are always well-ordered in practice. The policy process start in Stage 1 with a blank sheet of paper and in many cases the stages we identify overlap in time.

Also, there will not always be a single policy-making authority who directs the policy process from a central "control panel". The process rather is the outcome of many individual and group activities in the political and societal arena, regulated by democratic rules. The chosen presentation however is used to illustrate an in-built evaluation framework in a schematic way.

Taking this into account, the policy process encompassing design and implementation of the instrument or mix of instruments under review may consist of six stages:

1) Identifying and defining the environmental problem;
2) Discussing the need for policy intervention, and setting policy objectives;
3) Designing and assessing effective and efficient options (instruments or instrument-mixes);
4) Selecting, discussing and adapting instrument (mix);
5) Introducing instrument, implementing control and enforcement;
6) Possible modification after evaluation.

The procedure of evaluation of policy instruments according to the longitudinal approach also included six stages:

1) Description of the instrument under review and of the institutional context, including arguments pro and con, interests, etc, of the introduction of the instrument; definition of relevant internal and external factors influencing the performance of the instrument (baseline inventory);
2) Definition of operational evaluation criteria;
3) Construction of an evaluation model and definition of the data to be gathered;
4) Continuous collection of data and reassessment of influential factors; *ex post* evaluation;
5) Possible modification of the evaluation model, the evaluation criteria and data to be collected, *e.g.* of influential factors;
6) Conclusions, recommendations, and feedback into the policy process.

The policy process and the evaluation procedure are linked in the following way (Table 9):

Table 9. **Linked policy process and evaluation procedure**

Stage	Policy process	Link	Stage	Evaluation procedure
1	Identifying and defining the environmental problem			
2	Discussing the need for policy intervention and setting objectives			
3	Designing and assessing effective and efficient options (instruments or instrument-mixes)	→ ←	1	Description of the instruments and of the institutional context, definition of relevant internal and external factors; (baseline inventory)
4	Selecting, discussing and adapting instrument chosen	→	2	Definition of evaluation criteria
			3	Construction of evaluation model and definition of all data to be gathered
5	Introduction of instrument (mix), implementation of control and enforcement	→	4	Continuous collection of data and reassessment of influential factors, and *ex post* evaluation
			5	Possible adaptation of the evaluation model, evaluation criteria and data
6	Possible modification of instrument (mix) after evaluation	←	6	Conclusions, recommendations, and feedback into the policy process

Policy process Stage 1: *identifying and defining the environmental problem*

Signalising new environmental problems, the worsening of existing problems, perceived lack of policy progress and other factors (political fashion) precede new or modified policy intervention. In this stage (which is part of a continuous process), most of the efforts are devoted to research and monitoring. It takes time before experts agree on the situation (if ever), and provide solid material for further action.

Policy process Stage 2: *discussing the need for policy intervention and setting objectives*

Discussing the need for – additional – policy intervention, and setting – new – policy objectives ensues from evidence provided in Stage 1. Such action may start by responsible authorities, but also by other concerned parties (political bodies, pressure groups). Responsibilities for setting new objectives and for designing the further course of action to be followed may be in one hand, or may be divided among different authorities, depending on the institutional structure, and may differ across countries and types of environmental problems. Also definition of general policy objectives and of operational targets may be different competencies. Objectives and operational targets are the basis for definition of the criteria to be used in the evaluation procedure.

Policy process Stage 3: *designing and assessing effective and efficient options (instruments or instrument-mixes)*

Designing and assessing effective and efficient options (instruments or instrument-mixes) constitute a stage in the policy process that should be closely linked to the first stage in the evaluation procedure. Assessment of the environmental situation and expected developments over time requires a baseline inventory of the level of emissions, the use of resources, target groups and their composition, contribution of firms to total emissions, and of existing policy instruments. This should also include a complete assessment of all the stakeholders, including concerned government branches on various levels, and their roles and interests. The baseline inventory is also the background for *ex post* evaluation.

As regards economic instruments, OECD has developed guidelines for their application.[31] Suggestions for effective and efficient application of environmental charges/taxes, tradeable permits and deposit-refund systems were discussed with respect to their potential application in environmental sectors (water, atmospheric emissions, waste management and noise), as well as to key economic sectors (transport, energy, agriculture, industry).

Assessing the need for and impact of (new) policy instruments requires some form of *ex ante* evaluation, in which an estimation of relevant factors and their influence on the environmental problem, as well as an assessment of the impact of alternative courses of action, is made. A link between *ex ante* and *ex post* analysis should be established.

As already noted, *ex ante* (prospective) evaluation is by necessity a more restricted exercise than *ex post* (retrospective) evaluation, and the two approaches to evaluation differ in character. E*x ante* analysis attempts to predict the results of the instrument under review, given the limited knowledge about all the factors that will influence its performance. It assumes a manageable number of influential factors with predicted values. In *ex post* analysis the results can be found, but the difficulty here is to trace back the outcome to the functioning of the instrument. It has to sort out relevant factors from the vast array of factors that have developed over time. Therefore, *ex ante* and *ex post* analysis share the baseline inventory, but differ in the evaluation "model". The predicted values used in *ex ante* analysis can be used as a starting point for the inventory and assessment of influential factors in *ex post* analysis.

Operational policy targets are fundamental for selecting policy instruments. The adequacy of implemented instruments is reviewed on the basis of evaluation criteria. This implies a close link between these targets and the criteria for evaluation, to be defined in the second stage of the evaluation procedure.

Policy process Stage 4: selecting, discussing and adapting instrument chosen

If several courses of action are open for resolving the problem, a choice must be made. This is a process of selection (also based on *ex ante* evaluation), discussion, adapting and final choice. This part of the policy process may take up considerable time, because in this stage crucial steps are taken that will affect polluters for a longer period of time. A balance must be found between environmental interests, represented by some parties, and the interests of other parties concerned, including societal (target) groups and responsible authorities.

Several procedures are conceivable here. In case of serious problems, requiring strong instruments, a regular way is that a government or parliamentary committee proposes a single instrument or mix, based on a comparison of advantages and disadvantages of the possible courses of action. This proposal is discussed, and possibly amended, in political bodies, taking into account the results of opinions and lobbies executed. Finally, the government takes a decision, and preparation of implementation starts. This is typical for the, more consultative, European approach. In the USA, there is sometimes less influence from parties concerned in this stage than in Europe, which may result in trying to take action in the stage of implementation.[32]

Policy process Stage 5: introduction of instrument (mix), implementation of control and enforcement

Introduction of the instrument or mix requires a lot of practical work. This encompasses announcement, information, setting up of an organisational structure, regulation of control and enforcement, and monitoring. Practical problems may require small adaptations of the instrument.

Control and enforcement have to accompany the implementation stage. The section on "enforcement" in Chapter 10 (Key issues), contains a description of relevant authorities and activities. This is the main stage of the instrument's life-cycle, where data has to be collected for assessing its performance (Stage 4 of the evaluation procedure).

Policy process Stage 6: possible modification of instrument (mix) after evaluation

A major objective of evaluation according to an in-built framework is improving the design and implementation of reviewed instruments. Dependent on the outcome of *ex post* evaluation, modification of the instrument or of aspects of its execution are possible. This is the stage in the policy process that is closely linked to the final stage in the evaluation procedure, where the outcome of *ex post* evaluation is discussed and recommendations are drawn up. The more evaluation is a continuous process, the more likely is it that the reviewed instrument serves its purpose, provided that feedback is secured.

Evaluation procedure Stage 1: description of the instruments and of the institutional context, definition of relevant internal and external factors (baseline inventory)

At the stage of designing new policy instruments, a baseline inventory should provide a reference for evaluation of the instruments after their introduction. This inventory should contain relevant variables which follow from the institutional context of the intended introduction of the instruments. Depending on the policy context, such variables could include:

1) relevant economic activities;
2) their economic output;
3) relevant environmental characteristics (emissions, use of raw material, energy consumption, etc);
4) their market position;
5) applied technology;
6) availability of clean technology;
7) applied policy measures and impact in terms of reactions of target groups.

In the baseline inventory, also activities outside the jurisdiction of the responsible authorities (federation, state, province, municipality, river basin, etc.) with an environment impact that could interfere with instruments proposed (transboundary effects) should be taken into account.

Description of the institutional context is a major component in this evaluation procedure. It should provide an overview of circumstances and forces that are influential with regard to the instruments under design and its expected impact of effectiveness and efficiency. In the process of policy making, as well as in the process of policy implementation and operation, a number of barriers may arise, implying as many points of decision with an a priori uncertain outcome.[33] A problem must be signalised and the intended solution (*i.e.* introduction of an economic instrument) must be brought from the private or group agenda to the public agenda. The public agenda item must be elaborated into an official instrument design. This design must reach the stage of concluded policy. The policy must be brought to implementation. Finally, the instrument in operation must prove its effectiveness and efficiency in the real world, where it is subject to many factors capable of frustrating its operation.[34]

Around each of these barriers, stakeholders are operational, each of them trying to influence the outcome in a way favourable for their (private) purposes. Skou Andersen[35] discusses the role institutions play in the choice, implementation and enforcement of economic instruments (see also Chapter 8). Indeed, not only central government institutions and political parties are involved, but also regional and municipal authorities, water boards, waste management agencies, environmental pressure groups, and organisations representing industry, consumers and labourers may enter the stage. They act, in their own interests (interests of the groups they represent), in varying compositions according to the problem and instrument under discussion and the stage in the course of policy making and implementation. This not only may hinder introduction of instruments, but may also result in the building up of design failures of introduced instruments in the policy process, which impede effective and efficient functioning.

An inquiry of the baseline situation and of the institutional context should provide an overview of the environmental problem concerned, of the policy context (instruments already operational), and of the arguments for introduction of the economic instrument as a(n) (additional) solution to the problem. It also should provide an overview of the field of political and societal forces, executed by the stakeholders concerned, at the time of conceptualising the new instrument. These forces are not fixed, but may evolve over the stages described in Table 9. In an in-built evaluation procedure recording of this evolution is of decisive importance for the results.

The first stage of the evaluation procedure runs parallel to the third stage in the policy process: the design of the (mix of) instrument(s). In particular the baseline inventory should preferably be finalised previous to the instrument design, since parties at which the instrument is targeted may adapt their position in anticipation of the new instrument. The *ex ante* evaluation is an element of the policy process (*a priori* assessment of impact of various courses of action), as well as of the evaluation procedure. The *ex ante* analysis in the evaluation procedure should provide the reference for assessing the real impact of selected instruments in the *ex post* analysis.

Apart from influential forces related to the interests of *stakeholders*, a number of other factors may have an impact on the results of the newly introduced instrument. Such forces include changes in *economic factors* such as factor prices (labour, capital, management skills, raw materials, land). This will affect the economic position of the target group over time. At the time of a recession, reduced pollution may be attributed to lower production output, as much as to policy measures. *Consumer preferences* may change in favour of products that pollute less. Exogenous *technological change* may result in new investment in equipment with a more favourable pollution characteristic. Changes in the *international trade pattern* may result in import substitution. Another factor relates to environmental policy. New insights in environmental problems may result in aggravating, or relaxing, the objectives of the policy mix of which the instrument under review is a component.

The context of instruments should be identified and their impact on the outcome of the instrument under review established. Possible contextual factors for charges/taxes, tradeable permits and deposit-refund systems are given below as an illustration.

The context of *earmarked* charges normally consists of a set of well-established policy measures and activities for which financial sources are required. Earmarked charges are less an instrument of environmental policy than an instrument of *financing* environmental policy, although some systems have a regulatory impact as a side-effect. According to the polluter pays principle, contributions are demanded from those who have caused the problem or who benefit from the collectively organised solution. The main objective of earmarked charges is the creation of financial means, sufficient to meet the demand. A main condition is to spread the burden in an evenly manner, hence the commonly made choice of a charge base that somehow reflects the pollution load.

Incentive emission charges/taxes normally constitute an instrument additional to measures of a directly regulatory or of a "communicative" nature. Their main objective is contributing to attaining the goals of the policy mix, by means of internalising the price of the environment in the costs of emitting, discharging or dumping. Their proceeds are of secondary importance; the allocation of the proceeds however can be decisive for the acceptability and hence for the success of such charges.

The general framework of incentive charges is the environmental policy mix. If the evaluation is aimed at the economic component, effort must be devoted to disentangling the impact of the economic instrument and of the other parts of the policy mix. This is less relevant in the case of earmarked charges.

Table 10. **Contextual factors of emission charges**

Emission charges	
Factor	Example
Use of raw materials	S-content of mineral oil, in case of SO_2-charge
Applied production process; type of technology	Energy recovery, in case of NO_x-charge
Applied pollution abatement (add-on technology)	Scrubbers, in case of SO_2-charge
Available environmental technology	Residuals recycling, in case of waste disposal charge
Applied "good house-keeping" systems	Environmental Management Audit System
Factor prices	Labour, capital, raw materials
Costs of water pollution and waste removal	Wastewater treatment tariff
Market conditions	Consumer taste, (international) competitive position, economic boom or recession
Applied environmental policy measures	Emission standards, charges, tax allowances

Table 11. **Contextual factors of product charges**

Product charges	
Factor	Example
Product characteristics	Lead content of petrol, in case of tax differentiation leaded/unleaded petrol
Use of raw materials	Use of secondary material, in case of charge on virgin materials
Available substitutes	Use of reusable packaging, in case of charge on throw-away packaging
Factor prices	Labour, capital, raw materials
Costs of waste removal	Waste disposal tariff
Market conditions	Market position of (foreign) substitutes, consumer taste, (international) competitive position, economic boom or recession
Applied environmental policy measures	Product standards, charges, tax allowances

As regards the intended impact of incentive charges, the demand for or the production or generation of products or pollution on which the charge is imposed should decrease. Whether the quantitative effect is satisfactory depends on the defined objectives of the policy mix.

Some factors relevant in the context of emission and product charges are given in Tables 10 and 11. This list is an example only. It contains "technical" factors, but ignores contextual information, such as interests by stakeholders, concerned authorities, existing policies, etc, which has been indicated in this paper as of paramount importance for adequate evaluation.

The main purpose of *tradeable permits* is to support achieving environmental goals in terms of reduction of pollution. Major applications of tradeable permits are found in the field of air quality policy. Some systems exist in water quality policy. Other application are conceivable, *e.g.* with respect to the market penetration of products with more favourable environmental characteristics.

The framework of tradeable permits consist of a set of direct regulatory policies. In fact, tradeable permits can also be described as permission for evading (too rigid) regulations under very strict conditions. As such, tradeable permits may provide an escape route, allowing continued economic progress.

Like pollution charges, tradeable permits are aimed to promote least-cost solutions for the related environmental problem. Unlike charges, the costs of the system are unknown until permits are actually traded. Trade is a necessary, but not sufficient condition for success of the system. The volume of trade can give an indication of the performance of the system and thence of the efficiency of the solution it creates. The prices of permits on the market indicate the economic costs of the achieved solution.

New tradeable permit systems clearly mark the field of its operation, since initial permits must be allocated at the start. An operational system of tradeable permits should be open for new entry. If initial permits were "grandfathered", new entrants are at a disadvantage as they have to buy in. Thin markets may favour those who are already in, since they might be able to exclude competitors through strategic behaviour. This is not in the interest of economic policy objectives.

The relevant contextual factors in the baseline inventory of tradeable emission rights are similar to the factors of the baseline inventory of emission charges. Both instruments aim to affect the emission level of economic activities. The ultimate incentive of charges is to maximise cost saving in terms of a balance of applied abatement measures and the charge bill on residual discharges. Tradeable emission permits urge participants to find a similar balance between applied abatement measures and costs or revenues of bought or sold emission permits.

Deposit-refund systems are an instrument of waste management policy. They could induce safe disposal, reuse or recycling of products and could contribute to enhancing effectiveness of reducing the waste stream. Deposit-refund systems can be operated without a close relation with other policy measures, but can also constitute an alternative to policy regulation.

Objectives of deposit-refund systems generally include a previously set level of return of the products under the system. An important objective of these systems could also be the prevention of throw-away products on the market. Prevention of such products by regulation supports the success of deposit-refund systems.

The deposit and refund in the system should be set as to fulfil the goals of the scheme in terms of the rate of return, and to avoid unwanted effects. In practice, the refund generally will equal the deposit for non-durable goods bought by consumers. A handling fee could be calculated for retailers. For durable goods (cars), refunds could exceed deposit in order to make good lost interest.

A bracket for a feasible level of deposits and refunds is likely to exist, because both too high and too low levels may have unwanted effects: Too high levels may increase the price of the packed product (deposit included) to a level that incurs negative demand effects, or induces producers/packers not to accept empty containers. Too low levels may result in a low rate of return or cause financial deficits in running the system, since these must be covered from unredeemed deposits.

Participation of all groups concerned is of great importance for an effective and efficient operation. This includes the producers, packers, distributors, wholesale and retail traders, and the consumers.

Mandatory deposit-refund systems could cause trade barriers for foreign producers which can be seen as unacceptable distortion.

In case of mandatory deposit-refund systems, contextual factors in the baseline inventory constitute a set of variables related to consumer behaviour. A list is drawn in Table 12.

Evaluation procedure Stage 2: definition of evaluation criteria

Once the instrument design is available in its definitive form (Stage 4 of the policy process), criteria for evaluation can be defined. They have to be derived from the objectives of the relevant policy

Table 12. **Contextual factors of deposit-refund systems**

Factor	Example
Consumption of soft drinks	DRS on soft drink glass bottles
Consumer taste, *i.e.* appraisal of non-DRS substitutes	Drinks in throw-away drink packs
Composition of the household	On average more soft drink consumption in younger families
Distance to shops or recycling centre	On average larger distances in one-storey house areas
Availability of substitutes	Supply in neighbourhood and second-nearest shops
Costs of waste collection	"Pay-per-bag" systems may induce consumption of returnables
Level of deposit, and refund, if different	High level discourage consumption, but encourage return of empty bottles
Level of existing packaging charges, or other instruments	Exemption of charge on returnable bottles supports DRS

modification. Objectives were already formulated in Stage 2, but adaptation of the instrument under design may also affect the exact content of the objectives.

The full range of criteria which might be included in an ideal evaluation have been discussed in detail in Chapter 7. Operational criteria which can be used in concrete evaluation largely depend on the exact design of the instrument under review. A couple of possible specifications of the criteria of effectiveness and efficiency are listed below as an example.

Box 15 illustrates the link between the function of the instrument under evaluation, and the related need of specific data.

Evaluation procedure Stage 3: construction of evaluation model and definition of all data to be gathered

The *ex post* evaluation is carried out according to the evaluation model: a set of relations that link variables to be assessed to the instrument under evaluation. This is a model in terms of a (qualitative) logic train of thoughts, or in the form of econometric expressions, or both, linking those variables. Given the complicated policy design and implementation processes, much econometric modelling is not likely, however.

Constructing the evaluation model requires much attention. Since a basic character of the in-built evaluation framework is the gathering of data *en route*, it may not be clear in this stage how the model must look like. Possible guidance of an *ex ante* evaluation is limited due to its prospective character. The model may be subject to adaptation through the policy process up to Stage 5 where control and enforcement starts.

This implies also that data must be defined that has to be collected over time for "feeding" the evaluation model. Here an interdependence exist. The model should correspond with the evaluation issue, and should therefore be capable of processing the data that represents this issue. Constructing the model is limited due to time and budget constraints, however. This may make simplification necessary, resulting in a limited number of variables. Also data collection is likely to meet difficulties.

There are several approaches for evaluating the impact of imposed instruments: 1) a quantitative (econometric) approach; 2) a qualitative approach based on appraisal of circumstantial evidence; 3) a combination of 1) and 2). The quantitative approach has the advantage of a more exact outcome, but

Table 13. **Examples of operational evaluation criteria for selected instruments**

Environmental effectiveness	
Instrument	Criterion
Wastewater effluent charge	Reduction of aggregate discharges by target group of pollutant p with x per cent by year y
Product charge on throw-away packaging	Reduction of consumption of container type p with x per cent by year y
Tax differentiation of leaded/unleaded petrol	Abolishing the use of leaded petrol by year y
Charge on sand and gravel	Increase of the use of demolition waste as a substitute for sand and gravel with x per cent by year y
Tradeable emission right system for SO_2 from large sources	Compliance with target levels of SO_2 in the area covered by the "bubble" by the year y
Deposit-refund system for beer bottles	Return of empty bottles of 98 per cent
Economic efficiency	
Wastewater effluent charge	Minimal societal costs of collective and individual wastewater treatment
Product charge on throw-away packaging	Minimal costs of waste management, including operational costs of the DRS (if in place)
Tax differentiation of leaded/unleaded petrol	Minimal costs of introduction of unleaded petrol
Charge on sand and gravel	Minimal costs of the use of virgin materials and of demolition waste management
Tradeable emission right system for SO_2 from large sources	Minimal costs of SO_2-pollution abatement under the "bubble"
Deposit-refund system for beer bottles	Minimal costs of waste management, including operational costs of the DRS

Box 15. **The Dutch water pollution charge**

The Dutch water pollution charge was introduced in 1970. The revenues are earmarked for financing collective treatment of waste water from households and industry. Charge tariffs are determined by the revenues required, and differ across Water Board regions. Charged quantities of pollution are measured for the larger sources of wastewater. Table-based or fixed rates apply for smaller firms and industry.

Dutch water quality policy has resulted in substantial reductions of pollution in terms of BOD and of heavy metals in spite of healthy economic growth. It has been argued that this was due to incentive effects of the water pollution charge system. Bressers (1984) and Schuurman (1988) undertook evaluation studies and made plausible that this alleged impact of the charge occurred.

Evaluation of the incentive effects of the water pollution charge have to "disentangle" such effects from the impact of other policy instruments simultaneously in force. Evaluation has to address the impact on measured sources, where the chances of incentive effects are largest. Apart from the methodological problems, an additional obstacle appears to be that data from measured sources are not separately recorded. If the water pollution charge should have an incentive impact on polluters, it would concern those sources for which a direct relation exists between pollution and the charge bill. Small firms and households for which table-based or fixed charge rates apply are less likely to react to the level of the charge rate, since they have no means to influence it. Availability of separate data for measured sources would allow for a more exact cross-section analysis of sources and Water Board regions with different charge rates.

Source: A. de Savornin Lohman, "The Efficiency and Effectiveness of Water Effluent Charges in France, Germany and the Netherlands: a Synthesis of Available Evidence," paper prepared for the OECD Environment Directorate.

lacks in taking into account all relevant variables. The qualities of an in-built evaluation framework that facilitates keeping track of all evidence available for explaining why an imposed instrument has realised, or failed to realise, its purposes was discussed above. It is unlikely that an econometric model could contain all these variables, many of which are not quantitative at all (attitude, prestige, corporate image, etc). Both approaches should be used where possible, and could be mutually reinforcing.

Evaluation procedure Stage 4: *continuous collection of data and reassessment of influential factors, and* ex post *evaluation*

Continuous collection of data and reassessment of influential factors is an essential element in the in-built evaluation framework, and clearly marks its longitudinal character. Stage 3 has shown which data has to be collected, but changing conditions may lead to new relevant data of which the collection must be organised. Continuous collection and reassessment runs parallel to the introduction and enforcement of the instrument under review.

If "hard" data, for instance on costs of alternative abatement measures, are not systematically recorded, the evaluator has to rely on best guesses of those who were involved in policy design and implementation. Registration of discussions, negotiations and agreements and of relevant "soft" data may enhance the chance that such data can replace "hard" data that have not been collected.

After a prescribed period of time, the *ex post* evaluation is carried out. Data collected is brought together and processed and the evaluation model is "run". Evaluation certainly is not a mathematical exercise only. Some of the intended effects of economic instruments can be labelled "soft effects", which means that they cannot be traced back to the instrument by mathematical relations. An example is a changing attitude of target groups as a result of publicity around preparing and introducing the instrument.

Evaluation procedure Stage 5: *possible adaptation of the evaluation model, evaluation criteria and data*

The evaluation procedures should contain the stage of modification of the evaluation model, the evaluation criteria and of data to be collected. Since data collection and assessment of influential factors should be undertaken periodically, changes in circumstances might appear that necessitates reconstruction of the adopted evaluation model. That may induce the need of collecting other data. Changes in the (appraisal of) the environmental problem itself may result in modified evaluation criteria.

Modifications mentioned here are the result of changing circumstances, and should not be confused with the need for modification of the instrument under review, which may be the result of the *ex post* evaluation procedure.

Evaluation procedure Stage 6: *conclusions, recommendations, and feedback into the policy process*

The evaluation outcome may, or may not, result in recommendations for adapting the instrument under evaluation. With or without adaptations, the evaluation process could be repeated, either or not from Stage 3 in the policy process on in case of an adapted instrument design.

Chapter 10

KEY ISSUES IN EVALUATION

10.1 Who does the evaluation?

Organisational aspects

Ensuring the feasibility and success of in-built evaluation requires some institutional facility. For completing such an evaluation, an effort of several years might be necessary. Preparation, design, discussion, implementation and a reasonable period of operation of policy instruments can easily take up five to ten years or more. Without any form of institution such continuity can hardly be guaranteed.

The responsible agency could prepare and develop evaluation procedures which could be constantly checked and adjusted. Such procedures help in ensuring uniformity in the evaluation efforts, and could increase efficiency through repetition and learning.

Another major task of such an institution would be to keep record of all aspects relevant for the evaluation procedure. This would include modifications, changes, new developments, and judgements about the impact of these factors on the outcome of the instrument under review. Timely, additional research could increase the success of the final *ex post* evaluation.

The task of managing the evaluation could be assigned to an existing institution (such as the general accounting office in the USA and in some of the European countries), or to a new and dedicated organisation for which guarantees for continuity and independence are available. Existing institutions may have some efficiency advantages, if the work could be connected with existing practice. A new institution may have the advantage of independence and full dedication, but the necessary resources could impede this. Anyhow, budgets for the work must be made available.

Data collection

As has been suggested above, data collection is of paramount importance for success of an in-built evaluation framework. Data of various kinds has to be collected over a larger period of time. Data includes 1) hard data on *e.g.* numbers of firms, levels of pollution, (changes in tax rates), penetration of technology, constraints included in (international) conventions, but also 2) "soft" data on *e.g.* vested and new interests, (changes of) opinions of parties concerned, political and institutional factors, etc.

There should be a close link between the agency responsible for evaluation and the institution that is doing the data collection. There is an advantage in assigning the task of data collection to organisations already active in this field. As regards environmental taxes, two organisations could be considered.

Firstly, in most countries administering environmental taxes is the competence of the fiscal authorities. The data they collect only constitutes a subset of the data needed for evaluation, since the purpose of their activities is raising revenues in an adequate way (Box 16).

Box 16.   **The Danish waste tax**

The Danish waste tax was introduced in 1987. The tax is levied on waste that is landfilled or incinerated. The tax is calculated on the basis of the weight of the waste supplied at the entrance of the landfill of incineration plant. A refund of the tax is granted for waste that is carried off.

The tax rate amounts to ECU 28 per ton for dumping and ECU 22 per ton for incineration. An incentive impact resulting in reduced waste supply was suspected. Increased secondary use of demolition and building waste was supposed, but could not be proved. The responsible authority (Internal Revenue) records amounts of waste supplied and carried off by individual waste site, but is not interested in volumes of waste by type. Morevoer, data are kept for five years and then deleted, so that data for the years 1987-1990 are no longer available.

Currently, an attempt to evaluate the waste tax system is undertaken. One of the objectives of the evaluation is to verify the assumption of a reduced supply of building waste. Data has to be reconstructed by observing quantities of supplied and removed waste in waste sites which differ in types of waste that are dominantly handled. The evaluation is still in an early stage.

Secondly, central bureaux of statistics are experts in data collection, by profession. They have a very well-developed tradition in this field and probably are in a better position for collecting data that is needed for an in-built framework (additional to fiscal data). As an example, Dutch and French water quality statistics are actually to a great degree based on data derived from payment of the water charges. However, statistical bureaux will have strict conditions for data collection, due to their ambition of reliability and completeness. This almost certainly rules out collection of data with a "soft" character.

If data needed for evaluation is partly generated by the fiscal authority, partly by the statistical bureau, and partly by the agency for evaluation, a co-operation is needed actually between three different authorities which has to be facilitated, *e.g.* by the environmental authorities.

10.2 Methodological problems

E*x post* evaluation of policy instruments brings along some methodological problems.[36] This includes defining the baseline for evaluation, and disentangling the impact of the instrument under review from effects of all other influential factors.

Formulating the baseline, or assessing alternative developments, is a major issue in *ex post* evaluation. The actual situation found not only is the outcome of the installed policy instrument (mix), but also of other factors, or autonomous developments. To be able to sort out the instrument impact, the situation "without" has to be reconstructed (see Chapter 7). A first, and simple, approach is trend extrapolation, assuming that factors already active at the time of introducing the instrument, have remained unchanged since then. Secondly, econometric models, may offer a more sophisticated method, in which not the trend but estimated relations between explanatory and explained variables are the basis for reconstruction of the "without" situation. Thirdly, also linear programming techniques could work, based on rational decision-making among specified objectives and constraints. Finally, and probably most adequate for the in-built evaluation framework, are "judgmental" methods, that are better able to take "soft" influences into account.

Disentangling the effects of the reviewed instrument as part of a package of environmental measures is a second methodological problem. In some cases this can prove completely impossible; where the different policy measures have been introduced simultaneously, and where their incidence across the regulated subjects is the same, only the combined effect of the policy package can be evaluated, and the contribution of the component measures cannot be distinguished. For many purposes, evaluation information of this sort will still be of interest. However, where the objective of evaluation is to compare the performance of economic instruments and other environmental policy measures, cases where the separate contribution of economic instruments cannot be isolated are of little interest.

In other cases, there are, however, a range of possibilities for identifying the separate contribution made by economic instruments, even where such instruments have been employed as part of a package of measures. These turn on using differences either in timing of measures, or in their pattern of incidence, or both, to distinguish the contribution made by different types of measure.

For example, where data is available across regions or countries, then differences in the timing and strength of policy measures in different areas may allow the contribution of economic instruments to be distinguished from other measures. In the case studies discussed in Chapter 6, one example of this is the case of "pay-per-bag" schemes for charging for household refuse. Although these have almost always been accompanied by other measures (such as changes in kerbside recycling arrangements), differences across areas in the timing of introduction of these measures and differences in the level of the unit charge allow the contribution of the charge level to be identified, and separated from the effects of the recycling measures. A further example could be the scope for identifying the effect of the tax differential in favour of unleaded petrol. Different countries have introduced this differential at different times, and the size of the differential varies across countries. Although many countries have also encouraged unleaded petrol through non-economic instruments as well, these accompanying measures have varied across countries both in form and timing. Any effects on the diffusion of unleaded petrol related to the size and timing of the tax differential could generally be attributed to the effect of the tax differential rather than the accompanying measures.

Differences in the pattern of incidence of economic and other instruments are also potentially of use in separating their contributions to the overall impact of policy. A number of the case studies have described situations where some subjects are affected by the economic instrument but not by other parallel policies, or *vice-versa*. This difference was used by some of the evaluation studies of the German system of water effluent charges to identify the separate contribution made by charging to the pattern of abatement measures; where different abatement measures are taken by sources unaffected by the charge and by those subject to the charge, and where the burden of regulatory requirements is similar across the two groups, then the charge is likely to be the explanation for change in emissions behaviour.

The scope for disentangling the contributions of different policy measures is partly a function of the data available. Where disaggregated data is available, covering different areas, or different polluters, the scope for disentangling the separate effects of different measures will generally be greater. Where the only information available relates to aggregate emissions levels, identifying the separate contribution of economic instruments will generally be more difficult.

10.3 Observations on scope and limitations of evaluation evidence

The preceding sections have discussed evaluation criteria and some of the difficulties involved in *ex post* evaluation. In addition to these issues concerning methods of evaluation, there are also important issues concerning the value of evaluation studies. In the light of the conceptual discussion, and the evidence on the performance of actual instruments discussed in Chapter 3-6, what appears to be the "value added" by *ex post* evaluation evidence on environmental policies, as compared to other forms of evidence on the costs and benefits of different environmental policy instruments? Or, to put the question another way: what can evaluations tell us that we do not already know?

It might at first sight seem obvious that analysis of the costs and benefits of economic instruments based on actual experience should be much more informative, and much more reliable, than analysis which does not make use of actual experience. However, in practice, evaluation research appears likely to add significant value to our existing stock of knowledge in only a limited number of areas. Correctly identifying the issues to which *ex post* evaluation research, based on practical experience, can provide new or better information on the costs and benefits of economic instruments is an important issue, if resources and research effort are to be concentrated where they are most likely to be productive.

Whilst a full assessment of the costs and benefits of economic instruments would in principle include the whole range of effects of such instruments, the most important questions to be addressed by evaluation studies are those where *ex post* evidence will add significantly to what is already known from conceptual and theoretical arguments, and from *ex ante* studies and simulations.

In the case of emissions charges and other instruments which limit emissions by reference to a price, the priorities for *ex post* analysis should be:

– to measure the behavioural response in terms of the quantitative effect of the charge on emissions;
– to assess static cost effectiveness in terms of the pattern of emissions reductions across sources with different abatement costs; and
– to assess the administrative and compliance costs associated with the instrument.

In each of these cases, *ex post* analysis can potentially provide information which is not available from the *ex ante* perspective, and there is, at least in some cases, a reasonable prospect of drawing soundly-based conclusions from the empirical evidence.

In the case of *market mechanisms which limit quantities, such as tradeable permit mechanisms*, the effects which *ex post* research can best quantify include the key issue of the *efficiency of market transactions*, which may be assessed, in particular, from information on the volume and aggregate value of permit transactions. As with charges and other price instruments, issues of static cost-effectiveness and administration/compliance costs are also issues which *ex post* analysis may be useful in assessing.

Other effects, such as many of the wider economic effects set out in Chapter 7, can less usefully be evaluated from the *ex post* perspective, and are thus much lower priorities for *ex post* research. There are two main reasons for this.

In some cases, the *information* available for *ex post* analysis is no more extensive than that available *ex ante*, and therefore *ex post* evaluation provides information which is neither better – in the sense of more reliably-based – nor different than that provided by *ex ante* studies. An example of this would be analysis of the effect of emissions changes on the value of pollution damage. In general, the techniques, such as contingent valuation, for estimating the monetary value of pollution reductions can be conducted as easily in advance of any policy experience, as in the light of actual experience. Indeed, as the Norwegian case studies of environmental policy suggest, it may on occasions be easier to conduct contingent valuation studies *ex ante*, when the question can be posed in terms of the elimination of the current level of pollution in favour of zero pollution, rather than *ex post*, when pollution may have been eliminated, when the question has to be framed in terms of not having a hypothetical higher level of pollution; defining the hypothetical higher level of pollution so that the question can be understood by respondents may be more difficult than asking them to consider, *ex ante*, an alternative world with no pollution.

In other cases, *ex post* analysis may yield little useful data because the relevant *effects* may be so small relative to other sources of change, or so diffuse, that they are unlikely to be readily observable in actual data. Examples of this would be any effect of market mechanisms of the rate of innovation in pollution control (which is likely to take place over many years, and to be influenced by many other factors), and the effects of market mechanisms on macroeconomic variables such as inflation or unemployment. This is not to say that such effects are, in practice, negligible, but merely that they are unlikely to be feasible to quantify from actual observation of a single episode; various types of (*ex ante*) simulation model, in which other factors can be held constant, may give a more reliable quantification.

Chapter 11

CONCLUSIONS

11.1 What is expected from economic instruments and their evaluation?

There has been a vigorous debate in many OECD countries about the potential contribution which economic instruments could make to improving the efficiency and effectiveness of environmental policy.

- In comparison with existing "command-and-control" regulatory policies, economic instruments could in principle reduce the economic costs of achieving a given level of environmental protection. Viewed another way, economic instruments can permit a greater standard of environmental protection to be achieved without increasing the economic costs incurred.

- In addition, economic instruments may stimulate more rapid innovation in pollution abatement technologies than regulatory rules, because they provide an incentive for polluters to seek ways to reduce all units of pollution, rather than simply to undertake those measures needed to comply with the legal requirement.

- Also, some economic instruments such as taxes, charges and auctioned permits may raise revenues; these revenues can, in turn, permit other taxes to be reduced, or can be used to finance environmental policy measures or other government spending.

The arguments in favour of a greater use of economic instruments have been well rehearsed in both national and international policy debates, and have been influential in shaping the OECD's recommendations on the use of economic instruments. As citizens' demands for a cleaner environment grow, it becomes increasingly important that environmental policies should be employed that provide the desired standard of environmental protection without incurring excessive economic costs.

Many countries considering the possible use of economic instruments have also conducted analyses and studies of possible policies, which have used modelling and forecasting techniques to assess the likely costs and benefits. There has, for example, been extensive analysis in the context of global climate change policy of the potential costs and benefits of using taxes on carbon and energy to control carbon dioxide emissions.

The number of practical applications of economic instruments in OECD countries is growing, and further significant measures are planned by a number of countries. This experience provides the opportunity to learn more about how economic instruments function:

- Do they in practice have the effects that the theory and simulation studies predict?
- How do economic instruments fit in to the institutional structures and frameworks of existing environmental policies?

- What can practical experience show about the aspects of economic instruments which cannot easily be assessed in advance, such as the feasibility and costs of administration and enforcement?
- Do they have other side effects, or effects relating to other policy objectives?

Systematic analysis, or "evaluation", of practical experience can provide valuable information about the performance of economic instruments, to supplement the existing conceptual arguments and simulations of their likely effects.

Evaluations of practical experience with economic instruments can perform a number of different functions.

- Evaluation evidence on the performance of policy instruments can help to improve the administration of current policy;
- Evaluations can also improve the choice of instruments in future policy, by showing the advantages and disadvantages of particular instruments in actual operation;
- In addition, evaluations can provide evidence on the functioning of the political and policy processes, to ensure that they translate policy intentions into practice as effectively as possible.
- Evaluation may also contribute to better communication with and information of stakeholders and the public on the purpose, operation and effects of the policy.

In each of these ways, evaluation studies can contribute to better design and implementation of environmental policies in the countries concerned. There may also be important benefits to other countries, which can learn from the practical experience of countries which have implemented particular policies. Despite the benefits that could be gained from systematic evaluation of practical policy, few such evaluations of economic instruments have actually been conducted.

If attention is confined simply to studies which have set out to evaluate all relevant aspects of the costs and benefits of a particular economic instrument, based on *ex post* evidence, then the evidence evaluating the performance of economic instruments appears meagre. Few of the countries which have employed economic instruments have undertaken formal, *ex post*, analyses of their efficiency and effectiveness in practice.

This is, however, not a situation unique to economic instruments. Few environmental policy measures – indeed, few policies of any sort – are subject to systematic appraisal and evaluation of their operation and effectiveness. This raises questions about the obstacles to evaluation. Why is evaluation so rare, and what would be necessary for more evaluation studies to be undertaken?

Nevertheless, despite the lack of formal evaluation studies, much can be learned from practical experience about the performance of economic instruments in practice. As this report has shown, there is a substantial, albeit heterogeneous, amount of evidence bearing on the performance of economic instruments in OECD Member countries, from a range of sources, which is relevant to the question of whether the theoretical claims made for economic instruments are borne out in practice. This evidence shows that much can be learned from the study of practice; however, it also shows, that there is much still to be learned about the costs and benefits of economic instruments. More, and more systematic, evaluation work would make a major contribution to improving the efficiency and effectiveness of environmental policy.

11.2 Lessons from existing evidence

Although there has been little explicit evaluation of economic instruments in Member states, there is considerable evidence on various aspects of the performance of economic instruments. Some of the evidence has been summarised in this report, although it is certainly not comprehensive, either in its coverage of the economic instruments employed in the OECD area, or in the extent to which it has been able to identify all relevant data on performance held by governments, agencies and researchers.

Box 17. **Assessing the results of evaluation studies: some questions to consider**

Whilst the results of individual studies on the effectiveness of economic instruments are of interest in the particular policy context concerned, there is also much to be gained from comparative analysis of experiences, both with different types of mechanism, and in different countries. Evaluation studies will have rarely been undertaken to a common methodology across instruments or across countries, and comparisons will thus have to make use of a diverse set of studies and methodologies. Criteria are required to enable the results achieved from different evaluation studies to be compared. These might include:

- The representativeness of the case studied - are there any unusual features of the institutional context, for example, which might have made the impact of the measures greater or less than would normally be expected?
- The appropriateness of the methodology used - in particular, how realistic are the assumptions made about the "baseline" scenario.
- The strength of the evidence – *i.e.* how well supported are the findings? One aspect of this will be the extent to which judgement has been required to reach the results in any study.
- The extent of openness and independence in the conduct of the evaluation. Generally, evaluations which are conducted internally within organisations responsible for aspects of the policy are liable to run a risk that the objectivity of the findings may be questioned. In addition, external scrutiny of methodology and evidence can help to discover and correct methodological weaknesses. Relevant considerations in assessing openness may include whether the data are available for independent scrutiny, and whether there is any indication that the study could be replicated to assess its robustness.

Effectiveness and efficiency

Although it is very difficult to calculate the precise contribution of economic instruments to the efficiency of environmental policy, no systematic evidence can be found from the experience surveyed in this paper that the *ex ante* ideas about the efficiency of economic instruments are misguided. In many instances, the case for preferring economic instruments to regulation remains a "belief" – although it is supported in many cases by *ex ante* quantification and estimates. However, the case for economic instruments is a belief which is not, so far, contradicted by the bulk of the *ex post* evidence described in this report. Whilst the *ex post* evidence available so far cannot conclusively prove the efficiency of economic instruments, it is clear that it would be substantially more difficult to demonstrate the alternative thesis, that regulatory approaches are more efficient than economic instruments.

The evidence reviewed in this report does indicate that in relation to some of the relevant criteria, in many instances economic instruments can be shown to have been effective. Thus, the *charging and taxation measures* described have generally led to changes in emissions levels, and have not simply been absorbed as a cost by polluters, without any environmental improvement resulting. This appears true, even for some charging systems, such as the Dutch water charges, which were initially designed for revenue raising, rather than as incentive mechanisms.

There is also evidence on the extent to which *tradeable permit mechanisms* function according to theoretical expectations. In this case, much seems to turn on the restrictions imposed on trading, and on the extent to which rights and future entitlements are clearly defined. There are indications, too, from some of the studies (*e.g.* some of the fisheries quota markets, and the early Fox River tradeable permit system in the US) that permit trading may be affected by monopoly power in the permit market where there are too few participants.

However, whilst permit trading volumes may be an indication that economic efficiency gains are being achieved, relative to the same allocation of rights without trading, little of the evidence seeks directly to relate the observed outcomes from economic instruments to the underlying criterion of economic efficiency, which is the central theoretical justification for preferring economic instruments to conventional command-and-control regulation. In particular, there is little detailed evidence on the scale of the efficiency gains from permit trading, or on the extent to which charging systems succeed in equalising marginal abatement costs across polluters.

More could be done to investigate some of these key issues. In particular, a number of *ex ante* studies exist, which use data on the pattern of abatement costs across polluters in some particular situation to indicate the scale of efficiency gains which could result from achieving an efficient pattern of abatement across polluters, instead of the inefficient pattern resulting from some administrative rule. In principle, given appropriate data, such studies could also be carried out *ex post*, to assess the extent to which the actual pattern of abatement from using economic instruments achieved the efficient, optimal, distribution of abatement.

The major difficulty in conducting such studies is, of course, the availability of suitable data on individual emissions sources. Often this is difficult to obtain for reasons of commercial confidentiality. Also, however, retrospective analysis faces the further difficulty (encountered, for example, by the Norwegian evaluation studies) that relevant data about the costs involved in past abatement investments can no longer be found, due to the lack of detailed records, changes in personnel in firms and agencies through retirement and other causes, etc. Effective *ex post* evaluation thus requires advance planning, to ensure that appropriate data is collected, and records kept, to provide the necessary information base for later evaluation.

The effectiveness of economic instruments is likely to be only fully apparent after the instruments have been in operation for a considerable period of time, since then, and only then, do the full structural adjustments take place to the incentives the instruments provide. For example, in responding to higher energy prices, a substantial part of the effect may take a decade or more to emerge, since the response will be dictated by the pace of renewal of capital-using durable equipment, which may have an average life-span of some ten to fifteen years.

Capacity building

One effect of economic instruments, which was not widely anticipated, but which has been found through practical experience, is that they may have important *"capacity-building"* effects. The introduction of economic instruments requires government or environment agencies to develop better systems of measurement and monitoring, in order, for example, to levy emissions charges, and this means that they also have the information for better enforcement of regulatory policies too. The water charges in Germany were argued to have had a significant effect of this sort by Kraemer (1995), and similar effects were also evident in the Netherlands from the water charging system.

This capacity-building aspect of economic incentives is one example of a range of *"soft effects"* of economic instruments that may be important; they may, for example, help increase awareness of particular issues, and may thereby affect behaviour (as for example with the tax incentives for unleaded petrol, which may have stimulated fuel switching partly simply by bringing the leaded petrol issue to the attention of motorists).

Institutional context

It seems that existing institutions and the "meta-policy", or "style of governance" dictate to a significant extent whether a country will choose to employ economic instruments, or to rely on more conventional forms of "command-and-control" regulation. There have, however, been significant changes in the style and philosophy of government in some OECD countries in recent years, which have tended to increase the receptiveness of policy-makers to economic instruments as an alternative or supplement to regulation.

Nevertheless, it seems that introducing environmental taxes and charges is more likely to antagonise firms and consumers than introducing more stringent environmental regulations. This may simply be a matter of resistance to the unfamiliar; it may also reflect suspicion about the real motives of government in introducing new taxes or charges.

11.3 Why are so few evaluations undertaken?

Why is there so little systematic evaluation evidence on the performance of economic instruments in practice? Despite the vast number of economic instruments employed in the environmental policies of OECD countries, and the considerable interest amongst policy-makers and the wider public in their potential, the number of explicit evaluation studies which have been identified in the course of the OECD work programme has been very limited. What factors could account for this lack of evaluation studies?

A number of reasons might be suggested for the paucity of evaluation studies of economic instruments. Some concern the difficulties with evaluation research in general. Others relate to particular problems in the evaluation of economic instruments.

Most experiences are too recent

For many economic instruments it is simply too soon to investigate their effect on the efficiency and effectiveness of environmental policy. The number of economic instruments in the environmental policies of OECD countries has grown rapidly in recent years, and many are therefore only recently established. Where this is so, basic data on the operations of policy may not yet be available, and the necessary information base for evaluation would not therefore be available. In addition, at least some of the key issues in evaluating the efficiency and effectiveness of economic instruments concern effects which may take some time to become fully apparent. Thus, for example, firms' investments in pollution-control technologies may be made as part of wider investment decisions concerning assets with an average life-span of fifteen years or more; although environmental taxes or tradeable permits might affect investment decisions taken when the current capital stock comes up for renewal, little of the long-term effect of such incentive policies might be evident after only one or two years of operation.

Evolving role of economic instruments

The historical origins of some policy measures may have meant that their role as economic instruments with a potential incentive effect may only recently have become recognised. Thus, for example, the water charges in the Netherlands and France both began primarily as revenue-raising instruments. Where economic instruments have been established "by accident", as it were, their changed role has first to be recognised by policy-makers, before questions concerning their impact on the efficiency and effectiveness of environmental policies can be formulated and investigated.

Lack of evaluation culture and practice

In part, the lack of evaluation studies of economic instruments may reflect the fact that in many countries there is little tradition of evaluating government policies more generally. Whilst some countries have established procedures for evaluating the effectiveness of a wide range of government policies, and conduct evaluation studies as a matter of routine, this is the exception rather than the rule across the OECD as a whole. Economic instruments are therefore not alone in being subject to little *ex post* research and scrutiny.

Undertaking evaluation studies of economic instruments may be all the more difficult in a context where there is no tradition of policy evaluation:

- In this situation, setting up an evaluation study may be seen as a threat by those responsible for designing, agreeing and implementing the policy; by contrast, where evaluation is a matter of familiar routine, an evaluation of a new policy measure is likely to provoke a much less hostile reaction.

- Countries with no tradition of evaluation may have no established mechanism for using the results of evaluation studies. The gains from evaluation are likely to be small if there are no channels available for the findings to be used to improve the workings of the current policy, and improve the design of future policy measures.

- If evaluation is not a commonplace of the policy scene, there is a risk that adverse evaluation findings may provoke an extreme reaction, which may be out of proportion to the faults identified. Most evaluation studies would be liable to identify at least some faults and failings in the design of a policy measure; if political and public opinion is not used to evaluation findings there may be an excessively-hostile reaction in the media or from politicians to what are, compared to other areas of policy, comparatively minor criticisms. The fear of such a disproportionate reaction to evaluation findings may be a major obstacle to establishing a culture and tradition of evaluation.

Division of policy responsibility

The division of policy responsibility between different government departments or agencies may hamper evaluation, by making it more difficult to set up evaluations, and by making the conduct of evaluation more complex, than in situations where policy is the undivided responsibility of a single organisation. Often those departments which would be most concerned with aspects of the efficiency or effectiveness of an economic instrument are not in control of the implementation of the measure; thus, for example, charges may be operated by agencies which are separate from the environment and economic government ministries. The agency responsible for implementation may then have little interest in the achievement of the wider goals of efficiency or effectiveness, and therefore little interest in initiating evaluation studies. On the other hand, whilst the environment and economic ministries may be interested in the performance of the instrument, they may not have access to the operation of the policy, and indeed may have very little of the information which an evaluation would need. Often, therefore, evaluations will require interdepartmental co-operation to establish a framework for the various interested parties to co-operate in the evaluation. This has, for example, been a feature of the official evaluations of environmental policy in Norway and of economic instruments in Sweden. However, the need to establish such an interdepartmental framework may mean that evaluation requires considerable political and official support before it can get off the ground.

Lack of Data

A key reason for the lack of evaluation evidence on the performance of economic instruments is the lack of the data needed to conduct evaluations. As this report has observed, it is too late to start thinking about evaluation after an instrument has been introduced; "before" and "after" data will be needed to assess the difference which the new instrument has made. If there is insufficient forethought about the data needed for future evaluation research, it may be very difficult at a later date to reconstruct the information needed to assess the efficiency or effectiveness of economic instruments.

Technical Difficulties

Finally, there are undoubtedly conceptual and practical difficulties in evaluation which make it far from straightforward to assess the efficiency and effectiveness of economic instruments. Amongst the most intractable difficulties in evaluation are:

- The need to specify clearly what is the alternative by which the performance of the instrument is being compared. What would have happened otherwise? is the key test in assessing the impact of a policy measure. However, in a rapidly-changing economic system it may not always be easy to assess how pollution levels or environmental effects would have evolved if the economic instrument had not been employed. Simply comparing pollution levels before the instrument was introduced with pollution levels after does not demonstrate that the instrument had any effect on pollution levels; it is possible, for example, that changes in the available technologies (perhaps prompted by environmental policies in other countries) could have led to a reduction in pollution without the instrument.

- The difficulty of evaluating the separate contribution of an economic instrument when it forms part of a "package" of policy measures. This is the typical context in which economic instruments have been introduced; a relatively simple incentive may be backed up by various regulations to deal with other dimensions of the environmental problem. How to identify the contribution which the economic instrument has made, independently of the other measures, requires a technique to disentangle the separate contributions. Often, in practice this will not be possible, and it will be necessary to accept some limitations on the ability of the evaluation to reach conclusions about the economic instrument alone. However, as discussed in this report, there are also circumstances where methods can be found to disentangle some policy "packages".

- The difficulty of simultaneously achieving access to the data needed to conduct an evaluation, whilst at the same time maintaining a degree of objectivity and independence. Normally, much of the data needed for evaluation can only be obtained from those responsible for operation of the policy, and their co-operation will therefore be necessary for the evaluation. Access to the data may be more easily achieved where those operating the policy do not feel threatened by the outcome, and this may require that they have some involvement in, or control over, the evaluation process and outcome. On the other hand, there may be severe difficulties in maintaining an adequately-critical perspective where those responsible for conduct of the policy also conduct the evaluation; moreover there may be a perception of bias or a lack of independence in studies which are conducted "too close" to the officials affected, which may diminish the impact of the work.

11.4 Recommendations for future action

This report has shown that evaluations of actual practice in using economic instruments in environmental policy can shed valuable light on their efficiency and effectiveness of environmental policy. Ex *post* evaluation of actual practice can provide a valuable supplement to what is already known from theoretical arguments and simulation studies about the advantages and disadvantages of such instruments.

a) More attention to evaluation of economic instruments

There have, to date, been few attempts by those OECD countries employing economic instruments to conduct a systematic evaluation of their performance. There would be gains from more evaluation studies:

- They can provide evidence on the performance of policy instruments to help improve the administration of current policy.

– They can indicate the advantages and disadvantages of particular instruments so as to feed into future policy design.

– They can be used to provide evidence on the functioning of the political and policy processes, to ensure that they translate policy intentions into practice as effectively as possible.

More evaluation, in short, could contribute to better policy.

b) Some basic principles

Evaluations can perform different functions. They can, for example, be used to *modify current policy* to make it function better. Alternatively, or in addition, they can *provide information* which can be used in designing future policies. The political and policy systems and cultures of countries differ, too. Some OECD countries have extensive experience already of policy evaluation; others have administrative structures within which it would be relatively easy to introduce new evaluations; still others would need to establish new institutions for interdepartmental co-ordination and policy feedback in order to make effective use of policy evaluation.

For both these reasons, a single "blueprint", or set of principles, for evaluation of economic instruments is unlikely to apply to all cases. Evaluations will need to be designed to reflect the purpose of the evaluation, and the political and administrative context within which it will be conducted. Nevertheless, there are a number of issues which will require consideration in developing evaluation studies of economic instruments in environmental policy:

1) *When should the decision be taken to evaluate?* This report has argued that the sooner a commitment is made to evaluate, the better. The data needed for evaluation can then be collected as an integral part of the operation of the policy. Also, if evaluation is expected by all those involved in the operation of the policy, it may be seen as less of a threat.

2) *Who should undertake the evaluation?* Should the study be done "internally", by those involved in the operation of the policy, or should it be conducted by independent "outsiders"? There is a strong argument for the evaluation to be conducted independently, since this will help maintain the objectivity of the evaluation – and the perception of objectivity. However, outsiders will often be poorly informed about key aspects of the policy, and will therefore need to co-operate closely with those operating the policy.

3) *What mechanisms will be used to ensure that the evaluation feeds through effectively into future policy?* Publication of the findings of the evaluation may ensure effective dissemination of findings into the political domain, although selective publication decisions, taken once the evaluation findings are known, are likely to be viewed as more unreliable than when a prior commitment is made to publication, before the results are known. However, the issues are complex, and will need to be judged in the light of the political and administrative structures in each country. Excessive controversy over adverse evaluation findings could, for example, harden attitudes, and make reforms more difficult to introduce than where a more low-key approach had been taken to the dissemination of the evaluation results.

Greater efforts to evaluate the efficiency and effectiveness of economic instruments in actual practice would contribute greatly to improving future policy, by identifying the circumstances in which economic instruments are most likely to prove effective, and by providing information on the advantages and disadvantages in practice of employing the various different forms of economic instrument – taxes, charges, tradeable permits, etc. Greater experience with evaluation will also contribute to better evaluation design and practice. Although there are undoubtedly difficulties in conducting evaluation studies, and in integrating the results of evaluation research into administrative and policy processes, more extensive experience of evaluation of a range of policies, and in a range of institutional situations, will provide lessons which will help to improve the practice, and policy impact, of future evaluation work. Efficient and effective evaluation will, in turn, contribute to efficient and effective policy.

c) The case for in-built evaluation

If evaluations are not to be hampered by lack of the necessary data, there is a need for forethought and advance planning. Consideration needs to be given to the data requirements for future evaluation at the time initial decisions are being taken about the introduction of a new instrument. The most persuasive information on the performance of an economic instrument will come from analysing the changes that resulted from its introduction. A comparison of "before" and "after" data requires that data is collected before the policy is introduced; once the policy has been in operation for some time, it will be too late to consider evaluations of this form.

An "in-built" evaluation approach is thus desirable, in which decisions on future evaluation are made at the start of the policy process, and provision is made for collecting data and keeping records in a way which will facilitate the later evaluation of the policy.

An in-built evaluation approach, in which a commitment is made at an early stage to later evaluation of the policy, has the further advantage that it smoothes many of the potential institutional obstacles to evaluation. The individuals and agencies implementing the policy are aware from the outset that an evaluation will take place. When the evaluation comes to be undertaken, it is likely to meet less institutional opposition, and to be seen as less of a threat to those involved in the policy, than if proposals for evaluation are suddenly raised, after the policy has been up and running for some time.

d) The case for wider evaluation of environmental policies

Quite apart from the case for evaluating the performance of economic instruments, there would also be benefits from wider evaluation of the performance of environmental policy measures more generally. The costs and benefits of all forms of environmental policy measures could be evaluated along the lines suggested here. Some countries have already done this. This report has, for example, described the fundamental review undertaken by an interdepartmental group within the Norwegian government of the economic and environmental impact of the whole structure of environmental policy in Norway.

Many of the principles for evaluation set out in this paper would also be applicable to wider evaluations of environmental policies.

It would, for example, be desirable to look much more closely and systematically than has been the practice up to now at the performance in practice of regulatory policies, using an administrative rather than an incentive approach to pollution control. How far do such policies achieve the objectives they pursue, both in terms of environmental impact, and in terms of economic side-effects and administrative and compliance costs? How far are different approaches to regulation – based, for example, on emissions standards or technology standards – more or less efficient and effective, and what lessons can be learned from this for regulatory reform? In this report we have posed some difficult – but important – questions about the performance in practice of economic instruments. It is clear that a similar test, based on performance evidence, needs also to be addressed to the alternative approaches or policy packages available in environmental policy.

NOTES

1. OECD, 1994*b*; p. 17.

2. OECD, 1989; OECD, 1994*b*.

3. OECD, 1986.

4. Derived from the 1994 survey by OECD (1994*b*).

5. According to OECD Recommendation C(74)223 regarding the Implementation of the Polluter-Pays Principle.

6. Viz. OECD, 1994*c* (and its bibliography).

7. Viz. Bressers and Klok (unpublished).

8. OECD, 1994*b*.

9. For a more extended discussion of the case for and against the use of economic instruments in environmental policy see Helm and Pearce (1990) and the survey by Cropper and Oates (1992).

10. There are fewer measurement points; some boilers share the same chimney and measuring equipment, so that the total number of plants covered is about 120.

11. A small proportion of total payments is used to cover administration costs (Lövgren, 1993, Table 3).

12. This is evident when comparing Swedish emissions to figures from other European countries. In 1985, Sweden emitted around 292 000 tonnes of sulphur dioxide, while Germany (East and West) released 7.8 million tonnes, Poland 4.3 million tonnes, Britain 3.7 million tonnes, and Spain 2.2 million tonnes (UN ECE, 1993).

13. When the tax was introduced, the maximum (legal) sulphur content of coal and fuel oils was already low by European standards. The sulphur tax was designed to achieve further reductions from these already low levels.

14. Note that the taxable categories do not include crude oil, spilt oil, or bunker oil. The government recognises that the extension of the tax to new products may be considered at a later date. Coal and peat used for purposes other than fuel are exempted from the sulphur tax.

15. Note that even for light fuel oils of Class III, it is now quite common to have a sulphur content below 0.1 per cent in order to avoid payment of the sulphur tax.

16. The tax differentiation has not been revenue neutral.

17. Defined as facilities with a generator producing electricity for sale.

18. In the US there are a few cases where electricity generating plants have (re)located in states where the environmental standards would be less restrictive than in the state where most of the power is to be sold, whereas large-scale inter-state relocation in response to environmental policy measures has not been observed so far (Folmer and Howe, 1991). Note that although in the US there are minimum national standards for air pollution, individual states may toughen federal environmental regulations.

19. By putting the large, highest-emitting, plants into Phase I, the regulators tried to get early emission reductions from the plants that were thought to contribute most to environmental damage in the eastern half of the US and Canada.

20. Although industrial sources are not required to enter the programme, they may elect to do so as an opt-in source, to reduce emissions at costs lower than for utility plants, selling their reduction allowances to stations producing electricity.

21. 1 kwh = 3 412.13 Btu.

22. $1 968 per tonne exceeded, indexed to inflation. This amount was thought to be approximately three times the prevailing price of one allowance.

23. Since most mid-west utilities have not installed any significant pollution-control equipment to control SO_2, their marginal costs of reduction are considerably lower than the marginal costs of many other cleaner utilities.

24. As mentioned before, an allowance is not a property right, and can be limited, modified or revoked without compensation.

25. By-catch management problems may also distort quota prices, especially where, as in the New Zealand system, operators were required to balance catch and quota at the end of each month. Unexpectedly-high catches of particular species create an urgent need for quota; if the fish would otherwise be surrendered to the authorities, operators would be willing to pay up to the landed price for the necessary quota, since all of the costs of catching are, at that stage, effectively sunk costs. Recognising this risk in advance may also inflate quota prices above fishery rent levels since some operators may buy quota on the basis of the option value it offers.

26. Hong and Adams observe that since the charge schedules are non-linear, the charge level depends on the level of service contracted. Since this means that the unit charge level would potentially be correlated with the error terms in the garbage and recycling equations, a 2SLS technique was used for estimation, in which the unit charge variable was instrumented as a function of a range of household and locality characteristics.

27. Porter argued that the overall consumption of beer and soft drinks would probably change very little following the introduction of mandatory deposits; analysis of similar systems from Oregon and Vermont showed that average prices remained unchanged or declined slightly as a result of the introduction of mandatory deposits, perhaps broadly offsetting the impact on consumption of reduced convenience. It is possible that a mandatory deposit-refund system could induce structural change in the drinks industry, involving a shift to more and smaller brewers and soft drink bottlers. To the extent that this would increase real per unit production costs this would be a social cost of the mandatory deposit measure, although it might be partly offset by reductions in transport costs. In the study, Porter assumed that the size, structure and geographical distribution of plants would remain unchanged following the introduction of a mandatory deposit scheme.

28. In some cases, "clean" technologies may in fact be cheaper than other available technologies. In these cases, however, it might be desirable to investigate the factors that prevent clean technologies being chosen without any policy intervention, in order to identify the genuinely "additional" effects of the policy measures.

29. See also DHV, 1994.

30. Or: "environmental management process".

31. OECD, 1991.

32. Skou Andersen, 1995.

33. See Bressers *et al.*, 1990.

34. Viz. Bressers, Klok (unpubl.).

35. Skou Andersen, M., 1995.

36. Smith, 1994; OECD, 1994*a*.

REFERENCES

ANDERSEN, M. S. (1991), "Green taxes and regulatory reform: Dutch and Danish experiences in curbing with surface water pollution". Wissenschaftszentrum Berlin, Paper FS II 91-401.

ANDERSEN, M. S. (1994), "Economic instruments and clean water: why institutions and policy design matter". OECD Public Management Service, Meeting on Alternatives to Traditional Regulation, 5-6 May 1994, PUMA/REG(94)5.

ANDERSON, R.C., Hofmann, L.A. and Rusin, M. (1990), "The Use of Economic Incentive Mechanisms in Environmental Management", API Research Paper No. 051, Washington DC: American Petroleum Institute.

Apogee Research (1992), Incentive Analysis for Clean Water Act Reauthorization: Point Source/Nonpoint Source Trading for Nutrient Discharge Reductions, Apogee Research, Incorporated for US Environmental Protection Agency.

Applied Decision Systems (1974) "Study of the Effectiveness and Impact of the Oregon Minimum Deposit Law".

ARNASON, R. (1992), "I.T.Q. in Iceland", in OECD (1992), Property Rights Modifications in Fisheries, Occasional Papers on Public Management, Market-Type Mechanisms Series No. 3, Paris: OECD.

ATKINSON, S.E. and LEWIS, D. H. (1974), "A Cost-Effectiveness Analysis of Alternative Air Quality Control Strategies", Journal of Environmental Economics and Management, 1, 237-50.

BINGHAM, T. H. and MULLIGAN, P. F. (1972) "The Beverage Container Problem: Analysis and Recommendations", Research Triangle Institute.

BONGAERTS, J. and KRAEMER, A. (1989), "Permits and Effluent Charges in the Water Pollution Control Policies of France, West Germany and the Netherlands", Environmental Monitoring and Assessment, Vol. 12, pp. 127-47.

BOWER, B.T., BARRE, R., Kuhner, J. and Russell, C.S. (1981), Incentives in Water Quality Management: France and the Ruhr Area. Washington DC: Resources For the Future.

BRESSERS, J. Th. A. (1983), Beleidseffectiviteit en waterkwaliteitsbeleid: een bestuurskundig onderzoek, Enschede.

BRESSERS, J. Th. A. (1988), "A comparison of the effectiveness of incentives and directives: the case of Dutch water quality policy", Policy Studies Review, Vol. 7, No. 3, pp. 500-518.

BURRELL, A. (1989), "The demand for fertilizer in the United Kingdom", Journal of Agricultural Economics, Vol. 40, pp. 1-20.

BURTRAW, D. (1996), "The SO_2 emissions trading program", Contemporary Economic Policy, Vol. XIV, April.

CAMPBELL, H.F. (1990), "Resource Rent and Fishery Management", Paper presented at the Australian and New Zealand Southern Trawl Fisheries Conference, Melbourne, May 6-9,1990.

CAMPBELL, H.F. (1991), "Fishery Management through Property Rights: the New Zealand ITQ System", Paper presented at the Conference on The New Environmentalism: Applying Economic Solutions in the Real World, Sydney, March 18-19, 1991.

CARLIN, A. (1992), "The United States Experience with Economic Incentives to Control Environmental Pollution", United States Environmental Protection Agency, Economic Analysis and Innovations Division: Office of Policy, Planning and Evaluation.

CLARK, I.N., MAJOR, P.J. and MOLLETT, N. (1988), "Development and Implementation of New Zealand's ITQ Management

System", *Marine Resource Economics*, Vol. 5, pp. 325-349.

COOK, E. (1996) "Making a milestone in ozone protection: learning from the CFC phase-out", WRI *Issues and Ideas*, January 1996, Washington DC: World Resources Institute.

CROWLEY, R. W. (1992), "Canadian Experience", in OECD (1992), *Property Rights Modifications in Fisheries*, Occasional Papers on Public Management, Market-Type Mechanisms Series No. 3, Paris: OECD.

DELACHE X and HENRY C. (1994), *La fiscalité et l'environnement : le cas de la France*, Paris, OECD.

DENNIS, J. M. (1993). "Smoke for Sale: Paradoxes and Problems of the Emissions Trading Program of the Clean Air Act Amendments of 1990", UCLA Law Review, Vol. 40, pp. 1101-1144.

DILDANE, R. and RAINEY, R. (1974) "Impacts of Beverage Container Regulation in Minnesota", Minnesota Council of Economic Advisors and Minnesota Planning Agency.

ELLERMAN, A.D. and MONTERO, J-P. (1996), "Why are allowance prices so low? An analysis of the SO_2 emissions trading program", mimeo, Massachusetts Institute of Technology, Center for Energy and Environmental Policy Research.

ELMAN, B. S., TYLER, T. and DOONAN, M. (1991). "Economic Incentives under the New Clean Air Act", Office of Policy, Planning, and Valuation, US EPA, Washington DC.

Environmental Protection Agency (1992), "Solid Waste: Incentives that Could Lighten the Load", EPA *Journal*, Vol. 18, pp. 12-14.

FOLMER, H. and HOWE, Ch. W. (1991). "Environmental Problems and Policy in the Single European Market", *Environmental and Resource Economics*, Vol. 1, pp. 17-41.

FOSTER, V. and HAHN, R. (1994), "ET in LA: Looking Back to the Future", ENRP Project 88/Round II Project Report P-94-01, John F Kennedy School of Government, Harvard University.

FULLERTON, D. and KINNAMAN, T.C. (1994), "Household Demand for Garbage and Recycling Collection with the start of a Price Per Bag", NBER Working Paper No. 4 670. Cambridge, Mass.: National Bureau of Economic Research.

GRUBB, A. and OSÓRIO-PETERS, S. (1994), *Abfallwirschaft und Stoffstrommanagement. Ökonomische Instrumente in der Bundesrepublik Deutschland und in der EU*, ZEW Dokumentation Nr. 94-03. Mannheim: Zentrum für Europäische Wirtschaftsforschung.

GUDGER, C. and BAILES, J. C. (1974) "The Economic Impact of Oregon's Bottle Bill", Oregon State University.

HAHN, R.W. and NOLL, R.G. (1982), "Designing a Market for Tradeable Emission Permits", *in* W.A. Magat (Ed.), *Reform of Environmental Regulation*, Cambridge, Mass., Ballinger.

HAHN, R.W. (1989), "Economic Prescriptions for Environmental Problems: How the Patient Followed the Doctor's Orders", *Journal of Economic Perspectives*, Vol. 3, No. 2, pp. 95-114.

HAHN, R.W. (1991), "Meeting the Growing Demand for Environmental Protection: A Practical Guide to the Economist's Toolchest", Washington, DC: American Enterprise Institute.

HAHN, R.W. and HESTER, G.L. (1989), "Marketable Permits: Lesson for Theory and Practice", *Ecology Law Quarterly*, Vol. 6, pp. 361-406.

HAHN, R.W. and MAY, C. A. (1994), "The Behavior of the Allowance Market: Theory and Evidence", Centre for Science and International Affairs, Environment and Natural Resources Program, 94-02, Harvard: John F. Kennedy School of Government.

HAHN, R.W. and STAVINS, R.N. (1991), "Incentive-Based Environmental Regulation: A New Era from an Old Idea?" *Ecology Law Quarterly*, Vol. 18, pp. 1-42.

HARRISON, D., Jr (1983), "Case Study 1: The Regulation of Aircraft Noise", *in* Thomas C. Schelling (Ed.), *Incentives for Environmental Protection*, Cambridge, Mass., MIT Press.

HAUSKER, K. (1992). "The Politics and Economics of Auction Design in the Market for Sulfur Dioxide Pollution", *Journal of Policy Analysis and Management*, Vol. 11, pp. 553-572.

HONG, S., ADAMS, R.M. and LOVE, H.A. (1993), "An Economic Analysis of Household Recycling of Solid Wastes: The Case of Portland, Oregon", *Journal of Environmental Economics and Management*, Vol. 25, pp. 136-146.

Industrial Economics, Incorporated (1993), "The Benefits and Feasibility of Effluent Trading Between Point Sources: An Analysis in Support of Clean Water Act Reauthorization", Cambridge, Massachusetts; Industrial Economics, Incorporated.

KIP, E. (1994), "Financial instruments in the policy on waste materials: experiences and options" (in Dutch), cited in J. SCHUDDEBOOM and P.-J. KLOK, eds (1994), *Financial Instrument in Policy Process: The Dutch Case*, University of Twente, Centre for Clean Technology and Environmental Policy.

KLOK, P.-J. (1987), Loodvrije benzine en schone auto's, een toepassing van de instrumententheorie, Enschede.

KLOK, P.-J. (1991), "Een instrumententheorie voor milieubeleid", dissertation, Enschede.

KLOK, P.-J., LIGTERINGEN, J., PULLEN, H. and SCHUDDEBOOM, J. (1994), "Charges", *in* J. SCHUDDEBOOM and P.-J. KLOK eds (1994), *Financial Instrument in Policy Process: The Dutch Case*, University of Twente, Centre for Clean Technology and Environmental Policy, pp. 35-59.

KNEESE, A.V. and BOWER, B.T. (1968), *Managing Water Quality: Economics, Technology, Institutions*, Washington, DC, Resources for the Future.

KORB, B. (1996), "US Experience with Economic Incentives for Emissions Trading", OECD Workshop paper, Beijing 9-10 October 1996.

KRUPNICK, A.J. (1986), "Costs of Alternative Policies for the Control of Nitrogen Dioxide in Baltimore", *Journal of Environmental Economics and Management*, 13, 189-97.

LACASSE, F. (1992), "Lessons", *in* OECD (1992), *Property Rights Modifications in Fisheries*, Occasional Papers on Public Management, Market-Type Mechanisms Series No. 3, Paris: OECD.

LEE, D. R., GRAVES, P. E. and SEXTON, R. L. (1988) "On the Mandatory Deposits, Fines and control of Litter", *Natural Resources Journal*, Vol. 28, pp. 837-847.

LINDNER, B. (1990), "Something Fishy in the ITQ Market", Paper presented at the Australian Agricultural Economics Society 34th Annual Conference, University of Queensland.

LINDNER, R.K., CAMPBELL, H.F. and BEVIN, G.F. (1992), "Rent Generation during the Transition to a Managed Fishery: the case of the New Zealand ITQ System", *Marine Resource Economics*, Vol. 7, No. 4.

LABANDEIRA, X. (1994). "The Role of Environmental Taxation in the Control of Acid Rain. A Study for Spain", unpublished M.Sc. Dissertation, University College London.

LÖVGREN, K. (1993). "Economic Instruments for the Control of Air Pollution in Sweden", International conference on Economic Instruments for Air Pollution Control, 18-20 October, IIASA, Austria.

MALONEY, M.T. and YANDLE, B. (1984), "Estimation of the Cost of Air Pollution Control Regulation", *Journal of Environmental Economics and Management*, 11, 244-63.

McGARTLAND, A.M. (1984), "Marketable Permit Systems for Air Pollution Control: An Empirical Study", Ph.D. dissertation, University of Maryland.

MORTON *et al.* (1993), "Effluent Discharge Fees and Water Quality: A Preliminary Assessment", North Carolina: Research Triangle Institute.

OECD (1989*a*), *Economic Instruments for Environmental Protection*. Paris, OECD.

OECD (1989*b*), *OECD Environmental Data. Compendium 1989*. Paris, OECD.

OECD (1991), *Environmental Policy: How to Apply Economic Instruments*. Paris, OECD.

OECD (1992), *Reduction and Recycling of Packaging Waste*. OECD Environment Monographs, No. 62. Paris, OECD.

OECD (1993), *Taxation and Environment. Complementary Policies*. Paris, OECD.

OECD (1994a), *Managing the Environment. The Role of Economic Instruments*. Paris, OECD.

OECD (1994b), *The Economics of Climate Change*. Paris, OECD.

OECD (1995), *Environmental Taxes in OECD Countries*, OECD, Paris.

OECD (1996), *Implementation Strategies for Environmental Taxes*, OECD, Paris.

O'NEIL, W., DAVID, M., MOORE, C. And JOERES, E. (1982), "Transferable Discharge Permits and Economic Efficiency: The Fox River", *Journal of Environmental Economics and Management*, Vol. 10, pp. 346-355.

PALMER, A.R., MOOZ, W.E., QUINN, T.H. and WOLF, K.A. (1980), *Economic Implications of Regulating Chlorofluorocarbon Emissions from Nonaerosol Applications*, Report No. R-2524-EPA prepared for the US Environmental Protection Agency by the Rand Corporation, June.

PORTER, R. C. (1978), "A Social Benefit-Cost Analysis of Mandatory Deposits on Beverage Containers", *Journal of Environmental Economics and Management*, Vol. 5, pp. 351-375.

PORTER, R. C. (1983) "Michigan's Experience with Mandatory Deposits on Beverage Containers", *Land Economics*, Vol. 59, No. 2, pp. 177-194.

RAO, G. B. (1975) "An Economic Analysis of Energy and Employment Effects of Deposit Regulation on Non-Returnable Beverage Containers in Michigan", Michigan Public Service Commission.

REPETTO, R., DOWER, R. C., JENKINS, R.,and GEOGHEGAN, J. (1992), *Green Fees: how a tax shift can work for the environment and for the economy*, Washington, DC: World Resources Institute.

RESCHOVSKY, J. D. and STONE, S.E. (1994), "Market incentives to encourage household waste recycling: paying for what you throw away", *Journal of Policy Analysis and Management*, Vol. 13, No. 1, pp. 120-139.

Resource Futures International (1993), "The CRD User Pay Waste Management Initiative", mimeo.

RICO, R. (1993). "United States' experience in Designing and Implementing an Emission Trading System for Sulfur Dioxide", International Conference on Economic Instruments for Air Pollution Control, 18-20 October, IIASA, Austria.

RICO, R. (1994), "The US Allowance Trading System for Sulfur Dioxide: an Update on Market Experience", Acid Rain Division, US Environmental Protection Agency.

ROACH, F., KOLSTAD, C. KNESSE, A.V., TOBIN, R. and WILLIAMS, M. (1981), "Alternative Air Quality Policy Options in the Four Corners Region", *Southwestern Review*, 1, 29-58.

SCHUDDEBOOM, J. and KLOK, P-J. (1994), *Financial instrument in policy process: the Dutch case*, University of Twente, Centre for Clean Technology and Environmental Policy.

SCHUURMAN, J. (1988), *De prijs van water*, Arnhem.

SCOTT, B. (1992), "Australian Case", in OECD (1992), *Property Rights Modifications in Fisheries*, Occasional Papers on Public Management, Market-Type Mechanisms Series No. 3, Paris: OECD.

SESKIN, E.P., ANDERSON, R.J., Jr. and REID, R.O. (1983), "An Empirical Analysis of Economic Strategies for Controlling Air Pollution", *Journal of Environmental Economics and Management*, 10, 112-24.

SPRENGER, R.U., Körner, J., Paskuy, E. and Wackerbauer, J. (1994), "Das deutsche Steuer- und Abgabensystem aus umweltpolitischer Sicht – ein Analyze seiner ökologischen Wirkungen sowie der Moglichkeiten und Grenzen seiner starkeren ökologischen Ausrichtung", IFO Studien zur Umweltokonomie 18, Munich: IFO Institut fur Wirtschaftsforschung.

SPOFFORD, W.O., Jr. (1984), "Efficiency Properties of Alternative Source Control Policies for Meeting Ambient Air Quality Standards: An Empirical Application to the Lower Deleware Valley", Discussion paper D-118, Washington DC, Resources for the Future, November.

STERNER, T. (1994). "Environmental Tax Reform. The Swedish Experience", Studies in Environmental Economics and Development, Unit for Environmental Economics, Department of Economics, Gotheburg University

SWEDISH ENVIRONMENTAL PROTECTION AGENCY (1993). "Five Economic Instruments in Swedish Environmental Policy".

SWEDISH MINISTRY OF THE ENVIRONMENT (1991), *Economic Instruments in Sweden with Emphasis on the Energy Sector.*

TIETENBERG, T.H. (1989), *Marketable Emission Permits in the United States; A Decade of Experience*, Detroit, Michigan: Wayne State University Press.

TIETENBERG, T.H. (1990), "Economic Instruments for Environmental Regulation", *Oxford Review of Economic Policy*, Vol. 6, No. 1, pp. 17-33.

UN ECE (United Nations Economic Commission for Europe) (1993). "The State of Transboundary Air Pollution 1992 Update", *Air Pollution Studies* 9, United Nations, New York.

US EPA (1992). "Regulatory Impact Analysis of the Final Acid Rain Implementation Regulations", Office of Atmospheric and Indoor Air Programs, Acid Rain Division.

US EPA (1993). "EPA and Chicago Board of Trade Announce Results of First Acid Rain Allowance Auctions", *Environmental News*, 30 March.

VAN DYKE, B. (1991). "Emissions Trading to Reduce Acid Deposition", *The Yale Law Journal*, Vol. 100, pp. 2707-2720.

MAIN SALES OUTLETS OF OECD PUBLICATIONS
PRINCIPAUX POINTS DE VENTE DES PUBLICATIONS DE L'OCDE

AUSTRALIA – AUSTRALIE
D.A. Information Services
648 Whitehorse Road, P.O.B 163
Mitcham, Victoria 3132　　Tel. (03) 9210.7777
　　　　　　　　　　　　　Fax: (03) 9210.7788

AUSTRIA – AUTRICHE
Gerold & Co.
Graben 31
Wien I　　　　　　　　Tel. (0222) 533.50.14
　　　　　　　　　　　Fax: (0222) 512.47.31.29

BELGIUM – BELGIQUE
Jean De Lannoy
Avenue du Roi, Koningslaan 202
B-1060 Bruxelles　　Tel. (02) 538.51.69/538.08.41
　　　　　　　　　　　　　Fax: (02) 538.08.41

CANADA
Renouf Publishing Company Ltd.
5369 Canotek Road
Unit 1
Ottawa, Ont. K1J 9J3　　Tel. (613) 745.2665
　　　　　　　　　　　　Fax: (613) 745.7660

Stores:
71 1/2 Sparks Street
Ottawa, Ont. K1P 5R1　　Tel. (613) 238.8985
　　　　　　　　　　　　Fax: (613) 238.6041

12 Adelaide Street West
Toronto, QN M5H 1L6　　Tel. (416) 363.3171
　　　　　　　　　　　　Fax: (416) 363.5963

Les Éditions La Liberté Inc.
3020 Chemin Sainte-Foy
Sainte-Foy, PQ G1X 3V6　　Tel. (418) 658.3763
　　　　　　　　　　　　Fax: (418) 658.3763

Federal Publications Inc.
165 University Avenue, Suite 701
Toronto, ON M5H 3B8　　Tel. (416) 860.1611
　　　　　　　　　　　　Fax: (416) 860.1608

Les Publications Fédérales
1185 Université
Montréal, QC H3B 3A7　　Tel. (514) 954.1633
　　　　　　　　　　　　Fax: (514) 954.1635

CHINA – CHINE
Book Dept., China Natinal Publiations
Import and Export Corporation (CNPIEC)
16 Gongti E. Road, Chaoyang District
Beijing 100020　　Tel. (10) 6506-6688 Ext. 8402
　　　　　　　　　　　　(10) 6506-3101

CHINESE TAIPEI – TAIPEI CHINOIS
Good Faith Worldwide Int'l. Co. Ltd.
9th Floor, No. 118, Sec. 2
Chung Hsiao E. Road
Taipei　　　　　Tel. (02) 391.7396/391.7397
　　　　　　　　　　　　Fax: (02) 394.9176

**CZECH REPUBLIC –
RÉPUBLIQUE TCHÈQUE**
National Information Centre
NIS – prodejna
Konviktská 5
Praha 1 – 113 57　　　Tel. (02) 24.23.09.07
　　　　　　　　　　　Fax: (02) 24.22.94.33
E-mail: nkposp@dec.niz.cz
Internet: http://www.nis.cz

DENMARK – DANEMARK
Munksgaard Book and Subscription Service
35, Nørre Søgade, P.O. Box 2148
DK-1016 København K　　Tel. (33) 12.85.70
　　　　　　　　　　　　Fax: (33) 12.93.87

J. H. Schultz Information A/S,
Herstedvang 12,
DK – 2620 Albertslung　　Tel. 43 63 23 00
　　　　　　　　　　　　Fax: 43 63 19 69
Internet: s-info@inet.uni-c.dk

EGYPT – ÉGYPTE
The Middle East Observer
41 Sherif Street
Cairo　　　　　　　　Tel. (2) 392.6919
　　　　　　　　　　　Fax: (2) 360.6804

FINLAND – FINLANDE
Akateeminen Kirjakauppa
Keskuskatu 1, P.O. Box 128
00100 Helsinki

Subscription Services/Agence d'abonnements :
P.O. Box 23
00100 Helsinki　　　　Tel. (358) 9.121.4403
　　　　　　　　　　　Fax: (358) 9.121.4450

*FRANCE
OECD/OCDE
Mail Orders/Commandes par correspondance :
2, rue André-Pascal
75775 Paris Cedex 16　　Tel. 33 (0)1.45.24.82.00
　　　　　　　　　　Fax: 33 (0)1.49.10.42.76
　　　　　　　　　　Telex: 640048 OCDE
Internet: Compte.PUBSINQ@oecd.org

Orders via Minitel, France only/
Commandes par Minitel, France exclusivement :
36 15 OCDE

OECD Bookshop/Librairie de l'OCDE :
33, rue Octave-Feuillet
75016 Paris　　　　Tel. 33 (0)1.45.24.81.81
　　　　　　　　　　33 (0)1.45.24.81.67

Dawson
B.P. 40
91121 Palaiseau Cedex　　Tel. 01.89.10.47.00
　　　　　　　　　　　Fax: 01.64.54.83.26

Documentation Française
29, quai Voltaire
75007 Paris　　　　　Tel. 01.40.15.70.00

Economica
49, rue Héricart
75015 Paris　　　　　Tel. 01.45.78.12.92
　　　　　　　　　　Fax: 01.45.75.05.67

Gibert Jeune (Droit-Économie)
6, place Saint-Michel
75006 Paris　　　　　Tel. 01.43.25.91.19

Librairie du Commerce International
10, avenue d'Iéna
75016 Paris　　　　　Tel. 01.40.73.34.60

Librairie Dunod
Université Paris-Dauphine
Place du Maréchal-de-Lattre-de-Tassigny
75016 Paris　　　　　Tel. 01.44.05.40.13

Librairie Lavoisier
11, rue Lavoisier
75008 Paris　　　　　Tel. 01.42.65.39.95

Librairie des Sciences Politiques
30, rue Saint-Guillaume
75007 Paris　　　　　Tel. 01.45.48.36.02

P.U.F.
49, boulevard Saint-Michel
75005 Paris　　　　　Tel. 01.43.25.83.40

Librairie de l'Université
12a, rue Nazareth
13100 Aix-en-Provence　　Tel. 04.42.26.18.08

Documentation Française
165, rue Garibaldi
69003 Lyon　　　　　Tel. 04.78.63.32.23

Librairie Decitre
29, place Bellecour
69002 Lyon　　　　　Tel. 04.72.40.54.54

Librairie Sauramps
Le Triangle
34967 Montpellier Cedex 2　　Tel. 04.67.58.85.15
　　　　　　　　　　　Fax: 04.67.58.27.36

A la Sorbonne Actual
23, rue de l'Hôtel-des-Postes
06000 Nice　　　　　Tel. 04.93.13.77.75
　　　　　　　　　　Fax: 04.93.80.75.69

GERMANY – ALLEMAGNE
OECD Bonn Centre
August-Bebel-Allee 6
D-53175 Bonn　　　　Tel. (0228) 959.120
　　　　　　　　　　Fax: (0228) 959.12.17

GREECE – GRÈCE
Librairie Kauffmann
Stadiou 28
10564 Athens　　　　Tel. (01) 32.55.321
　　　　　　　　　　Fax: (01) 32.30.320

HONG-KONG
Swindon Book Co. Ltd.
Astoria Bldg. 3F
34 Ashley Road, Tsimshatsui
Kowloon, Hong Kong　　Tel. 2376.2062
　　　　　　　　　　Fax: 2376.0685

HUNGARY – HONGRIE
Euro Info Service
Margitsziget, Európa Ház
1138 Budapest　　　　Tel. (1) 111.60.61
　　　　　　　　　　Fax: (1) 302.50.35
E-mail: euroinfo@mail.matav.hu
Internet: http://www.euroinfo.hu//index.html

ICELAND – ISLANDE
Mál og Menning
Laugavegi 18, Pósthólf 392
121 Reykjavik　　　　Tel. (1) 552.4240
　　　　　　　　　　Fax: (1) 562.3523

INDIA – INDE
Oxford Book and Stationery Co.
Scindia House
New Delhi 110001　　Tel. (11) 331.5896/5308
　　　　　　　　　　Fax: (11) 332.2639
E-mail: oxford.publ@axcess.net.in

17 Park Street
Calcutta 700016　　　　Tel. 240832

INDONESIA – INDONÉSIE
Pdii-Lipi
P.O. Box 4298
Jakarta 12042　　　　Tel. (21) 573.34.67
　　　　　　　　　　Fax: (21) 573.34.67

IRELAND – IRLANDE
Government Supplies Agency
Publications Section
4/5 Harcourt Road
Dublin 2　　　　　　Tel. 661.31.11
　　　　　　　　　　Fax: 475.27.60

ISRAEL – ISRAËL
Praedicta
5 Shatner Street
P.O. Box 34030
Jerusalem 91430　　　Tel. (2) 652.84.90/1/2
　　　　　　　　　　Fax: (2) 652.84.93

R.O.Y. International
P.O. Box 13056
Tel Aviv 61130　　　　Tel. (3) 546 1423
　　　　　　　　　　Fax: (3) 546 1442
E-mail: royil@netvision.net.il

Palestinian Authority/Middle East:
INDEX Information Services
P.O.B. 19502
Jerusalem　　　　　Tel. (2) 627.16.34
　　　　　　　　　　Fax: (2) 627.12.19

ITALY – ITALIE
Libreria Commissionaria Sansoni
Via Duca di Calabria, 1/1
50125 Firenze　　　　Tel. (055) 64.54.15
　　　　　　　　　　Fax: (055) 64.12.57
E-mail: licosa@ftbcc.it

Via Bartolini 29
20155 Milano　　　　Tel. (02) 36.50.83

Editrice e Libreria Herder
Piazza Montecitorio 120
00186 Roma　　　　　Tel. 679.46.28
　　　　　　　　　　Fax: 678.47.51

Libreria Hoepli
Via Hoepli 5
20121 Milano　　　　Tel. (02) 86.54.46
　　　　　　　　　　Fax: (02) 805.28.86

Libreria Scientifica
Dott. Lucio de Biasio 'Aeiou'
Via Coronelli, 6
20146 Milano
Tel. (02) 48.95.45.52
Fax: (02) 48.95.45.48

JAPAN – JAPON
OECD Tokyo Centre
Landic Akasaka Building
2-3-4 Akasaka, Minato-ku
Tokyo 107
Tel. (81.3) 3586.2016
Fax: (81.3) 3584.7929

KOREA – CORÉE
Kyobo Book Centre Co. Ltd.
P.O. Box 1658, Kwang Hwa Moon
Seoul
Tel. 730.78.91
Fax: 735.00.30

MALAYSIA – MALAISIE
University of Malaya Bookshop
University of Malaya
P.O. Box 1127, Jalan Pantai Baru
59700 Kuala Lumpur
Malaysia
Tel. 756.5000/756.5425
Fax: 756.3246

MEXICO – MEXIQUE
OECD Mexico Centre
Edificio INFOTEC
Av. San Fernando no. 37
Col. Toriello Guerra
Tlalpan C.P. 14050
Mexico D.F.
Tel. (525) 528.10.38
Fax: (525) 606.13.07

E-mail: ocde@rtn.net.mx

NETHERLANDS – PAYS-BAS
SDU Uitgeverij Plantijnstraat
Externe Fondsen
Postbus 20014
2500 EA's-Gravenhage
Voor bestellingen:
Tel. (070) 37.89.880
Fax: (070) 34.75.778

Subscription Agency/ Agence d'abonnements :
SWETS & ZEITLINGER BV
Heereweg 347B
P.O. Box 830
2160 SZ Lisse
Tel. 252.435.111
Fax: 252.415.888

**NEW ZEALAND –
NOUVELLE-ZÉLANDE**
GPLegislation Services
P.O. Box 12418
Thorndon, Wellington
Tel. (04) 496.5655
Fax: (04) 496.5698

NORWAY – NORVÈGE
NIC INFO A/S
Ostensjoveien 18
P.O. Box 6512 Etterstad
0606 Oslo
Tel. (22) 97.45.00
Fax: (22) 97.45.45

PAKISTAN
Mirza Book Agency
65 Shahrah Quaid-E-Azam
Lahore 54000
Tel. (42) 735.36.01
Fax: (42) 576.37.14

PHILIPPINE – PHILIPPINES
International Booksource Center Inc.
Rm 179/920 Cityland 10 Condo Tower 2
HV dela Costa Ext cor Valero St.
Makati Metro Manila
Tel. (632) 817 9676
Fax: (632) 817 1741

POLAND – POLOGNE
Ars Polona
00-950 Warszawa
Krakowskie Prezdmiescie 7
Tel. (22) 264760
Fax: (22) 265334

PORTUGAL
Livraria Portugal
Rua do Carmo 70-74
Apart. 2681
1200 Lisboa
Tel. (01) 347.49.82/5
Fax: (01) 347.02.64

SINGAPORE – SINGAPOUR
Ashgate Publishing
Asia Pacific Pte. Ltd
Golden Wheel Building, 04-03
41, Kallang Pudding Road
Singapore 349316
Tel. 741.5166
Fax: 742.9356

SPAIN – ESPAGNE
Mundi-Prensa Libros S.A.
Castelló 37, Apartado 1223
Madrid 28001
Tel. (91) 431.33.99
Fax: (91) 575.39.98

E-mail: mundiprensa@tsai.es
Internet: http://www.mundiprensa.es

Mundi-Prensa Barcelona
Consell de Cent No. 391
08009 – Barcelona
Tel. (93) 488.34.92
Fax: (93) 487.76.59

Libreria de la Generalitat
Palau Moja
Rambla dels Estudis, 118
08002 – Barcelona
(Suscripciones) Tel. (93) 318.80.12
(Publicaciones) Tel. (93) 302.67.23
Fax: (93) 412.18.54

SRI LANKA
Centre for Policy Research
c/o Colombo Agencies Ltd.
No. 300-304, Galle Road
Colombo 3
Tel. (1) 574240, 573551-2
Fax: (1) 575394, 510711

SWEDEN – SUÈDE
CE Fritzes AB
S–106 47 Stockholm
Tel. (08) 690.90.90
Fax: (08) 20.50.21

For electronic publications only/
Publications électroniques seulement
STATISTICS SWEDEN
Informationsservice
S-115 81 Stockholm
Tel. 8 783 5066
Fax: 8 783 4045

Subscription Agency/Agence d'abonnements :
Wennergren-Williams Info AB
P.O. Box 1305
171 25 Solna
Tel. (08) 705.97.50
Fax: (08) 27.00.71

Liber distribution
Internatinal organizations
Fagerstagatan 21
S-163 52 Spanga

SWITZERLAND – SUISSE
Maditec S.A. (Books and Periodicals/Livres
et périodiques)
Chemin des Palettes 4
Case postale 266
1020 Renens VD 1
Tel. (021) 635.08.65
Fax: (021) 635.07.80

Librairie Payot S.A.
4, place Pépinet
CP 3212
1002 Lausanne
Tel. (021) 320.25.11
Fax: (021) 320.25.14

Librairie Unilivres
6, rue de Candolle
1205 Genève
Tel. (022) 320.26.23
Fax: (022) 329.73.18

Subscription Agency/Agence d'abonnements :
Dynapresse Marketing S.A.
38, avenue Vibert
1227 Carouge
Tel. (022) 308.08.70
Fax: (022) 308.07.99

See also – Voir aussi :
OECD Bonn Centre
August-Bebel-Allee 6
D-53175 Bonn (Germany)
Tel. (0228) 959.120
Fax: (0228) 959.12.17

THAILAND – THAÏLANDE
Suksit Siam Co. Ltd.
113, 115 Fuang Nakhon Rd.
Opp. Wat Rajbopith
Bangkok 10200
Tel. (662) 225.9531/2
Fax: (662) 222.5188

**TRINIDAD & TOBAGO, CARIBBEAN
TRINITÉ-ET-TOBAGO, CARAÏBES**
Systematics Studies Limited
9 Watts Street
Curepe
Trinadad & Tobago, W.I.
Tel. (1809) 645.3475
Fax: (1809) 662.5654

E-mail: tobe@trinidad.net

TUNISIA – TUNISIE
Grande Librairie Spécialisée
Fendri Ali
Avenue Haffouz Imm El-Intilaka
Bloc B 1 Sfax 3000
Tel. (216-4) 296 855
Fax: (216-4) 298.270

TURKEY – TURQUIE
Kültür Yayinlari Is-Türk Ltd.
Atatürk Bulvari No. 191/Kat 13
06684 Kavaklidere/Ankara
Tel. (312) 428.11.40 Ext. 2458
Fax : (312) 417.24.90

Dolmabahce Cad. No. 29
Besiktas/Istanbul
Tel. (212) 260 7188

UNITED KINGDOM – ROYAUME-UNI
The Stationery Office Ltd.
Postal orders only:
P.O. Box 276, London SW8 5DT
Gen. enquiries
Tel. (171) 873 0011
Fax: (171) 873 8463

The Stationery Office Ltd.
Postal orders only:
49 High Holborn, London WC1V 6HB

Branches at: Belfast, Birmingham, Bristol,
Edinburgh, Manchester

UNITED STATES – ÉTATS-UNIS
OECD Washington Center
2001 L Street N.W., Suite 650
Washington, D.C. 20036-4922 Tel. (202) 785.6323
Fax: (202) 785.0350

Internet: washcont@oecd.org

Subscriptions to OECD periodicals may also be
placed through main subscription agencies.

Les abonnements aux publications périodiques de
l'OCDE peuvent être souscrits auprès des
principales agences d'abonnement.

Orders and inquiries from countries where Distribu-
tors have not yet been appointed should be sent to:
OECD Publications, 2, rue André-Pascal, 75775
Paris Cedex 16, France.

Les commandes provenant de pays où l'OCDE n'a
pas encore désigné de distributeur peuvent être
adressées aux Éditions de l'OCDE, 2, rue André-
Pascal, 75775 Paris Cedex 16, France.

12-1996

OECD PUBLICATIONS, 2, rue André-Pascal, 75775 PARIS CEDEX 16
PRINTED IN FRANCE
(97 97 01 1) ISBN 92-64-15360-8 – No. 49187 1997

DATE DUE